Crisis
Real Estate
Investing

Increase and Protect
Your Assets
from Potential Disaster

Hal Morris

BEAUFORT BOOKS
Publishers
NEW YORK

To Connie, Debbie, and Craig.
The perfect wife, daughter, and son.

ACKNOWLEDGEMENTS

This book, like any other, has many debts and a long ancestry. Many people have shared with me their experiences that has resulted in the urgent advice you will find in this manuscript. I have profited immensely from many distinguished thinkers and doers from both Wall Street and real estate.

I would like to thank the following individuals who contributed to my development: Dr. & Mrs. Harold W. Morris, Duane Gomer, Hugh Wilson, Jack Jennings, Rafe Cohen, Ted Rutherford, Don Nickelson, Sommers White, Richard Chaput, John Dickson, Caroline Manuel, Danny Wheeler. Charles A. Burton, Brad Johnson, Robert Wolenik, Mike Ferry, Tony Antoun, Rose-Marie Sines-Morrisey, Jerry Ducot, Jack Liebau, Paul Smith, Jackie Sanders.

Copyright © 1982 by Hal Morris

Library of Congress Cataloging in Publication Data
Morris, Hal.
    Crisis real estate investing.
    1. Real estate investment.   I. Title.
HD1382.5.M67   1985   332.63'24   84-24400
ISBN 0-8253-0282-X

Published in the United States by Beaufort Books Publishers, New York.

Printed in the U.S.A.   First Beaufort Edition

10 9 8 7 6 5 4 3 2 1

CONTENTS

FOREWORD

On a cold, winter night in February men and women thronged into a meeting room at the Marriott Hotel in Bloomington, Minnesota. Every available seat was filled by 7 o'clock. At seven-thirty the crowd was still pouring in. The room was soon jammed; standing room was at a premium and people were still buying tickets to stand outside the door and just listen. After a long business day, on a Monday evening with the temperature 30° below why would people stand for over an hour and a half?

These people were there to hear how to deal with the realities of today's new real estate market and how they could attain financial freedom through a simple easy-to-follow five-year plan. These people had all turned out without any newspaper advertising, just word of mouth, and two radio interviews with the speaker, Hal Morris, and written invitations that read:

"FIVE YEARS TO FINANCIAL FREEDOM"

Was this some revolutionary new breakthrough in the world of investments? No, it was the essence of simplicity. One lady asked the speaker as she left, "Do you think this plan is sophisticated enough?" Sophisticated enough for whom? No, it is not sophisticated. It just works. It just makes sense. It will just improve the quality of your lifestyle. It will just permit you to begin to do what you want to do when you want to do it. So, lady, if you want a complicated, intricate, sophisticated plan, this is not for you.

This book is a result of many people throughout the country asking to have the steps involved in the Five Year Plan spelled out in book form. The recommendations in this book are not experimental or speculative. They have worked for thousands of people throughout the United States. They represent a sound, solid approach to financial planning. As Jack London has stated, "The best measure of anything should be: does it work?"

—Brad Johnson

1

A Real Estate Disaster in the Making?

Facts that are not frankly faced have a habit of stabbing us in the back.
—Sir Harold Bowden

It came about so quickly that almost no one could believe it. Prices for homes all across America went up dramatically year after year. One region reported 15 percent a year appreciation, another called it 21 percent, and still a third, 23 percent. Imagine, the value of a house going up by nearly a quarter of its price every year!

And then one day it just stopped.

Inflation was still bothersome, but high interest rates were calming it. And the high interest rates also calmed real estate. Where before buyers had waited in line for a chance to buy a home—they actually had auctions where as many as 1500 people competed for as few as 49 homes—now there were seemingly no buyers at all.

Sellers put their homes up for sale for 90 days, and then for six months, with little result. Builders saw their profits eaten up in interest charges on unsold houses. Brokers saw their volume cut in half. Investors began to scratch their heads and wonder just how appreciation would fare with the lull in the market.

Inflation soared, then slowed, but interest rates soared even higher. Savings and loan associations, which had been the bread and butter of real-estate financing, began refusing to fund all but the best-qualified borrowers. Disintermediation *was a word that even the man on the street began to understand. It meant more people were taking money out of savings and loans than were putting it in.*

My friend Harry went down to one of the largest savings and loans in the country and asked for an 80-percent mortgage on his new home. You know what they told him? They told him that they weren't making any mortgage loans anymore—they were making loans on cars!

Sellers, realizing that buyers simply couldn't get financing to purchase their homes, began handling the financing themselves. It was called creative financing, *but it really meant* seller financing. *And sellers soon found that when they handled the mortgage there almost always was a discount involved; at first they got their price, but later on when they wanted cash they had to take less.*

Investors, seeing that prices for homes were no longer appreciating rapidly, began to hold back. Why should they invest in property when that property was likely to show a loss? Only a fool would invest in something that not only was illiquid, but also was failing to appreciate.

Those who had already bought saw that they were in a terrible bind. Often mortgage payments were twice what the property could be rented for. Both investors and residents had hoped that they could sell quickly at a profit to make up for those high payments. But now selling seemed difficult, if not impossible.

Foreclosures jumped to a rate higher than at any time since the Great Depression. Sellers, many of whom were investors, saw the handwriting on the wall. If they didn't sell quickly, they would surely be forced to take an even bigger loss in the future.

They cut their prices to get out of their homes at a loss. But still the buyers were few and far between. Even at a reduction of 5 percent, the houses were priced so high that 95 percent of all Americans couldn't afford them. And those who could were thinking twice. With prices coming down, why buy today when you can buy the same property for less tomorrow?

Prices began plunging almost as fast as they had gone up. Instead of a 15 percent appreciation rate, prices stopped dead. Then the country experienced a 10-percent depreciation rate on houses. The home that was worth $100,000 in January was only worth $90,000 by December.

Real-estate brokerage firms went bankrupt. Savings and loan associations, not able to compete with banks for commercial and consumer loans and not having the funds to offer mortgages, closed their doors in droves. The Federal Savings and Loan Insurance Corporation was called upon to cover small depositors (those who had $100,000 or less on deposit). Within a few months, the FSLIC fund of $7 billion was gone and the FSLIC appealed to the Treasury and Congress for more money.

Investors, seeing that real estate had become an albatross, bailed out. They quickly cut their prices 20 or 25 percent, or let their property go into foreclosure. Suddenly foreclosure rates rose to levels as high as the Great Depression and prices fell almost as quickly. Within a few years the price of real estate had tumbled by nearly 50 percent!

The real-estate market was in chaos. No one would buy and everyone wanted to sell. The financial institutions of the country, from savings and loans to banks, were in collapse as depositors made run after run to get out their money, believing the worst was at hand. The economy as a whole turned down and the President announced that we definitely were not yet in another Great Depression!

It was the domino theory all over again. A house of cards had been blown over. It was 1929 revisited, only this time instead of the stock market it was real estate.

Will it happen?

You just read a fictional scenario. It hasn't happened yet. But many disturbing things *are* occurring.

I originally intended this book to be about creative investing in real estate. I was going to tell you about a lot of techniques that I don't think anyone else has ever talked about for buying homes as investments: how to buy them, how to refinance them to get profits out, and why *not* to sell.

But before I could begin I realized that the real-estate market was in turmoil. The volume of resales was down by 40 percent. The number of new homes being built had been slashed in half. For the first time since the Great Depression, there was a chance that the year-to-year median price for homes would go down! Savings and loan associations had stopped making first mortgage loans ... because they didn't have any money! Interest rates were soaring to 17 percent and beyond!

In this climate an old-fashioned book about real estate investment would not do because it could not address the real issue of the day. *The real issue of today is a real-estate market in crisis!*

But, were my perceptions askew? Was I just reading scary headlines in the news, written by editors who wanted to sell papers? Underneath, was the real-estate market really as badly off as the figures made it seem? Or was it doing just fine despite the bad publicity? It would not be the first time that the media created a phony crisis.

To find out, I visited five people, all friends I had gotten to know over the last ten years but had not seen recently. I picked these five because of their relationships to real estate: They were a banker, a builder, a savings and loan president, a real-estate broker and a mortgage banker. What better way to learn the true status of the field than by talking with the people most intimately involved.

(**Note:** These are real people, not phantoms created out of thin air. I have changed only the names and, in some cases, the locales.)

GEORGE THE BANKER

Back in 1974 I went to George and said to him "If your objective were to make as much money as you could, and you didn't care what area it was in (as long as it was legal, of course), what would you do?" George thought a while, then said "I would buy foreclosed properties."

George was very right. Back in 1974 we were heading downward into a big recession and foreclosures were up everywhere. It was possible to buy for very little and get a real bargain.

George told me of one large piece of commercial property in Redondo Beach, California, that his bank took back. As part of the foreclosure proceedings they offered the property for sale to anyone "on the courthouse steps." No one showed up to bid, so the bank took possession, put the property on the market, and within three weeks sold it for $100,000 more than it cost them.

Of course, that was 1974. I recently took George to lunch (I think everyone should take their banker to lunch at least once a year!) and asked him what the market was like for him today. George just shook his head. "The pressure is building on all sides. Real-estate prices are going to drop as much as 30 percent."

I was shocked at George's pessimism. I asked him what his problem was. After all, he had been so optimistic in the past.

George's problem was straightforward. His bank portfolio on that day had $30 million outstanding in construction loans. Of that $30 million, maybe $1 million was good.

How can that be, I wanted to know. George was an excellent banker. How could he have made such poor loans?

George explained that the loans weren't poor when he made them. They were made to builders who had good track records, and were based on realistic projections of the value of the property. But then times changed—dramatically and quickly. Interest rates soared. Buyers couldn't qualify for mortgages. Builders couldn't sell their projects.

In his case, builders who had been reliable clients of the bank for decades were simply walking away from the projects, leaving them half-finished. They were saying that if they finished them they would lose more money than if they just dropped them.

His bank was having to foreclose, take over the half-finished property, find another builder, and hire him to finish. There was no way the bank could come out with a profit. It was simply a matter of spending more money to lose a little less at the end.

"And that's not half the trouble," George lamented. "In about a fifth of the cases, the builder is also going into bankruptcy. That means that the property gets tied up and we can't foreclose. It means we don't get any interest and we can't even get to our money. It's tied up in a half-built building involved in a bankruptcy and we can't touch it!"

The Bottom Line

"Right now," George concluded, "in Santa Clara County, California, foreclosures are up 300 percent over just a year ago. We have 697 properties in foreclosure and, of those, 25 percent will go to sale!"

George threw his hands up in the air. "It's not just high interest rates, it's difficulty in getting buildings finished on time. Do you realize that ten years ago a builder's time to get a project from conception to sale was only about six to eight months. Today it's three years. *Three years!* Think of it. By the time the builder goes through all the required government approvals, the market he originally designed the project for no longer exists!

"There was a recent newspaper article on San Francisco developer M. Sherman Eubanks and how his sub-division project has been delayed for *ten years!* The first eight years because much of the land scheduled for development was turned into a public park. That was bad enough, but the last two years he has spent over $800,000 because his property is the home of a rare butterfly and it is a federal offense to kill one. He still cannot start construction until they figure out a way to prevent the tractors and other construction equipment from running over the butterflies' caterpillars. The butterflies only have a lifespan of one week!"

George handed me a breakdown sheet prepared by Ira Norris, who has been a builder for fifteen years. It compared building costs and times in 1966 and 1981. Here is what it looked like:

	1966	1981
Subdivision processing time	4–6 months	1–3 years
Fees (per lot)	$200–$300	$3000–$10,000
Environmental impact reports	no	yes
Design review (some jurisdictions)	no	yes
Archeological review (some jurisdictions)	no	yes
Rent control (some jurisdictions)	no	yes
Growth management ordinance (some jurisdictions)	no	yes
Moratoriums (some jurisdictions)	no	yes
Limitations on filings/permits (some jurisdictions)	no	yes

"See," said George. "Three years and in most cases $10,000 *per lot* just in government costs. Ira wants to know if I can imagine General Motors or Levi Strauss bringing their plans for a new product to a public hearing and waiting anxiously for the public debate to end so that a local board can vote on whether they may proceed!"

George continued ruefully. "Government overregulation stifled builders. Then when the market got tight, like it is now, they collapsed. And that left me with 29 out of 30 million dollars in bad loans."

George the Banker said he knew other bankers who were in far worse straights. They had troubled portfolios in the billions of dollars. But it was small consolation that he was in trouble for only $29 million.

"You know," George mused, "someone recently asked me when things will get back to normal. I had to answer that this *is* the new normal."

After talking to George, I wanted to hear the builder's side of the story.

HARRY THE HOMEBUILDER

I knew Harry when he was a stockbroker. During the 1970s he got out of the market and moved into building. He put up condominiums and made a lot of money. I met Harry at his office after work.

A few years ago Harry came up with what he thought was a super project. It was to be 32 condos in a prime location. These homes had everything going for them. They were going to have the amenities of a pool and a recreation room. They were going to be spacious. And they were going to be affordable. For the area, Harry figured that they would be priced slightly below existing condos. They should sell in a minute—with lots of profit for everyone concerned.

But then Harry ran into the problems of modern day construction. From the time he began until the time he was ready to bring the project on-line, it took him three-and-a-half years!

When Harry's condos finally came on-line, the market they were planned for no longer existed. He had expected to sell them inexpensively to a mass market. But, over the three-and-a-half years, inflation had pushed his costs sky high. Now he had to sell them for a much higher price. Then high interest rates came along, and the combination of high prices and interest rates kept people from qualifying for mortgages.

It wasn't that people did not want to buy Harry's condos. They did. He had a great real-estate broker working for him and a constant stream of lookers. It was just that no one *could* buy. (Back in 1970, 46.3 percent of American households could buy the median-priced home. In 1980 it was down to 20 percent. Today, who knows?)

Meanwhile, Harry was sitting on a time bomb. He had borrowed money to construct the condominiums. In fact, the huge construction loan the project had required was costing him interest charges of $40,000 a month! (Prime was 7½% when he began, but 20% when it came time to sell.)

Forty thousand dollars may seem very high. But he had planned on selling the condos quickly and paying off the construction loan at once. He would have had more than enough money to pay any "carrying" charges along the way . . . before today's market.

Now, Harry was in trouble. He had to make those huge monthly payments and, since he wasn't selling any condos, there wasn't any money coming in.

Harry finally decided, in desperation, to auction off the condos. He paid for advertisements in the local paper and then one Sunday morning he put them on the auction block to the highest bidder.

He was only able to sell ten this way, at an average price of 30 percent less than he was asking. But, before these deals could close, six fell out of escrow! The hopeful buyers couldn't qualify for the new mortgages.

Harry had only sold four through his auction. Using his own credit, Harry was able to buy four more himself. This paid off part of the construction loan and he rented them out to help make his regular mortgage payments. But, there were still 24 unsold, and these were costing him $30,000 a month in interest.

Harry slowly paced around his office, stopping to gaze at the scale model of his development. "It's three-and-a-half years of my life, and it's all going down the drain," he said. "I've got about $60,000 left in assets, so I can hold out for two more months. After that it's all over. I'll go into foreclosure and there's nothing to keep it from happening. What am I supposed to do—go back to the stock market?"

"Did you see the letters to the editor Sunday? Look at this article that a fellow builder wrote the *L.A. Times.*

> I am not a protester. I am not anti-government and I am not against government controls in most areas of industry. I am violently opposed to the imminent prospect of being forced out of business. I am violently opposed to being put in a position of losing everything which I have worked 40 years to gain.
>
> I am in the business of housing. We build homes and we build them in the lower spectrum of cost. Granted, we are a small business. We have only built $14-million worth of homes in five years. I have been in the construction industry for over 20 years. The greatest pleasure in my working life was to establish my own corporation in 1976. That business is on the

verge of following many others into oblivion and, worst of all, not because of bad judgment on my part, as principal, but because of decisions rendered at the government level.

I undoubtedly speak for thousands, perhaps millions, of Americans who, like me, are being crushed by the juggernaut of "inflation control." I have had enough. The "new" Chrysler Corp. is boasting of profits. The oil and petrochemical industries are more profitable than ever. Consider the Dupont/Conoco merger, the largest corporate merger in history. How did this occur? Is not the stock value of Conoco rather inflationary? Where does it stop? When will we not hear of more ways to save the ailing auto industry? When will we not hear of the fantastic profit-taking by the oil companies and by Wall Street?

Wall Street and the automobile industry are not the backbone of this country. We take the pulse of the economy on Wall Street, therefore, it is not the most vital organ. We the people, we the small businesses of America, are the backbone and we are being forced to step aside, to stand in line to file bankruptcy, and to extend the unemployment lines.

I stated before that I have had enough. This is an understatement. If the "Fed," Wall Street and the government can move to force people like me to close up, they, or the Executive Branch of the Government, can also move to prevent the literal bankruptcy of the country.

Companies like mine and people like me are told we must suffer, we must tighten our belts, but we can only take so much. I am currently paying 21% interest on a loan that one year ago was at 12¾%. This loan was to build a mere 20 homes. We cannot sell the homes. How many veterans can afford to pay 15½% interest? How many others can afford to pay the FHA rate of 16%? Who can afford to pay the "best market rate" of 16¾%? How many savings and loan institutions have been forced to merge or cut back drastically in order to stay in business?

We want to survive. I do not pretend to know the answers as to how to control inflation. I do know that you do not kill a patient to cure his cancer. Killing the economy and the construction/housing industry cannot be the answer. The Monroe Doctrine (America for the Americans), has not been enforced. How about a Reagan Doctrine, Americans for the Americans?

The interest rates must be controlled by the Executive Branch or Congress. The bureaucrats are playing monopoly and it must be stopped. While they are strangling small and medium business, they are openly permitting our industry to be consumed by the Canadians, the Japanese, the French and the Middle East. These foreign entities do not rely on the domestic dollar and are not concerned about our interest rates. They bring their own capital with them. Do we want American industry controlled by foreign interests or do we want Americans to do as we have done for 200 years and be what we have struggled to be: independent, aggressive, imaginative and industrious?

We have endured and suffered long enough. This country and this industry cannot wait any longer. We are very tired of hearing about more ways and means of aiding the auto industry. The housing industry comprises probably 40% to 50%, directly and indirectly, of the working class of this country. We need housing to survive. Give us the means to produce and sell affordable housing and we will give the government, the economy and America back to the Americans.

I write as an avid Republican, a beleaguered businessman, a frustrated builder, and an American who cares.

WILLIAM J. BOLICH
Carlsbad

When I left Harry's office, I don't know who was feeling grimmer, Harry or me. He had his own personal financial problems, but I was aware that he was far from being alone. Perhaps the *majority* of U.S. builders were in similar straights. Up close, firsthand, I was beginning to get a feeling for the magnitude of the real-estate crisis we were in.

Since most real-estate mortgages come from savings and loan associations, my next call was on Sam, the president of an S & L.

SAM THE SAVINGS AND LOAN PRESIDENT

Sam has been president of his moderate-sized savings and loan association for nearly fifteen years. During that time he has weathered a few recessions, including the hard times of 1974 and 1975. But, Sam says, he has never seen anything to match this.

Over lunch I asked Sam what was happening in his industry. He looked at me sadly and predicted "It's going to be a catastrophe." Sam pointed out that on that day something like 400 to 500 savings and loan associations, including his, were on the Federal Savings and Loan Insurance Corporation's target list of S & L's in serious difficulty. These were associations whose net worth was close to zero. If they were to continue in business they might not have sufficient assets to pay off all their depositors. (All Savers certificates have been created recently to help this situation.)

Sam said that during the past year some two dozen S & L's had either closed their doors or been forced to merge. This was more than the total number of closures and forced mergers since the Great Depression. And the troubles were only beginning. Sam pointed out that the FSLIC only had about 7 or 8 billion dollars in assets. This is the insurance fund available to cover depositors in the event of an S & L's insolvency. (If just those S & L's in New York state that are in trouble went under, the entire fund would be wiped out.)

I asked Sam to explain how it happened. How could such a strong industry, in only a year or two, come to the very brink of disaster? Sam said it came down to three words: "High interest rates."

"It's not the high interest rates that you and I pay when we borrow. It's the high interest rates that depositors demand on their savings accounts. We're in competition with the money market mutual funds. They can pay 15 to 18 percent interest on their accounts and they require little or no minimum balance. You can keep your money in for only a day if you want, then get it out by writing a check! We can't come close to offering that. We pay a lower amount of interest, have high minimum balances and require long terms. We are forced to lend long and borrow short. We just can't compete."

I nodded that I understood. But Sam shook his head. "We're going broke as the depositors are pulling out. That's the reason we can't make real-estate loans. We can't tie up our money in longterm accounts. Longterm accounts? Heck, now we don't have any money to tie up at all!

"Hundreds, perhaps thousands, of S & L's are facing massive disintermediation right now. That means more money going out than coming in. As more goes out, our net worth goes down. When it gets to zero we either have to merge or go out of business."

"You know what?" Sam looked me right in the eyes. "My S & L can only continue for seven months longer at the present rate of withdrawals. At that time we won't have any net worth. The Federal Deposit Insurance Corporation will come in and liquidate us and pay off our depositors—if they have any money left."

I still remember Sam's words as I left. "If things don't change soon, the troubles the S & L's are in today will make 1929 look like a Girl Scout cookie drive!"

FAY THE REAL ESTATE BROKER

Fay is a particularly successful broker. She has everything that personality profiles say makes for success in real estate: a dynamic personality, sincerity, aggressiveness and smarts. Fay started as a salesperson back in 1970. She worked her way up to broker, opened her own office, and by 1980 had thirty-one major real estate offices in Florida. She had sold franchises and had other brokers working for her. She was rapidly developing a real-estate empire.

Then today's market hit. When I caught up with Fay in a coffee shop down the street from her main office she was almost in tears. She told me the story of her airplane!

"We bought it two years ago. It was a great investment, it seemed. We got a tax credit and depreciation. The plane saved us money in flying costs when compared to commercial airlines. But that's all past. Our volume is down by more than 50 percent. We're just not closing deals. We get lots of buyers, but no one can qualify for the new mortgages and only so many owners can handle the financing themselves. The volume is way down. And for those who close, there is little or no cash. Sellers are accepting anything of value as a down payment—motor homes, boats, diamonds. One even accepted a cow as part of the purchase price!"

She sighed. "And I've got a director of training, a general manager, a VP of personnel, a VP of marketing, a VP of public relations, a VP of franchising, and a plane!"

Fay put her hand on my arm. "Do you have any idea how much all of those salaries and plane payments come to?" I shook my head. "Plenty! And every one of my offices except the investment division is showing a negative cash flow. I am having to support those offices to keep them going."

I asked Fay why she didn't close down. She was trying to, she said, but she was locked into longterm leases. If she closed down she wouldn't have phone bills and utility payments, but she would still have to pay the rent unless the landlord could rent to someone else—and that was hard right now.

What about the investment division? Why not expand that? Fay just hung her head. "It is in the most trouble of all."

"I thought you said it was showing a profit."

"It has a positive cash flow right now. But it is a time bomb. I have a guaranteed investment plan I offer to investors. I guarantee to manage the properties bought by my investors and to make up any negative cash flow on any projects. If tenants don't pay, or if the mortgage is higher than the rents, I make up the difference.

"I've been able to keep going thus far because I've used the money from new investors to support the older projects. The whole idea was to sell after a year or two for a big profit. I would get out of my guarantee, the investor would get his money back, and I would make two commissions plus some profit. It was great. Only nothing is selling!

"Each time a new property comes into the investment division, I have more negative cash flow to take care of later on. Sure, there is some positive flow from the commission, but without being able to sell, that negative could go on for years. In a few months, if investors stop buying, I'm dead and so is my investment division."

As I left Fay I reflected that she was not alone. Many brokers across the country had made similar guarantees on investment property. Even those who hadn't were seeing their volume of sales (which really means their income) slashed. In the last twelve months, 30 percent of all real-estate agents went out of business.

ZEKE THE MORTGAGE BANKER

Fay had mentioned that most of the sales closing now were handled through seller financing. One alternative to seller financing—and sometimes used with it—was a "hard money" second. This was a second mortgage borrowed, not from the seller, but from an individual investor. It was arranged through a mortgage broker. I decided to see one of them.

Zeke and I met early one morning in his office. He poured us both coffee and we sank into plush chairs. Everything about Zeke's office indicated wealth. I knew he had been doing very well. Rumors were that he was making in excess of half a million dollars a year in profits. I asked Zeke how it was going. "It's hard. But if it's bad for me, you can't imagine how bad it is for a friend of mine." He raised one hand, five fingers. "I walked into his office the other day. He raised his hand like this and said 'That's how many days I have left. Five days, and then it will all come crashing down.'

"I said he must surely be mistaken, or exaggerating. 'Not at all,' he assured me. 'I've already written bad checks. My trust account is over a million dollars overdrawn. I figure it will be about five days more before the bank closes my line of credit and then it will be over.' "

I asked Zeke to explain further about this friend.

"It's a combination of expanding too fast and then having the market come crashing down." Zeke indicated that his friend had been offering second mortgages on property. He never cared whether the buyer qualified for anything; it was the property that had to qualify. If, when his second mortgage was added to the existing first, the total mortgages were no more than 80 percent of the value of the property, he would make the loan. If not, he wouldn't.

"It seemed perfectly safe," his friend had said. "We had a 20 percent margin. If a borrower went into default, we could foreclose, take the property back, and resell. We had 20 percent over the amount we were into the property for, as a buffer. It should have worked out." (Note: Today there is private mortgage insurance available on seconds on select property.)

Zeke continued. "He charged 12 points (or 12 percent of the loan) as a fee. When the loan was made he got 12 percent. On a $10,000 mortgage that came to $1200. Plus his company serviced the loan, for which he charged a fee. And finally, if there were any late charges, he got those. But best of all, he put up no money! Investors did that. They put up all the money that he lent out on second mortgages." I asked Zeke what went wrong with his friend.

"Two things. The first was cheating. He had a loan portfolio of over $100 million. He was making loans of $5 million a month. He couldn't handle it all, so he had 'financial counselors' do some of it. One day one of his trusted employees came in with a mortgage package. It included a description of the house on which they were making a loan, a photo, the appraised value by an independent appraiser, and other documents. He should have just signed it and thought nothing more. But, he told me, it stuck in his mind. So he waited. The next day the counselor urged him to sign the package, and my friend wanted his commission.

"Again he didn't sign. That night on the way home he drove by the house on which he was about to lend money. He could not believe what he saw. A house that had burned down! The photo was of the house next door. Somehow that counselor had gotten together with the appraiser and they were arranging a loan which they never intended to repay. They would take the money and run!

"The next day he fired the counselor, then began going through the files. About 5 percent of all those loans had been fabricated. They were on nonexistent property. Those poor investors! They had all had the right to examine the property and each investor had lent the money for a separate house. There was no pooling of money. But they had all trusted my friend because he had guaranteed the mortgages. He had told them that if there was ever a default, or if the borrower didn't pay, he would make up the negative cash flow."

I sighed. It was just like Fay the Broker and her property. Zeke continued the sad story.

"My friend began disposing of the bad loans. But the market closed down too fast. Suddenly, he went from having had only seven properties in foreclosure to where he had 67 properties in foreclosure. The borrowers were not paying, and he was supposed to make up any payments not made by the borrowers. He could have done it if new investors were lending more money. But now new investors are getting shy of the market and are not coming in. He has been making up the payments to his investors out of his own funds."

That much I understood. "But how," I asked Zeke, "could his trust fund be a million dollars overdrawn when it was other people's money?" He shook his head.

"I can't believe it. All the money that came in on mortgages went into that one fund, and from it he paid everyone out."

"You mean he commingled investors' money."

"Worse. He put his own money in there."

This was indeed bad. Commingling is illegal.

"It happened too quickly. He was just starting business in 1979 and suddenly he was doing as much as $5 million a month. He didn't have time to set up bookkeeping systems—he couldn't handle all the money. He couldn't loan it out fast enough! Investors were throwing it at him and he couldn't find enough borrowers. Things just got out of hand."

While this was a personal disaster, the fallout is a catastrophe for the real-estate industry. With high interest rates on new mortgages, about the only way sellers could sell was through the second-mortgage market. With all the adverse publicity over this sort of thing, sellers and investors are now pulling back. They have seen others get hurt and they don't want to get hurt themselves. The second mortgage market is drying up.

When second mortgages dry up, the last source of good financing for real estate goes with it. And when it goes, the volume of sales declines precipitously. Few will be able to sell. And prices could plummet as desperate sellers compete with one another for the few remaining cash buyers. (As I write this, more than fifty of the largest mortgage brokers in California alone are under investigation for similar practices.)

The five examples I have presented are real people and they represent the spectrum of real estate. All are facing an unprecedented crisis.

Yet there is one area I have not covered, and it is the largest area and the one that covers most of the readers of this book. It is the area of *the buyer and the seller and the investor.*

The best way I can illustrate the plight of buyers/sellers/investors is to tell the story of a trip I made recently to appear on the KCBS Lila Peterson Show in San Francisco.

The minute I got into town I bought a copy of the local afternoon paper, the *San Francisco Examiner.* I searched through the classified ads for the cheapest home advertised in San Francisco. On that day the cheapest home advertised was $79,500. It was a one-bedroom, one-bath condominium.

Assuming that the buyer had a $20,000 down payment, that would require a $60,000 mortgage. At the station, Jim Reilly, of Lawyers' Title Insurance Company, met me and passed along a list of all lenders' current quotes for the San Francisco Bay Area.

(I didn't know what the quotes were going to be. Each market is different. When you go to Minnesota, you don't know what the market there is going to be. If you go to New York, that's different. Los Angeles is different. And so on.)

I picked Bank of America. It is not only the largest bank in California, but also the largest in the country. On that day B of A was quoting 18 percent interest, three point plus $200. (Eighteen percent is the interest rate and three points is the bonus the lender wants for funding the loan. Three points translates into 3 percent of the loan, which in this case amounted to $1800.)

In order to qualify for that mortgage, assuming a standard 4 to 1 income-to-monthly-payment qualification, it would have required an income of $53,000 a year to get that mortgage!

I then checked the statistics on the average income in the San Francisco market and found that only 3.7 percent of the population would qualify (have enough income) for that conventional mortgage. Imagine what that means. *On that day, 96.3% of all the people in the San Francisco Bay Area could not qualify to buy the cheapest home offered for sale.*

Buyers are locked out of the market. But what about sellers? The situation comes closer to home when you recognize that chances are your own house has declined in value during the past year!

That's a tough fact to swallow, but it is very likely true. For the first time since before World War II, housing prices are declining in some parts of the United States.

Think of that. We have only seen housing prices rise. Now they are dipping downward.

"The great 1970s bull market in real estate is over," says David Saulman, economist at UCLA's business forecasting project.

I think that is a fascinating statistic. But I know many people will dispute it. They have seen prices go up and up in their own neighborhoods. They have seen their friends sell their houses at increasing values. "Maybe prices have gone down somewhere else, but not in my neighborhood," I've heard them say.

Really?

I say that unless you are living in a truly exceptional area, prices have gone down even in your neighborhood!

Of course that decline may be disguised, unless you know where to look. The reason is that *houses aren't declining–terms are.* Here is what you should look for.

In sales over the last year in your neighborhood, how many buyers put *cash* down to a new first loan? (If you don't know, a quick check with a local broker probably can give you the information. Fast.)

I'll wager very few, if any, buyers put down cash in the last year. In most cases buyers couldn't afford the horrendous interest rates for new first mortgages which at times were over 17 percent. Buyers simply couldn't qualify for a new loan at that rate of interest.

In order to get rid of their property, sellers had to help buyers out by carrying some of the financing themselves. Over the last year, in the vast majority of cases, buyers didn't go out and secure new first mortgages from savings and loan associations, banks or other institutional lenders. Instead they simply took over the seller's existing low-interest first mortgage and gave the seller a second.

When a seller accepts a second mortgage as part of the purchase price, he or she is actually *cutting* the price of the property.

Here's how it works.

The only thing that's as good as cash, is cash itself. A second mortgage is a promise to pay cash at some future date, usually three to five years from the present. A second is just paper. Of course, the borrower pays interest on that money.

But, what if the seller has an emergency and suddenly needs cash, right now? What if the seller, a husband and wife, have taken back a $50,000 second mortgage on a house that sold for $100,000, thinking to hold it for three years. But the wife suddenly discovers her husband has cancer and she needs the money for medical expenses?

She has a promise to pay in three years, but she needs cash now. So she tries to convert that second mortgage to cash. She goes to someone who has cash, to "sell" her second.

Do you know what she would be told?

She would be told that, depending on the interest rate of the second and the other terms, its cash value would be between 5 and 35 percent *less* than its face value! *To convert a second to cash means taking a discount.*

Let's take a typical discount of 20 percent. Two months after she sold her house, our seller has to have cash. So she sells her $50,000 second for 20 percent less than the face value.

$$\begin{array}{ll} \$50,000 & \text{second mortgage} \\ \underline{20\%} & \\ \$10,000 & \text{discount} \end{array}$$

Instead of getting back $50,000 in cash, she only gets back $40,000 for her second. She has lost $10,000.

Did she lose that money, in truth, on the second?

Not really. She lost it on the sale of her house! If she had been able to sell for $100,000 *cash* (buyer giving her cash down to a new first mortgage—all cash to seller), she would indeed have been getting her price.

But because she was handling the financing herself, she in reality accepted $10,000 less than her asking price. True, she did receive $100,000 for her house *on paper*. But as she found out two months later, she had actually received only $90,000 *in cash*.

The vast majority of homes sold in the last year were sold this way. Many did achieve their reported prices—on paper. But in terms of cash, their real prices were anywhere from 5 to 35 percent less.

Prices of real estate, particularly homes, are already sliding when we factor in the terms.

THE LOOMING DISASTER

Some very smart people I know say that the process is going to accelerate. They say that the decline will increase rapidly in the next year or so, as those buyers who accepted second mortgages in the past begin finding their short-term seconds coming due.

Consider those 20 to 40 percent of buyers who got seconds over the last two or three years. Most of those seconds were written for a short term—3 to 5 years was common. Those second mortgages are now coming due. Right now, today.

Imagine that you bought your home three years ago with a $30,000 second due in three years. You figured you would live in your house and when the three years were up, you'd refinance.

Well, it's time. Have you looked at the cost of refinancing today? Interest rates are bouncing around in the 14 to 18 percent area for new first mortgages, if you can qualify, and in the 18 to 22 percent range for new seconds. Not only that, but there are *points*. To go out and get a new second, you're going to have to pay the discount up front—right at the time you obtain the money!

If you are a borrower who bought with a big second three years ago, you could be in trouble right now. You have to come up with cash to pay off your second—come up with cash at the very time that it costs more to borrow money in this country than any other time in this century.

So, what can you do if you can't borrow? Naturally to save your equity you'll try to sell. But, to sell you need a buyer who has "all cash." (You have to have cash to pay off your second.) But, as we've seen, in order to get all cash, you have to lower your price.

Some of the smartest people around say that it may already be happening. The bottom may be falling right out of the real estate market, if not the entire economy. These people say that the time to get out is now, at any cost, even a substantial loss.

(This is the exact opposite of the inflation philosophy. Remember, in inflation we try to buy quickly because we know that tomorrow the price is going to be higher. These very smart people are saying that we should sell today, quickly, because tomorrow the price is going lower.)

BUT ARE THEY RIGHT?

Are these people I'm talking about—people you undoubtedly have heard yourself—correct? Are their evaluations of the housing market and the economy in general correct? Are we falling over the edge of a precipice and had we better grab for any twig to support us? Is tomorrow to be down instead of up? Here's a sample of what is being said:

> ... you are perceptive enough to sense that something is terribly wrong out there, and you are one of millions of Americans with a growing sense of unease about the future. The institutions you always trusted are now giving you a queasy

feeling. You are making money, but you seem to have less, and you know all is not well. I congratulate you for your insight. I share your feelings. Those who are making and influencing our economic policy are either acting in their own economic or political self-interest, are fools, or just plain wrong. The course that they have plotted can only end in fiscal chaos . . . Howard J. Ruff, in *How to Prosper in the Coming Bad Years.*

In sum, both volume-price curves and 'breadth' price ratios are flashing warnings. They're telling us that the top of the real estate market is approaching. While we can't be certain that a collapse is imminent, once the top has been made and the decline begins, the panic stage that follows could be so precipitous that sales may be impossible. For this reason, we feel comfortable in recommending that investors start liquidating holdings even though the top could be as much as a year away. Charles D. Kirkpatrick II, "Bearish on Real Estate," *Barrons Magazine*, July 23, 1979.

"It's not a good time to speculate on real estate. Sell your house and rent." Richard Russel, publisher of *The Dow Theory Letters.*

"The real-estate bubble is about to burst." Michael K. Evans, *Los Angeles Times*, June 16, 1981.

"Condo mania is slowing down in such major markets as California, New York City, Chicago, Washington, D.C., and Philadelphia . . . More apartments are on the market . . . they take longer to sell . . . Many sellers have had to lower prices . . . there are predictions that prices will drop by as much as 45 percent, which in some cases will occur almost overnight." *Dun's Business Month*, September 1981.

2

A Real-Estate Turnaround

Understanding and appreciating the realities of the new real estate market is a good starting place in your success plan!

· · · · · ·

Back in 1974 the United States had a major recession. In fact, it was the most severe recession since the Great Depression. During that period of time, interest rates almost doubled. Housing sales plummeted. Builders and real-estate agents went out of business. Condominiums and new tract houses were lined up around the country, and they couldn't be sold because no one would get involved in real estate. Nearly everyone felt the bottom had fallen out of the real-estate market.

But nearly everyone's perceptions were wrong. What they were seeing was not the beginning of the end, but the beginning of the greatest real estate boom the country had seen in a century. The years 1974 and 1975 were about the last times anyone could buy real estate truly cheap in that decade. From then on prices skyrocketed right up through the 1980s.

The point is that some people feel history may be about to repeat itself. Just as 1974 was the last chance for the 1970s in terms of getting in on real-estate values, so *right now* may be the last chance for the 1980s.

POSITIVE FACTORS

The market we are experiencing certainly is in crisis. But it may be just the falling out necessary in order for real estate to take off once more. We may not be seeing the beginning of the end. We may be witnessing the start of a whole new boom. I think there are good reasons for believing this.

1. History repeats itself. We have already alluded to this. We may be seeing a repeat of the 1974 recession. Now as then sales slumped and supply dipped. But as soon as the economy recovered, people poured back into real estate. As soon as our economy recovers and interest rates and inflation drop, we may see the same thing occurring.

2. Housing demand is staggering. We have to ask ourselves, why is the housing market in a slump today? Is it because people don't need or want housing? Is it because there have been too many houses built and there just aren't enough buyers to go around?

Everyone knows better than that. Today we actually have a *housing shortage!*

The proof is in the rental market. Nationwide, rental vacancies are at their lowest levels in decades. In every city I've visited, I have seen rentals in short supply. Nationwide, the overall rental vacancy rate is less than 5 percent—the lowest level in the 35 years that statistics have been kept. In Los Angeles it is less than 1 percent!

What does a low rental vacancy rate mean? It means that people who want to buy houses, can't. Therefore, they are forced to rent. Many renters are house buyers in disguise.

As soon as (1) prices get low enough for those renters on the sidelines to jump in, or (2) those on the sidelines get income increases so they can buy, we may see a new housing boom take off. It could be as simple, as inevitable, as supply and demand.

What we may really be seeing today is a retrenching of the market, a pulling back to a more stable price range. Not a collapse, but the groundwork being laid for another advance. The evidence of the past indicates that, when interest rates increase, appreciation slows down. *When rates decline, there is a price explosion!*

3.　**There are new buyers in the market.** The newest factors in the housing markets are the singles and seniors. In the singles market we see that many households no longer have both parents living on the premises. More and more people are choosing not to get married or are divorced and choosing to live alone. The result is the percentages of separate housing are increasing dramatically.

The senior market is also booming. Seniors are living for years and years longer, and that too is creating a strong demand for housing.

Finally, there are all the baby-boom children. During the 1970s roughly 32 million Americans reached the age of 30, the prime buying age for first-time buyers. That's 32 million buyers!

Guess how many Americans are projected to reach that same age of 30 during this decade. The answer is astonishing. It's 42 million! That is nearly a 50 percent increase. Twelve million *more* Americans will reach the age of 30—the age when they want to buy—during this decade than last.

All of these singles, seniors, and new families need housing. Go into any real estate office and ask if there is any shortage of buyers.

The answer will be no. There's a great shortage of buyers who can qualify for purchase. But not a shortage of buyers.

Just let the interest rates—and the accompanying monthly payments—take a dip, so that more people can afford the housing that's out there and we could see that large volume of resale homes disappear overnight.

4.　**Real supply is short.** New housing starts have been cut to about a third of what they once were. The reason, as we have seen, is that buyers simply cannot afford to purchase. No builder is purposely going to construct a house that he can't sell. But what happens when interest rates drop, *or incomes rise,* and people are able to afford housing again? As I noted, the existing surplus will be used up very quickly.

And it will be a long time before new houses are built! Remember, it takes three years from the time a project is conceived to the time houses actually come out the other end of the pipeline. What will happen during the three-year period once people can afford to buy?

The answer is that prices will escalate. Few houses, lots of people buying, and up go prices.

A 90-YEAR PERSPECTIVE ON NEW HOME PRICES

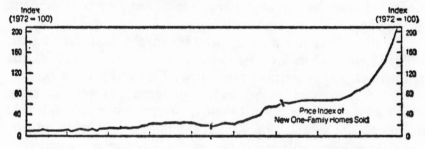

5. **Offshore investors are flooding in.** Many people other than Americans are investing in U.S. housing and other U.S. real estate. The United States is the best place in the world to live. Given a choice, more people choose the U.S. than any other country. There are many reasons for this.

One reason is that we have a stable economic system. It might not seem so when we look at double-digit inflation and high interest rates. But, compared with other countries, our inflation and interest rates have traditionally been low. In England, for example, an inflation rate approaching 20 percent has been the case for many years. Comparing costs of goods and services shows that prices are 80 percent higher in Japan, 50 percent higher in Britain, and over 40 percent higher in France and

West Germany. In Italy inflation has skyrocketed, as it has in most of the countries in South America. In Israel, inflation has been over 100 percent for at least the past three years.

Another attraction to living here is that the U.S. has not fought a war on its own soil in this century and, excepting an all-out nuclear shoot-out, is not likely to. There is almost no other country that can make that statement. While the oil-rich countries of the Middle East have great wealth, they do not have great political stability. In every one of them the possibility of revolt or outside invasion is a constant threat. That is why the sheiks and other wealthy individuals come to the U.S. to spend their money. And what do they buy? You guessed it. They buy U.S. real estate.

Even those countries in Western Europe, such as Germany and Switzerland, that have long and stable economies find that their citizens are coming here to buy. Having a Russian bear right next door is quite an incentive to move across the ocean!

Finally, the last big incentive to foreigners is our *cheap prices!* As high as the prices seem to us, by comparison to the rest of the world, they are cheap. The very best investment you can make may be in your own back yard!

Americans have become accustomed to having The Big Three at low cost. What I call The Big Three are:

> Housing
> Energy
> Interest rates

Well, times are changing. We have already seen that the days of low-cost energy are gone. Interest rates are also rising. (Right now the federal government is borrowing billions of dollars. This not only forces up interest rates, but also takes money away from business, home owners, and other segments of the private sector.) And our housing costs have gone up as well.

Yet our housing, when compared to the rest of the world, is cheap. For example, if we were to go to Hong Kong, where some of the world's highest priced housing exists, you might find that the typical three-bedroom home is selling for $300,000! At the same time, the median price for a similar home in the U.S. is about $65,000.

In Switzerland the story is not a whole lot better. A one-bedroom there might cost $200,000! And in most of the world there simply is no longterm financing. Typically, the buyer pays *all cash* or obtains short-term bank financing for usually no more than half the cost of the home.

Closer to home, in Canada, the loans for first mortgages are currently for 1 to 3 years at 20 to 23 percent.

The point is that, when housing prices and financing are taken together, property in the U.S. is a bargain. Just ask anyone who comes here from overseas. Often they are amazed at what they can buy . . . for so little!

People come to the United States, therefore, because of stability, security and cheap prices. And they compete with us for housing. Is there any possible result except stronger demand?

6. Government regulations may ease. Many of the smartest people I know believe that government overregulation is strangling the real-estate market. Duplication and incidental filings have upped the cost of bringing a house to market by at least 25 percent and increased the lead time to at least three years. This has cut down construction and led to a dwindling supply.

But some of us sense a new shift in the political winds. Both in Washington and in state and local governments, people are awakening to the real cost of overregulation. They are beginning to see (as Thomas Jefferson pointed out) that the best government may be the least government.

Overregulation has not brought about the great benefits it promised. Our air is not appreciably cleaner, our views not much better, and our population not that much healthier, better fed or better housed.

Rather, overregulation has created a bureaucratic nightmare. Hundreds of thousands of people have been given artificial jobs at public expense overseeing regulations that, in many cases, are neither necessary nor wise. The taxpayer has had to bear the burden of overregulation.

Overregulation has increased the cost of housing and the home buyer, instead of getting a better product in a more beautiful environment, finds that he or she cannot afford to buy at all!

The public and the policymakers are awakening. There is a move afoot to slice through the red tape, to cut it out and go back to the old marketplace way of doing business.

Regulation will not be done away with entirely. But I do expect to see, within the next few years, a big effort made to do away with *unneeded* regulation. I expect to see, in community after community, the wise and the affected rise up against rent control, against overregulation of buildings and land, against the bureaucratic nightmare, for one reason—their own self-interest. People will rise up because they want to save their own money. They will rise up because they want homes to be affordable again.

I can see a time in the future when, instead of more and more government regulation, we will have no more, and may even have less.

7. There are still healthy lenders. The S & L's are the backbone of the real-estate industry. They are the ones who supply more than half of all the money to finance homes. And they are the ones who are in big trouble.

Do I expect a government bail-out?

Certainly not. The government is cutting corners and trimming the budget in Washington and in the various states. There is no fat left to bail out the savings and loan industry.

Do I see a savings and loan collapse?

Certainly not. Those in government may not always be wise, but they are never immune to public opinion. And public opinion would never tolerate a financial collapse of the savings and loan industry. People in America have faith in their financial institutions, and they want their government to keep that faith. If there is a savings and loan association that is in trouble, the government will either merge it with a healthier institution or dissolve it and pay off the depositors. Never, never, never will the government allow the public to lose faith in the financial institutions. The lessons of the Great Depression are not that far in the past.

No bail-outs, but no collapses either. The All Savers certificates, plus the ability of S & L's to cross state lines to acquire failing S & L's, among other techniques, will permit their survival.

The savings and loans are going through a tough period right now, but what I see happening is a gradual resurgence of their strength.

One of the important factors in this is that they will soon be relatively free from government regulations themselves. Current indications are that by 1985 there will be *no regulations* governing the amount of interest a savings and loan association may pay a depositor.

While that at first sounds like it could mean higher interest rates on mortgages, as the savings and loans pay higher amounts on deposits, the opposite could be true. As the savings and loans are able to compete with money market mutual funds, depositors will come back to them. They will start bulging with money once more, and when they do, they will be able to lend that money out again.

The money will, of course, be more expensive—the days of single-digit mortgages are gone forever. But, unlike today, the money will be readily available.

8.   Interest rates WILL drop. It may seem that they are going to be high forever, but we must remember that all things pass. We have had a few years of high rates. But, prior to that, we had nearly fifty years of low rates.

As inflation temporarily ebbs, so will high interest rates. Healthy lenders will also contribute to periods of relatively lower interest rates. And, as I pointed out earlier, there are literally millions of people waiting on the sidelines, ready to jump into the real-estate market the minute rates decline.

It is popular to say that the real-estate market is in desperate straits today. Doug Casey, in his book *Crisis Investing*, suggests that the real-estate market will collapse because of a lack of financing. In the book *The Coming Real Estate Crash*, the authors suggest that the many similarities between today's market and other markets that have collapsed (going back to the tulip market in Holland hundreds of years ago!) indicate a crash. And there are numerous other gloom-and-doom forecasters. (If the world is really coming to an end, why do Howard Ruff and others sell lifetime subscriptions to their newsletters?)

Getting back to reality, I think we have to look at the real-estate market in America as unique. As we did in the last chapter, we have to look at the downside—the reasons it is failing, and failing badly.

But, as we have just done here, we also need to look at the market's strengths and its potential for the future.

I agree that things do look grim. But I think that if we are honest with ourselves, we think rationally, and then we have to admit that this may be a unique time of opportunity.

3

The Last Train Out
for the 1980s

**Certainly you can have a crash in housing; it is thinkable, but
unthinkable, like nuclear war.**
—Adam Smith

WHAT IS A CRISIS?

The word *crisis* evokes fearful images for us. We see the collapse
of the current order as being inherent in it. When it's a real-
estate crisis, we see a collapse of the market.

In reality, though, what is a crisis but a turning point?

If we were to plot the current real-estate crisis on a graph,
it might look something like this:

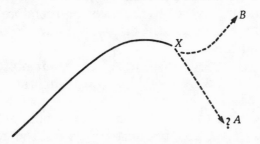

The solid line represents the real-estate market. As you can see,
in the past the trend had been up for a long time. The *X* repre-

35

sents today, and shows that we've turned down. Now is the time of crisis.

A and *B* represent the two different directions that real estate can take. It can continue to get worse and fall toward *A*. Or it can reverse the trend of the moment and start back upward toward *B*.

If the market were to turn upward to *B*, I think that we all would say to ourselves "Hey, it's time to get on the bandwagon again. We've got to go out there, buy, buy, buy, and get rich."

But if the market were to continue downward toward *A*, it would be a different story. Here's where all the gloom and doom would enter. Here's where some people would say "Sell today because the price will be much lower tomorrow."

I want to address both possibilities in a moment, but right here I think what's important to understand is that the real-estate market *will not* "crash" in the sense that most of us understand the word. The price of houses and other real estate *will not* continue downward forever.

There is *never* going to come a time in the future when the price goes down to zero. It just won't happen. Even during the greatest depression this country ever saw, in the 1930s, prices dropped to perhaps 50 or 60 percent of earlier values, and then only in certain areas. Never did real estate go for free.

If the market plummets, surely it will eventually bounce back. Some day in the future it will turn upward. If you think about it, you'll see that it has to happen. We went through all of the reasons for fundamental market strength in the last chapter. Some day they will prevail.

Of paramount importance to the investor, therefore, becomes the question, where are we in the crisis right now? Where is real estate as you read this?

Is it still heading down toward *A*? Or has it bottomed out already and headed upward toward *B*. Most important, what do we do in either case?

I'll get to the what-to-do question in just a moment, but first let's consider how we can tell exactly where the real-estate market is at any given time. As I'm writing this I could tell you very precisely where the market is. But, that might not do much good if you read this a month or a year from now. You will need to judge for yourself where the market is. And doing that is not hard at all.

One of the best ways *not to know* is to listen to the commentators of radio, television and the other news media. Most of these people know little or nothing about the real-estate market. Most of the time they have one or two statistics, which they may be using out of context to prove a point that may not be true.

The best way to know where we are in the crisis is to look at those market indicators that give us the accurate information. Basically there are eight indicators to watch. They tell us very precisely what the real-estate market is doing.

1. New housing starts
2. Resale volume
3. Median prices for resale of homes
4. Mortgage interest rates
5. Inflation
6. Delinquency rate of home mortgages
7. Foreclosure rates
8. Increases or decreases in government regulation of new housing

Let's consider each of these separately.

NEW HOUSING STARTS

Every time a builder begins work on a new home, he must obtain a building permit from the local government. These permits are recorded and statistics are kept by the Commerce Department and other agencies. Once each month the number of new homes started is released to the public.

In good years, housing starts are between 1.3 and 1.7 million annually. Anything below 1.3 is considered bad. Recently the figures have been far below 1.3.

Given the current crisis situation, it may be best to check not just the annualized starts, but the direction over a period of several months. If, for example, in May the annualized figure is 0.7 million, in June it's 0.8 million, by July it's 0.9 million, and by August it's up to 1.2 million, indications are that the market is experiencing a phenomenal recovery. You don't have to wait to reach the magical 1.3 number to know that things are improving, and *fast*. It's an indication the housing market is quickly turning around. On the other hand a similar movement in the other direction would signal a worsening situation.

New housing starts are a significant indicator because they quickly give us the overall health of the builders. They quickly tell us whether builders see enough potential in the market to risk their money on new housing. The figure, however, is somewhat deceptive because housing "starts" don't mean houses sold, or even houses built. Starts only means that builders started work. Thus it measures the builders' perception of the market.

RESALE VOLUME

This is an excellent indicator of the state of the housing market from moment to moment. It is a statistic that tells us how many houses were actually sold in the resale market.

In general, the greater the volume, the better the market. The lower the volume, the more trouble the market is in. The resale market is enormous, with often 3 or 4 million homes sold each year. Just as for the new housing starts, figures are usually given for the last month and on an annualized basis.

If you see sales volume picking up quickly, it's a good sign that a market turnaround is underway. Reduced sales volume means trouble. Beware, however, of seasonal changes. Generally the summer months always show greater volume, the winter months less.

The resale figures are compiled by local Realtor® boards across the country. National figures are compiled by the national office in Chicago. The figures can be obtained many ways. Often they are reported in newspapers or magazines.

In addition, most areas of the country have a legal or business paper that reports vital economic statistics, and will carry resale figures. It's well worth a few dollars to subscribe to one of these.

Finally, if all else fails, you can call your local Board of Realtors®.

They will almost always be happy to give the figures to you.

MEDIAN SALE PRICES FOR HOMES

This is another figure supplied by Realtor® groups. But, it is a statistic often misused, so we must be careful in its application.

The median sales price is the "middle" price. It is the price above which half the homes were sold and below which the other half were sold in the latest reporting month.

Many people take this to mean that it is an index of prices in the housing market. It is not always that.

When prices are going up overall, we tend to see a general increase in the median sales price. Through the 1970s we saw substantial median price increases year-to-year. This was widely interpreted, generally accurately, to mean that the price of all homes was going up.

Recently, however we've seen a decline in the median sales price. Does that mean that the prices of all houses are declining?

Not necessarily. Remember, the indicator is for the mid-price of homes SOLD. A lowering of the median price may merely mean that in today's market, more lower-priced homes are being sold than higher-priced homes. It can merely mean a changing in the direction of buyers. (Buyers can't afford the mortgages on higher-priced homes, so they are purchasing lower-priced ones.)

A lowering of the median price, with a high volume of homes sold, probably is an indication more of a change in buyer preference than a change of the market. A sharp drop in median price accompanied by a drop in sales volume, however, could mean that the market is in very serious trouble.

THE MORTGAGE INTEREST RATE

This is the most important indicator. It is the interest rate charged by major lenders for first mortgages on homes. Within the past few years it has been as low as 11 percent and as high as 17.5 percent.

This figure is widely reported in the press. It's almost harder to miss it than to see it! If you have any doubts, just call up two or three local S & L's or banks or your real-estate broker. You'll quickly find out what it is.

In today's market, a drop in the mortgage interest rate will probably signal the start of an upturn more clearly than any other indicator. In the summer of 1980, interest rates that had been hovering around 15 percent dropped suddenly to 12 percent during a two-month period. During that same period, housing sales volume almost doubled and median price appreciation accelerated!

The mortgage interest rate is the biggest single indicator to the housing market. If it comes down and stays down, we almost certainly will see the other indicators—and the market—turn upward.

If, however, mortgage interest rates remain high or get higher, we may see the "patient" become moribund.

INFLATION

Inflation is most conveniently measured by the Consumer Price Index (CPI). This is published monthly and widely disseminated in the press and on television.

I include inflation here, not because it directly affects the real-estate market (although it does in terms of the cost of building), but because it indirectly affects interest rates.

Interest rates are high, presumably, because the Federal Reserve is using high interest rates to combat inflation. If inflation falls and remains down, interest rates can be expected to follow suit. Watching inflation, therefore, is a good indicator of what interest rates are likely to do several months into the future.

DELINQUENCY RATES ON HOME MORTGAGES

When a home buyer fails to make a mortgage payment on time, the lender sends out a notice and assesses a late charge. When the borrower fails to make several payments, the lender not only assesses a late charge, but declares the borrower in default. Depending on the state, that gives the borrower anywhere from a few weeks to half a year or more to make the mortgage current.

The delinquency rate on home mortgages is a compilation of all the defaults in a particular month across the country. It does not count the one-month late payment with late charge. It does count the defaults.

Both the government and the home building industry watch delinquency rates closely. They are reported, but are rarely picked up by the media. To find them, you will probably have to subscribe to a local business newspaper or check with your local Homebuilders' Association.

This rate is important because it indicates how well borrowers are able to make mortgage payments and it also indicates the priority mortgage payments have in borrowers' minds.

During the period of 1978 through 1980, delinquency rates were at an alltime low. The reason was that borrowers with then-existing mortgage interest rates found it easy to make their payments. And because they knew that housing prices were accelerating, their incentive to keep up mortgage payments was high.

Recently, however, with high interest rates and lower appreciation, the incentives and the ability to make mortgage payments have declined. Thus we have seen an enormous increase in delinquencies. In some areas the rates have jumped 200 and 300 percent.

A continuing increase in delinquency rates is a further indication of a downturn in the real-estate market. A slowing or a reduction in delinquency rates, however, would indicate a tightening up and improvement of the market.

THE FORECLOSURE RATE

When a borrower is delinquent on a mortgage, he or she has a period of time in which to make good. If the missed payments are made up, the mortgage is reinstated and all is as it was before. If the payments are not made up, ultimately the property is foreclosed. The lender takes it back.

In good times, the foreclosure rate is virtually zero. Whenever a borrower gets into trouble, all she or he has to do is advertise the house for sale and some investor will pop right in and pick it up.

In bad times, however, the foreclosure rate soars. It means that no investor can be found to bail out the home owner. The property has gone to sale and the bank has taken it back.

Any increase in the foreclosure rate is an almost certain sign of trouble in the real estate market. A big foreclosure rate is a sure sign of disaster. If the foreclosure rate should ever reach as much as 5 percent of the total volume of home sales, we would be reaching a condition almost equivalent to the housing collapse that occurred during the Great Depression. It would mean that one in 20 houses were being lost.

Most recently, the *delinquency* rate was up to about 5 percent, but the *foreclosure* rate was still around 1 percent. It's a critical figure to watch.

GOVERNMENT REGULATION

This is the toughest indicator to follow, but it's an important one.

As we saw with Harry the Builder, government regulation is adding enormously to the cost of building new homes. The next chapter shows that government regulation, in the form of rent control, is adding to the price of homes and acting to reduce the number of rental units purchased.

More government regulation is bad for real estate. Less government regulation is good.

But, how do we measure government regulation?

Unlike the other indicators, there is no single index to watch. Rather, it has to be a "gut feeling." It's a matter of watching the business and real-estate sections of the general papers and keeping a close tab on building-industry news by subscribing to several of the building-industry journals.

They all tend to announce new and stiffer government controls, as well as any relaxing of existing controls. More government regulation, along with a decline in the other seven indicators, means the real-estate industry is in deep trouble— far into the future.

Relaxed controls, along with upward indicators, means that the market may be headed for longlasting good times.

Government regulations is at best an uncertain indicator of longterm trends. But it is an important one.

These, then, are the eight indicators that tell us where we are in the current real-estate crisis. But once we've checked them out and ascertained our current position, *what do we do?*

WHAT TO DO?

If we as investors look at the statistics and see that the market is turning up, very likely we will want to jump on board and take advantage of it. Of course, we can always say "It's too difficult," or "It's too risky" and move to the sidelines. But *in an upward market, most investors get in, not out.*

If we see that the market is turning down, we have the same two alternatives.

(1) We can move to the sidelines and stop playing the game. If we have property, we can dispose of what we have at any cost or loss, take our money and go elsewhere. If we don't own property, we simply don't buy any.

(2) OR, we can continue to play. But now we take advantage of our understanding of the market. We try to take advantage of the crisis.

In either an upward or downward crisis, if you are the sort who wants to take his or her marbles and go home, feel free to do so. I'll understand. Just close the book at this point and read no further.

But if you do continue to read, I'm going to assume that you're not ready to quit yet. I'm going to assume that you want to continue with the game, if you can see profit and advantage for you.

"But, Hal," I hear a reader from Bend, Oregon, protest, "I can see getting in if the market's going up, but what if it is actually declining? You don't expect us to buy property during falling prices, do you?"

Yes, I do!

Remember, prices aren't going to fall forever. They will bottom out and turn upward. If you understand that, then you can make money even in a falling market. Doing it is known as *dollar cost averaging* and it's done in stocks and commodities all the time.

DOLLAR COST AVERAGING

I'm going to assume a period of six years. During the first three years, real-estate prices fall 10 percent a year. During the last three years, they appreciate 10 percent a year, so that after the full six years we are almost back to where we started.

Say that the average house costs $70,000 before the down cycle begins. Assuming three years of 10 percent drops, then three of 10 percent appreciation, here's what the prices would look like:

$70,000	Original price	
63,000	First year	10% drop
56,700	Second year	10% drop
51,030	Third year	10% drop
56,133	Fourth year	10% appreciation
61,746	Fifth year	10% appreciation
67,920	Sixth year	10% appreciation

Given this scenario, how would a smart investor take advantage of it?

The smart investor would buy a house each year. Assume that you were able to buy a house each year for five years, starting with the first year that prices dropped. Looking back at the prices in the table, the first house would cost $63,000, the second $56,700, the third $51,030, the fourth $56,133, and the fifth $61,746. Over the course of five years you would have invested a total of $288,609.

Well, you might ask, where is the profit in that?

The profit is there, believe me. Assuming that the houses you bought all move up and down right along with the overall real-estate cycle, at the end of the fifth year you would own five houses all worth $67,920. That is, each one of them is worth roughly $68,000.

$$\begin{array}{r} \$68,000 \\ \times 5 \\ \hline \$340,000 \end{array}$$

The five houses are worth roughly $340,000. Yet your investment was only about $289,000. *By dollar cost averaging, we have shown that you have a profit of approximately $51,000.* This is in addition to all the tax advantages and equity return on mortgages that you have accomplished. (As we'll see in later chapters, you will make money based only on tax advantages over the five years, even if there should be no appreciation at all!)

Dollar cost averaging will allow any investor to make a profit on the down cycle of a real estate market. What is more important to understand is that, while we chanced to pick a six-year cycle, *it doesn't really matter how long the cycle is or how far it drops.* Not only that, by using this method, we don't even have to predict the bottom! As long as we regularly buy each year on the way down, one of our purchases will be at the bottom. Then, when prices turn up, we'll find that we are making money.

Dollar cost averaging allows the little man to do in real estate what giant investors do in commodities and stocks.

"Hey, Hal, hold up a minute." It's the fellow from Oregon again. "I own four properties now. If things start getting really bad, wouldn't it be better for me to sell out and then buy back once prices drop way down?"

It's an interesting idea, but not a good one, for two reasons.

The first is that, unless you're very lucky or very psychic, you won't know when we've reached the bottom. You could be actually selling out at the bottom! I don't think you'd like that.

The second is that, with the real-estate commissions and closing costs that occur on sale, it simply isn't economical to bail out, planning to get back in later. If you want to continue playing the game, then you should take your lumps and hang in there. You'll make out fine once the market rebounds. Nine times out of ten it will cost you more to sell out now and buy back later.

It really is possible to make money in real estate during a down cycle. And it really does make sense to hold on during such a period.

As I said earlier, there definitely is reason for hope in our current real-estate crisis. But there is even more than hope. To see what I mean, let's examine the word *crisis*.

The Chinese word for *crisis* is a composite that carries two meanings. The first part connotes *danger*, and that certainly applies to our current situation. This is a dangerous time, and the person who ignores the danger could stumble and possibly sustain serious injury.

However, the second part of the Chinese word stands for *opportunity*.

This is the part of the crisis that we are just now beginning to look at. Yes, there is danger. But there is also opportunity. Let's look at the opportunities that this real-estate crisis may offer.

1.   There is still good financing available today. Billions of dollars in longterm, fixed-rate mortgages are still held by home-owners, and buyers can still come in and buy these properties "subject to" the existing financing.

This is a point that has been overlooked by many and is, I think, the reason that we may now be in a crucial period for home purchasing.

Tomorrow's financing is already descending upon us. It is based on fluctuating interest rates. When we get a new mortgage in the future, we will never know for sure what the interest rate will be. That rate could be raised or lowered every six months by the lender, depending on what happens in the short-term interest market. There won't be any way for us to lock into a long-term fixed interest rate.

Think what that means to you as a buyer. You buy a home at 12 percent but, because the short-term market goes wild, the next year you're paying 18 percent!

By contrast, in the existing home market of today, millions of homeowners have mortgages that they obtained in past years when interest rates were fixed. This financing is still available on many resales. It offers an opportunity that will be gone in just a few years.

Once this great financing is gone, or replaced by higher-value mortgages, buying and making a profit will be much harder.

2. The Federal National Mortgage Association (FANNIE MAE), which is a secondary lender (it buys mortgages from banks and savings and loans), currently has a huge portfolio of $48.1 billion in fixed-rate mortgages. And all of these are at an average interest rate of 9.1 percent! And (if they were issued before November 10, 1980) *all of these are assumable!*

This represents something like 5 percent of the entire housing market in this country. These low-interest, fixed-rate mortgages, *which are assumable,* are out there waiting for investors to take advantage of them.

3. Sellers are willing to assist in financing today. Think back to the housing market of just a few years ago. Then it was a seller's market. Buyers were clamoring for any house that was offered for sale. Sellers in some areas were actually getting *more* for their house than they were asking! Some sellers were pulling their houses off the market because they saw greater opportunity in holding than in selling.

And, in those days, what did every seller want? He or she wanted *cash*! The buyer had to arrange a new mortgage and pay the difference in cash. Seller financing was almost unheard of. Why should a seller help a buyer with the financing when another buyer was just around the corner waiting to come in with cash?

But today it's far different. Today, sellers are desperate to sell and buyers with cash are almost non-existent. What that adds up to is that sellers are very willing to help buyers make the purchase. They will carry back second and third mortgages. Often they will arrange for these mortgages to have no payments until they come due three to five years in the future. In many cases these sellers will sell for nothing down!

What this all adds up to is an unprecedented buying opportunity!

4. **There is a sense of fear on the part of many.** They have read about indications of a crash. For sellers, this means they are anxious to sell. It means that all of a sudden there are a lot of distressed sellers. Today we are seeing more probate, foreclosure and trust-deed sales than at any time since the early 1970s.

Yet, those who believe that the market is going to turn up (for reasons we have already given) are scooping up this distressed property. They are acting the same way that investors who are now millionaires did during the Great Depression, and again during the recession of 1974–75.

THE LAST TRAIN OUT FOR THE 1980s

Yes, there is a real-estate crisis. Yes, there is danger. But yes, yes, yes, there is also opportunity!

Today we may be witnessing the last great buying opportunity in real estate.

Real estate is the only investment I know of today that offers the small investor the ability to control huge assets with very little risk. You can't do it in stocks, in commodities, in bonds, in gold, in silver, or any place else. And this opportunity is in its twilight.

The real-estate world is changing. Tomorrow we will no longer have the financing that is still in place today. Tomorrow it will be far, far harder for the small investor to get started. Tomorrow will be the day of the real-estate barons.

Today is still the time of the little guy.

Essentially, this chapter has been about timing. When should I invest? Here is my answer.

Invest now!

The time to invest is *during* the crisis. The time to invest is when people are worrying that the market is going to collapse—that real estate is soon going to be worthless.

As I noted earlier, we really can't know if we're at the bottom or not. We won't know until much later, when we look back and say, "Hey, that was the bottom six months ago. Everything's been going up since then." Of course, by then it's too late to profit by it.

TAKE ADVANTAGE OF THE CRISIS!

While everyone else is moaning and groaning about how terrible real estate is, *buy*. When everyone else is selling at fire-sale prices, *buy*. When no one thinks too much about that super-terrific financing that's still available, *buy*.

Today may be the last opportunity for you. Today is the last train out for this decade.

4

How to Stop Foreclosure

If you ever need a heart transplant, hold out for a lender's heart . . . 'cause it ain't ever been used.

In the remainder of this book I am going to show you where the real-estate opportunities are today and how you can take advantage of them. You will see how to control property with low down payments and little or no negative cash flow. You will see how to become financially free in just five years!

Before we can move toward our goals of real-estate profit, however, we need to know where we are right now. Where are you in the real estate market?

To help you find out, I have developed the questionnaire beginning on p. 52. It is simple and easy to fill out. Usually it is surprising. It will help you to rank yourself with everyone else in real estate.

I think the questionnaire helps us to be honest with ourselves about a lot of things. It helps us to pinpoint what we have realistically. Even more important in many cases, it helps us to identify our goals.

Now I want you to try a little test. I want you to think of the real-estate market as a giant pile of investors, all struggling to make money and achieve their goals. Almost all of them have

INVESTMENT AND ESTATE
PLANNING OBJECTIVES

(Rank in order of importance)

1. Long-term growth _____   4. Minimizing taxes _____

2. Current income _____   5. Hedge against inflation _____

3. Retirement income _____   6. Other *(please specify)* _____

CURRENT SITUATION

A. CURRENT ANNUAL INCOME   B. CURRENT ANNUAL
                                              TAXES

		Sole proprietorship or partnership income		State income tax	$_____
Salary	$_____				

Real estate _____   Federal income tax $_____

Investments _____ Other _____   Tax bracket (%) _____

                                   Total $

C. MONTHLY LIVING EXPENSES _____   Monthly cash available _____

D. ASSETS _____

Property	Cost or Other Basis	Loan Balance	Present Fair Market Value	Registration 1. Husband or Individual 2. Wife 3. Joint Tenant 4. Tenancy in Common
Savings account	$_____	$_____	$_____	_____
Checking account	_____	_____	_____	_____
Home	_____	_____	_____	_____

Business _____ _____ _____ _____ _____

Securities _____ _____ _____ _____ _____

  (Other real estate)
  (List below):

_____ _____ _____ _____ _____

_____ _____ _____ _____ _____

_____ _____ _____ _____ _____

_____ _____ _____ _____ _____

_____ _____ _____ _____ _____

_____ _____ _____ _____ _____

_____ _____ _____ _____ _____

_____ _____ _____ _____ _____

What assets do you have that you could trade or exchange (real estate, boat, motor home, diamonds, etc.)

_____

_____

_____

(Continue on separate sheet if necessary)

Property	Cost or Other Basis	Loan Balance	Present Fair Market Value	Registration 1. Husband or Individual 2. Wife 3. Joint Tenant 4. Tenancy in Common
Other *(List):*				
Automobile _____	_____	_____	_____	_____
Jewelry _____	_____	_____	_____	_____
Collectibles (stamps, etc.) _____	_____	_____	_____	_____
	_____	_____	_____	_____
	_____	_____	_____	_____
Total	$_____	$_____	$_____	_____

E. LIFE INSURANCE _____

Type of Policy	Total Insurance	Insured	Beneficiary	Cash Value	Annual Premium
_____	$_____	_____	_____	$_____	$_____
_____	_____	_____	_____	_____	_____
_____	_____	_____	_____	_____	_____
_____	_____	_____	_____	_____	_____
_____	_____	_____	_____	_____	_____
Total	$			$	

RETIREMENT SITUATION

Social security	$_____	Annuities	_____
Pension or profit sharing plan	_____	Trust beneficiary	_____
		Other	_____
Investments	_____	Total	$

MISCELLANEOUS DETAILS

Indicate Any
Particular Problems   (any possible problems lawsuits, health etc.)

Total liabilities $_____   _____

Anticipated
  inheritance $_____   _____

List gifts that you
  would like to
  make to any
  individuals.   _____   _____

                        _____   _____

                        _____   _____

                        _____   _____

GOALS

Each Individual is to write down or answer the following without consultation with each other.

1. Things I have wanted to do but have never done.

---

2. Things I have wanted to be and have never been.

---

3. Things I have wanted to have and have never had.

---

4. Places I want to go and have never been.

---

5. One-year goals.

---

6. Five-year goals.

---

a single goal: financial independence. I want you to find your place in the pile.

TOP OF THE PILE

These are the investors who got into real estate some time back. You own your own home, plus other real estate. It could be some rental houses or an apartment building or two. Maybe a commercial center of an office building is part of your portfolio. To a large degree, you have "made it" in real estate.

MIDDLE OF THE PILE

You are someone who owns his or her own home. But, in terms of real estate, that's about it. You may have a few bucks in the bank, some life insurance, and a few other assets. But, although you've got a foot on the first rung of the ladder of financial success, you still have a long way to go. You would like to grow a lot bigger.

UNDER THE PILE

You're just starting out. You haven't had time to acquire any assets or wealth. You're renting and don't own your own home. You have little or no money in the bank. You may have a good job, but you're spending your money as fast as you make it (a good portion of it in taxes). You haven't done any asset building. You would like to get that foot on the first rung of the ladder, but it looks mighty difficult. You would like to cut your income taxes. You would like to get off to a good start.

Where are you in the pile? Are you on top, in the middle or underneath?

Be honest! You won't get to a better position until you honestly admit where you are now.

Let me tell you a few things about these positions in the pile. In one respect, the person on the bottom is in the best position! You know why? Because the only way to go is up!

The person in the middle or at the top can indeed move further up, but they can also fall. This is particularly true for the person on top. If you're at the apex of the heap, chances are you have been having some sleepless nights lately. During this crisis, if you are heavily leveraged in real estate (as most on the top are), you are worrying a lot about losing what you have. You've got two worries, compared to the person underneath—you want to protect what you've got as well as move on up. The person on the bottom only worries about moving up.

WHAT TO DO?

If you are the worried person at the top, in just a few paragraphs I am going to show you how to *keep what you've got.* We will talk about solutions to two of the biggest problems during this real-estate crisis; (1) What to do with large negative cash flows (having to take money out of your own pocket to keep your property away from foreclosure), and (2) large second mortgages coming due.

Once I have given some strategies for those of you on top and in the middle, then I'm going to point out how to take advantage of the opportunities in today's real-estate market no matter where you are in the pile.

You're going to see how, even if you have no assets, have no cash to put down, have no income to handle negative cash flows, you can control real estate. We'll talk about one individual who started with nothing at all and in the last two years took control of 22 properties—and now has $1500 in positive cash flow going into his pocket every month!

We are going to take a long, hard look at financing techniques that will help you get started during this crisis, so that you can move up and achieve financial freedom through real estate within five years. *In the last chapter of the book we will even talk about the 20 top spots for investing in real estate in the United States.*

But first, if you already own property, let's get to the solutions to your two biggest problems.

NEGATIVE CASH FLOW PROBLEMS

Typically this hits the person who has several properties, all with negative cash flows. Our investor, who I'll call Pete, could handle one or two negative cash flows, but suddenly he finds that he has seven or eight, and he cannot handle them all.

Here's how it happened.

Pete got started in real estate about three years ago. He bought a home for $60,000 with 10% ($6000) down. Another 10 percent of the purchase price came from a second mortgage for $6000 at 12%, and he borrowed the rest as a first mortgage of $48,000 at 11%.

$ 6,000	cash down		
6,000	second mortgage	at 12%, payable	$ 60 per month
48,000	first mortgage	at 11%, payable	457 per month
$60,000	purchase price		$517 monthly payment

Pete also has additional monthly payments of $100 in taxes and insurance, making his total monthly payment $617 per month. When he bought the property, Pete could only rent it for $450 per month. That meant that he had a negative cash flow of $167 per month:

$617 expenses
− 450 income
$167 negative cash flow per month

Deducting all the interest, the taxes, and a sizeable amount for depreciation helped Pete to offset this loss. But, putting that aside for a moment, let's remember his negative cash flow was $167 per month.

Now it's two years later. Pete is renting the same property for $625 per month. Instead of a negative cash flow, he's getting a *positive* cash flow because he raised the rent. And he still has the same tax benefits.

Additionally, his property—instead of being worth $60,000—is worth $80,000. Old Pete's doing great! So he decides to refinance.

$80,000	current value
× 80%	percent of value mortgaged
$64,000	new mortgage
− 6,000	pay off existing second
− 48,000	pay off existing first
$20,000	cash left after refinance

In two years Pete has generated $20,000 in cash from his property. Now he decides to pyramid his money. He goes out and buys *seven* more houses. On each deal he puts no money down.

He uses the $20,000 to pay his closing costs, which leaves him $10,000 in a slush fund to help cover the negative cash flow.

The new homes he buys cost an average of $80,000 apiece, and the deals are structured like this:

$ 8,000	third mortgage carried by seller
8,000	second mortgage purchased from mortgage broker
64,000	first mortgage from savings and loan
$80,000	purchase price

Pete's payments look like this:

Third mortgage	due in three years, no payments		
Second mortgage	at 18% payable at	$100	monthly
First mortgage	at 14%, payable at	758	monthly
plus taxes and insurance		150	monthly
		$1008	
Income		− 700	
		$ 308	negative flow

Pete has a negative cash flow *on each* of these seven new properties of $300 a month. He also has a negative cash flow of about $200 on his first property *because* he refinanced and got a new and higher-interest-rate mortgage. If we add up all his negative cash flows we find the following:

$$
\begin{array}{rl}
\$300 & \text{negative} \\
\times \quad 7 & \text{no. of properties} \\
\hline
\$2,100 & \\
+ \quad 200 & \text{from first property} \\
\hline
\$2,300 &
\end{array}
$$

Pete had a total negative cash flow of $2,300.

Why did Pete get himself into such a predicament?

The answer is simple. On his first property, Pete made $20,000 in cash in only two years of ownership. If he could do the same in the next two years with seven more properties, he could make at least $140,000. *Pete did it to make money.*

The trouble is, Pete didn't realize just how bad the negative cash flow was going to be. Also, he didn't count on prices not appreciating. Remember, we are assuming a further downtrend in the market.

How is Pete going to meet his $2300 in negative cash flow each month? He figures he can make up about $500 of it per month from his salary. There is only about $5000 left in his slush fund from the refinancing of his first house. When that is gone, what is Old Pete going to do?

Even with the $500 he can make up from his income, and the $5000 in the slush fund, he can only go for four or five months more before he runs out of money.

Is Pete up the creek without a paddle? Is he going to lose all of his properties? Is he going to lose some of them? Is he going to be a distressed seller? Is Pete washed up?

Pete's situation, though exaggerated to make a point, is not far from that of a lot of investors who have either been on the top of the pile for a while or have just scrambled to the top. For one reason or another, they all have big negatives. Even though they control a lot of property, that property is threatened by the excessive negative cash flow.

Pete doesn't have to come out a loser. I'm going to give him five solutions to his cash flow problem. If he uses them, he'll transform a crisis into a positive turning point.

(Note: if you're in a position similar to Pete's, listen up. This will help you. If you're not, you might want to read carefully anyway. Some of these solutions could help you get out of other real-estate problems, or even help you get into the field.)

Solution 1

The first thing Pete should do is make a list of everyone he knows who fits the following three criteria:

1. Has a tax problem because of high income
2. Is not currently an investor
3. Has a strong cash-flow situation

There are lots and lots of people who fit these criteria. Pete found two of them at the country club he belongs to. They both happened to be doctors. They had large incomes from their profession. That income was in the form of a strong cash flow. Yet, because they didn't have time to go out and find investments and manage them, they simply didn't invest. This meant that they were paying huge taxes to Our Favorite Uncle.

Pete proposed the following to each of them:

1. We'll form a limited partnership. A limited partnership is a partnership where some of the partners (in this case, the doctors) have limited liability. They can participate in profits and in tax write-offs. But they can't be sued, even for a personal injury. And normally they can't lose any more money than they invest. A general partner, on the other hand (in this case, Pete), manages the property, has overall liability, and can be sued (thus potentially can lose more than he invests).

2. The doctors would receive 100% of the tax write-off. That means that they would be able to deduct from their income taxes:

    a. *All* the interest on the mortgages of all Pete's
       properties.
    b. *All* the taxes on all the properties.
    c. *All* the depreciation on all the properties.
    d. *All* the negative cash flow.

3. **In exchange, the doctors would have to come up with all of the money to pay the negative cash flow,** or $2300 per month.

4. **When it eventually comes time to sell the properties, the profits will be split 50/50.**

5. **Pete would manage all the properties.** Do you think those doctors would go for a deal like that? Do you think they would invest in properties that were, in effect, losing over $2000 a month? Do you think they would put their good money in after Pete had already almost gone broke on the houses? Do you think they're crazy?

Yes! Crazy like foxes.

Here's why. Those doctors with their big incomes were paying Our Favorite Uncle 50 percent of everything they made. When state income taxes were thrown in, the figure was even higher. But if they put $2300 a month into a "losing" operation, such as the houses Pete owned, right away they saved on their income taxes. The $2300 was immediately tax deductible. In a 50% tax bracket, instead of putting up $2300 a month, they were really putting up only about $1150 a month. The government was putting up the other half (in funds that would otherwise have been collected as taxes).

Then there was depreciation on eight houses. Do you have any idea how much depreciation there is on eight houses? Let's see:

	$80,000	value
−	15,000	land (cannot be depreciated)
	65,000	building (can be depreciated)
÷	15 yrs	depreciation term (shortest used)
	4,333	yearly depreciation per house
÷	12	made monthly
$	361	per month

That's right! There is $361 per month depreciation on each house! (This is using a straight-line method. An accelerated method of 175% is now allowable, and that would increase the depreciation far more.)

$$\begin{array}{r} \$\ 361 \\ \times\ \underline{\quad 8} \\ \$2,888 \end{array}\ \begin{array}{l} \\ \text{total depreciation on all eight} \\ \text{houses} \end{array}$$

Those doctors could write off another $2,888 each and every month because of depreciation. In the 50 percent tax bracket that meant a savings in cash to them of $1444. Let's look at the total savings now:

$1150   *cash savings* because of negative cash flow
  1444   *cash savings* because of depreciation
$2594   total cash savings
− 2300   negative cash flow
$ 294   *cash into doctors' pockets* to buy eight houses per month!

That's right, it was paying those doctors $294 per month to buy those houses! And they got even more from savings on their *state* taxes! (And you wondered why they jumped at the chance to get in on Pete's deal!)

(**Note:** The depreciation probably would come back at the doctors as capital gain when the property is sold. Also, the payments on the houses must be made monthly, yet depreciation only comes once a year at tax time. Some may wonder if this causes a cash-flow problem? It doesn't. The doctors either produce withholding on their W-4 forms or on their estimated tax, so they receive tax write-off benefits monthly too.)

Old Pete didn't have to ask twice. The doctors jumped at his offer. Their tax situation and their need to invest and not have management headaches made them perfect partners.

The doctors really didn't care if the market was going down. They figured that someday it would come back up. And as long as it wasn't costing them anything, they'd wait. Chances are that in a few years rents would increase.

(Note: Our real-estate crash never mentioned rent decreases—with property as scarce as it is, rents are bound to increase).

If and when rents went up by $300 per month, the doctors would not have to make up any negative cash flow at all. And yet, they would still be getting tax benefits from depreciation. **They would be making a profit on no investment even before the properties were sold!**

A word of caution. In recommending this strategy, I always suggest contacting friends first. Putting an ad in the paper is a last resort, and may not work in some states that severely regulate partnerships.

Solution 2

All of us know some people who are really difficult to be around. Well, what is true for people also hold true for property. Properties tend to take on personalities. Some are easy-going and never demanding. They are always rented. The tenants always pay on time without complaints. There is never anything to be fixed. They are just the sweetest properties you could ever hope to meet.

But some properties are the other side of the coin. Their personalities are mean and ugly. There are constant vacancies. When they are rented, the tenants are always late with the rent. Sometimes you have to go to court to get them out. The plumbing is always broken. The roof leaks. The fence falls down. The garage door won't open. The built-in electric range burns out.

Let's say that we have seven or eight properties that we bought a few years ago. We have some equity in each. We still have some negative cash flow. But, because of our own equity position, we don't like the idea of giving away part interest in a limited partnership. What might we do in this circumstance?

If it were me, I'd pick the least glamorous property—the one with the worst personality—and sell it. I'd dump it, even at a loss, which might be the case in a falling market.

What I'd do is get out of the worst property with as much cash as possible. And then I'd use the cash to pay the negative cash flow on the other properties. I would buy time. I'd sacrifice my worst property in order to hang onto the others.

Why? Simple. As I noted before, even in a real-estate crash, the prices don't continue downward endlessly. They continue down until the financing and the economy as a whole stabilize. Then they turn around and head back up. If we can simply hang on to what we've got during this downward cycle, we'll be sitting pretty when the market comes back up.

(Some might argue that it would be best for us to bail out—sell the whole lot, even at a loss—and then, once the market turns around, buy back in. I don't think so. With commissions and closing costs so high, we'd lose more that way than by holding on through the worst of it.)

Getting rid of the property with the worst personality has a name. I call it *dumping the dog*.

Solution 3

This is a solution that will work in some markets when interest rates make sense. It won't work particularly well at the very time I'm writing this. But, it may work by the time you read this. The solution is to *refinance*.

If our friend Pete had some equity in his properties, if he had bought them a few years earlier and had been able to take advantage of price appreciation before our hypothetical crash, then when times got tough he could refinance. He could get new and bigger mortgages and use the cash to help make the payments. He could buy time in this fashion much as he could by dumping the dog, except by refinancing he wouldn't have to sell anything.

The trouble with this solution, of course, is high interest rates. When rates are high, it really doesn't pay to refinance. The carrying charges simply become prohibitive. What's the point of refinancing when you go from an old 10% mortgage to a new 17% one?

In the right market, refinancing works.

Solution 4

But, what if Pete is in the same situation as the first house we talked about back in solution 1. Now he has equity, real equity. He has between $20,000 and $40,000. But prices are dropping and he's lost his job, so he can't handle the negative, small though it may be. Refinancing (with him out of work and unable to handle the negative and without a bigger equity) is out of the question. What should Pete now do in a declining real-estate market?

Sell, of course. What else can he do?

Pete should sell immediately. And he should offer "soft terms." By that I mean he should sell for nothing down!

I realize that may come as something of a shock to some readers. Most readers think in terms of buying with nothing down. But selling? Only a fool sells to a buyer who puts up no cash.

Really? Well, Pete's no fool. He finds a buyer who will purchase for nothing down. But he insists that the buyer offer some other security. He ties up the buyer's other assets to be sure that the sale is secure.

Here's what I mean. Pete is going to sell his investment house for $80,000. He owes $65,000 which means that he has an equity in the property of $15,000:

$80,000   sales price
− 65,000   owed against property
$15,000   equity

Pete is looking for a buyer who can assume the $65,000 in existing debt. Then Pete will give this buyer a $15,000 second mortgage. The buyer will have to put nothing down. The only money he will have to come up with is closing costs. And given the fact that there is no new loan, these should be low.

Normally in such a deal, the great danger is that the buyer will feel no obligation to hang onto the property. If times get tough—if he can't rent or if the negative cash flow gets too hard—he'll walk away.

But not in Pete's deal. Pete's buyer is going to have to be very special. For one thing, he's going to have to have a strong positive cash-flow position from his personal job or business.

That's so he can handle the stiff payments that will occur under the first and second mortgage when Pete sells.

Second, he'll have to have some other assets that Pete can tie up.

It took Pete a month to find his potential buyer. It was an attorney who owned another house across town that happened to have a lot of equity in it. Here's the deal that Pete proposed:

$65,000	existing financing on Pete's houses
15,000	"blanket" mortgage covering both
	Pete's house and the attorney's other property
$80,000	sale price

What's a *blanket mortgage* and why did Pete insist on it?

A blanket mortgage is simply a loan that covers more than one piece of property. In this case it covers the attorney's other house as well as the house Pete is selling. It works like this. *Both* properties are liable for repayment of the $15,000. If the attorney were to walk away from Pete's house without keeping up the mortgage, Pete could foreclose not only on his own house, but also on the attorney's. Pete had effectively tied up the attorney's other assets. It wasn't likely that he would drop Pete's property when he knew he could lose his other equity property as well.

For Pete, the advantages are obvious. But, what about that attorney? Why would he give up the security in his other property to buy this one?

The answer is simple: *no money down.* The attorney would be buying a property on which he would have a strong negative cash flow, on which he would get good depreciation and write-off (remember the doctors from Solution 1) and on which the tax savings alone would allow him a small profit.

Additionally, if he held onto Pete's house until the next upswing in the market, he stood a good chance of making a healthy profit. All of this on *no investment* of his own. He wasn't putting anything in except closing costs.

The attorney was glad to go along. After all, he wasn't trying to steal Pete's house. He wasn't trying to buy it for nothing, live in it for a few months not paying the payments, and then move out. He legitimately intended it as an investment. As long as he was sure he would come out in the end, why should he mind putting up some other property as security?

Had Pete been aggressive, he would have realized that getting other assets wasn't limited to real estate alone. He could have tied up virtually anything, from diamonds to rare coins.

Also, it wasn't necessary to have a blanket mortgage. Pete could have taken a first or second mortgage on the other property instead of his and it would have worked out just as well.

All that Pete was doing was being sure that the buyer had enough assets to warrant the purchase. It's something that any prudent seller would do. And it's something that no honest buyer should object to.

At this point you may ask, How come he sold for nothing down? He had a big equity position in the property. Why didn't he sell in the normal way, for cash down?

The realities of today's market are that if you have a negative cash flow on a piece of property, you cannot expect a buyer to pay cash. In a market that is volatile, such as we're assuming here, there is even less reason to believe you can find a cash buyer. Besides, could it not be that the loss really occurred when you bought?

Solution 5

My next solution for a big negative cash-flow situation is one that I'll go into in much greater detail later in the book. It has to do with options. I call it *option to equity.*

Pete does something totally different, something that *works.*

Pete takes out an ad in the local newspaper. The ad states, "For rent—$800 per month."

The $800 happens to be enough to eliminate the negative cash flow on Pete's house. But even on a good day with the sun shining he can't hope to rent that house for more than $600 per month. That, after all is his negative cash-flow problem. He's bringing in $600 and paying out $800. So what is Pete up to?

When the potential tenants call, Pete begins talking with them and right off the bat explains that the house he has really is only worth $600 in rent.

But, if a tenant will rent that house for $800 per month and sign a 3- to 5-year lease, he'll give back the $200 a month difference plus a percentage of the profits after the end of the lease. He starts by offering the first interested tenant 10 percent of the profit.

Do you think a tenant would be interested?

Pete had them standing in line. After all, he had advertised for a tenant who could afford to pay $800 per month to begin with. Now, for virtually nothing, he was offering to refund that tenant the excess rent over what the house should get, *plus* give that tenant a portion of the profits.

The only thing the tenant would lose would be living in a slightly less expensive house. The tenant stands to gain!

Solution 6

You could try this.

You could advertise "rent to own" for $800 per month. When a tenant appeared, you could give that tenant a 12-month lease at the higher rental with an option to buy, at the end of the lease, at a price 10 to 15 percent higher than today's market.

The tenant might be eager. He or she could be locking into the purchase of a home.

The contract should include a provision that, if the tenant does not exercise the option after 12 months, he or she can try again with a new lease/option. My experience has been that most tenants in transactions like this do not exercise the option. Many times they want to renew the lease with another option.

It's important, in such a case, *not* to record the option. This is in case the tenant chooses not to exercise it. We can then get a new tenant under the same plan and without there being the "cloud" on the title that recording would make.

Unlike the previous solution, the tenant here feels that he or she is the owner-to-be of the property.

THE BIG SECOND MORTGAGE PROBLEM

Those big second mortgages sure looked good and seem so beneficial when you bought, but now they are coming due. Many of you at the top, or in the middle of the pile, are facing that second mortgage with more than a little consternation. Hang on, help is on the way.

Johnny bought a property just a few years ago. He was able to buy it only through a lot of heavy financing. In addition to a big first, he had the seller carry back a *large second mortgage*. The mortgage was for 12%, *all due in three years*. Johnny put very little down on the property. That big second is now giving him trouble.

Johnny figured when he bought his house that it would be easy to refinance in a few years. By then appreciation would have increased his equity. Lenders would be eager to give him a big new first mortgage, big enough to pay off his existing first and any big seconds he had. Here's the deal Johnny worked out:

$25,000	second mortgage
5,000	cash down
50,000	first mortgage
$80,000	purchase price

While the first mortgage was long term, that $25,000 second only had three years to run. Johnny figured that by year 3, his property would easily be worth $100,000. At that time he could refinance and get a big new 80% loan. That would have given him $80,000 in cash: enough to pay off the existing first, that big second, and even give him his original cash back again.

But Johnny didn't count on a downturn in the real-estate market. He didn't figure on a crisis. Instead of prices increasing, they started down.

As if that weren't trouble enough, interest rates were so high that refinancing became virtually impossible. Even if Johnny could have qualified for a 17% new first mortgage, he couldn't handle the negative on it.

Now it's two years later and Johnny is feeling very down-hearted. He's really worried about that second mortgage. In just 12 months he's going to owe that original seller the $25,000 (by the way, it was an interest-only second, so Johnny hasn't paid anything on principal). The way he sees it, he's going to lose the property, the $5000 cash he originally put up, as well as the neg-ative cash flow he's been paying for the past two years.

Of course, if it were just this one house, Johnny might wash his hands of it and say it was a lesson learned the hard way. But Johnny was on top of the pile. He owned eleven houses! And because he bought them for little down, they ALL have big sec-onds coming due! A big real-estate entrepreneur, Johnny is sud-denly about to fall. From the top of the pile, he's ready for a nosedive.

There are many people from the top or the middle of the pile who are in a position similar to Johnny's. Like Johnny, they too are looking for solutions. Here is what is recommended for them.

Johnny's basic assumptions were (1) that if he could hold on long enough, he would end up rich; (2) he didn't want to sell because he understood that with commission and closing costs and so forth, selling now and getting back into the market when prices turned around was just too costly. He wanted to hang on. He didn't want his big seconds to knock him out of the game.

Solution 1

Johnny's problem is made somewhat easier by the fact that he owes all of his big seconds to the original sellers of the proper-ties. This is not unusual. Perhaps 75 percent or more of all second mortgages in the country are owed to sellers.

Here's what Johnny can do.

Prior to the note's coming due (perhaps 12 to 14 months before it's due, in fact) Johnny should approach the lender (the old seller) and make him or her this offer.

1. I will increase the interest rate I'm paying on this second by three percentage points (if it were 10% he'd go to 13%, if it were 11% he'd go to 14%, and so forth).
2. This increase in interest will take effect *immediately. It will apply right now, even over the last year of the mortgage* during which I'm required only to pay the older, lower interest rate.
3. I will do these things IF you will extend the term of the second mortgage for an additional 3 to 5 years.

Johnny is buying time.

The lender, if he or she doesn't have any immediate use for cash, may very well go along with the offer. After all, it means getting a higher interest rate on the existing mortgage, bringing it closer to market rates. And it means a secure source of income from the second for three or more years into the future. It could be a very good deal.

For Johnny, it's an excellent deal. He's buying three to five more years for only 3% additional interest. What's 3%? On his $25,000 mortgage it's only $63 a month!

It's far cheaper than any refinance could be (if he could arrange it) and he's able to hang onto the property.

Other approaches for Johnny:

1. Pay a one-time fee for an extension.
2. Offer a shared-appreciation mortgage at same interest *plus* a percent of the profits.

Solution 2

The next solution could be used if the lender refused to renegotiate. This one would work whether the second was given by the original seller or was a hard-money second (a second mortgage obtained from the mortgage broker).

If Johnny has owned his property for a couple of years, chances are that if he didn't have that second on board he would not have negative cash flow. Without the second payments, he would have positive cash flow.

He should find a rich partner. Here's what he could offer a partner. He could offer an equity position—half or more of the equity in the property down to the first—in exchange for which the new partner would put up enough cash to pay off that big second coming due. (This is similar to Solution 1 that Pete used.)

In Johnny's case, where he has very little real equity, he would probably have to offer a potential partner a larger percentage of the equity. But that partner coming in (once the second is paid off) will have positive cash flow PLUS depreciation and other write-offs. He would probably end up getting tax-free cash out of the property. For the partner, it could be a good deal.

If Johnny had more equity in the property, the deal would be even nicer. If Johnny's second were $25,000 and he had $25,000 in equity, he could easily offer a partner a 50/50 split. With the partner getting cash flow and Pete handling management, it would be a highly workable arrangement.

Johnny's partner had to be someone who:

1. Had a substantial amount of cash on hand.
2. Wanted to invest in passive investments because of lack of time or motivation to be an active investor.
3. Wanted a cash-flow return.

Many other Americans who are nearing retirement age and are looking for good solid investments fill this need perfectly. Many young professionals with large incomes also would qualify.

Solution 3

Because I believe in win-win business solutions, *I do not recommend this*. However, honesty compels me to include it.

It is sometimes the case that investors are simply unaware of the first two solutions. They have procrastinated and suddenly find that their second is due and now the lenders want all their money.

At this point perhaps the only solution left is to "prepare for war."

In many states it is possible to transfer title to someone else *without* the consent of the lender. Let's assume our investor is Johnny. What he might do is form a limited partnership and transfer title to the property to the partnership. Then he could bankrupt the partnership.

This all comes down to a little-known and little-used part of the bankruptcy law, which permits a real-estate partnership to file bankruptcy without any taint on the limited partners.

While in bankruptcy, the lender *may not* complete foreclosure proceedings.

Johnny would have some more time. He would buy it in a way that's very expensive for the lender, yet not terribly expensive for him. By transferring title to the partnership, he has avoided personal bankruptcy and kept his own record clean. By having the partnership go into bankruptcy, he prevented the lenders from:

1. Getting his money
2. Foreclosing on the property
3. Or even gaining sufficient control to rent the property out for income.

All Johnny has to do is to pay his own attorney's fees (to keep the partnership in bankruptcy) and to prove via an independent appraisal that there's equity to protect in the property.

Of course, this maneuver won't last forever. Usually it's good for only about two to three years. In the meantime, however, Johnny doesn't have to make any payments on the mortgage.

What's the ultimate advantage to Johnny?

The advantage is that, if the market turns around during that period of time, Johnny may eventually be able to sell for sufficient money to pay off his back mortgage payments and make a profit. Johnny has bought time.

Probably Johnny will never need to go through with all this. Simply educating the lender to *what he could do* might be enough of an incentive for that lender to extend the second mortgage at an increased interest rate. The seller who carried back a second now looks at an option of a higher interest rate and an extension *or* (1) legal expenses while your partnership is in bankruptcy, (2) with a two- to three-year wait anyway, and (3) no increase in interest rate and no income.

Does this work?

I know from firsthand experience. I gave this technique at a seminar one day where in the audience was a young man who owned a property on which I had a second mortgage. Unknown to me, he set the wheels in motion; he asked me for an extension. I refused, not realizing what he was going to do. It is now two years later and I have received no payments and he is not making any payments on the first.

Solution 4

This is the last alternative. It should be used only if all else fails. It is intended to save Johnny's credit.

In the event that Johnny finds he is going to lose the property and cannot save it, he should give the lender a *deed in lieu of foreclosure*.

He goes to the lender and says he can save them both time and money: He'll save them the additional time the mortgage has to run plus any additional attorney fees. He'll deed the property back to the lender at once. In many cases, for the convenience, the lender will accept.

Johnny will still lose the property, but he'll save his credit. He can go out and borrow to buy again.

There is one case I know of where the lender refused to accept a deed in lieu of foreclosure. There was bad feeling between the investor and the lender, and the lender *wanted* the foreclosure to ruin the investor's credit rating.

What was the investor to do?

In this case, she took a very creative way out. She had a friend who already had several foreclosures on his name. He had terrible credit and no chance of seeing it get better for some time.

She went to this friend and offered him $100 in cash if he would allow her to transfer the property to his name.

The friend needed the $100 and accepted.

One day before foreclosure, she transferred the property. The next day the property was sold at a foreclosure sale.

But, the foreclosure did not go on her name. It did not taint her credit record. She was able to go to the credit reporting agency and establish that she had transferred title prior to the sale. She had a letter from her friend corroborating this. Her credit was cleared.

(Note: The above solution could also work for negative cash flows if the situation got bad enough.)

I hope that, if you have loans coming due, these last few pages have given you hope. The world is not ending, there are indeed many things you can do about *negative cash flow:*

1. Find a partner
2. Dump the dog
3. Refinance
4. Advertise "rent to own" and do a lease option
5. Sell for nothing down
6. Give an option to equity

And there are also solutions when you have a big *second mortgage coming due:*

1. Offer the lender an increased interest rate 12 months before the second comes due—rate to be effective immediately in exchange for an extension. Or offer to pay points or pay a one-time upfront fee.
2. Take in an equity partner.
3. Go to war, threatening to file bankruptcy *after* forming a limited partnership for the property.
4. Find someone else to take the credit loss.

HOW TO STOP FORECLOSURE

There are times when many face the ultimate disaster of property ownership—losing the property through foreclosure.

Thousands of builders, homeowners, and investors are currently faced with that grim prospect. In order to stop foreclosure you should follow the following steps.

1. Find out how the foreclosure laws work in your state. You probably have a mortgage or a trust deed. They are both widely used as security by lenders but have vastly different impacts on your options in responding to a foreclosure. For example, a judicial foreclosure requires a lawsuit, trial, and can take many years before you have lost your right to redeem your interests. In many states the court calendars are crowded and, after the trial and the sale of your property, you still have one year to pay the amount that was due plus interest, costs and attorneys' fees. In Hawaii some judges are not permitting sellers who carried back financing to foreclose as long as the buyer has made a good faith effort to secure new financing and they continue to make the interest payments on the loan.

2. Communicate with your lender. Many sellers sold to get out from under negative cash flow and do not want to foreclose. If you are working on a sale, call them every day with an update. When you have a contract to sell, send a copy of the agreement. This will work with banks as well as with private lenders. The bank does not want your property. What they want to do is avoid having the bank examiner force them to set money aside in case of a loss. Some banks will even make arrangements for another lender to bail you out.

If you call the loan officer every day and tell him "I had another prospect in to see the property again today, etc.," he will sense your sincerity and say, "Hey, call me in 30 days if you have something." I cannot overemphasize the point to communicate, communicate, communicate.

3. Start your planning before you go into foreclosure. The best way to stop foreclosure is to make your payments. If the

property is worth saving, pull out all the stops. Sell your motor-
cycle, boat, jewelry, stamps, any assets you can to stop foreclosure. One couple saved their property by having a garage sale.
Borrow on your life insurance policy, from your credit union, a
friend or relative. Ask your boss for an advance or borrow against
a year-end bonus. Take a second job. Have your spouse go to
work to supplement your income. Offer the lender a bonus to
extend the loan or a percentage of the future appreciation. Go
in with a partial payment and explain when you will be able to
make another. Do not make a commitment you cannot keep.
Some holders of seconds and thirds have accepted partial payments for several years because they did not want to assume the
payments on the other loans. Check your credit card balances.
It is possible to have 13,000 different VISA cards and most
permit the card holder to increase the credit line by $500 every
six months with a toll-free phone call.

4.   Make an emotional appeal to the lender . . . CRY! Take
your family with you to meet the lender. If it is a private party,
you want both husband and wife to see you. Explain your situation and then have your wife cry. Do the same thing with
your banker but save your most emotional appeal for the President or top decision maker.

**5.   If foreclosure is filed, request an itemization of amounts
due.** The failure of a beneficiary to respond to your request can
be grounds for stopping the foreclosure sale later on.

**6.   Get a good attorney who understands foreclosure laws
and bankruptcies.**

7.   Examine the Notice of Foreclosure. If it is not accurate,
it can be rescinded and the lender can be forced to start all over.
If the notice says the June payment was not made when it was
really July, the lender can be restrained from proceeding because
you found a goof.

**8.   Ask the holder of your second to lend you money to
cure the default on the first and add that amount to his loan.**

9. See if you have any grounds to get an injunction to stop the foreclosure. Was there any undue influence or fraud when you got the loan? Did the seller tell you the property could be used for commercial purposes when it turned out to be residential?

10. Sit down with the lender and discuss the possibility of your filing bankruptcy. The lender may *PAY YOU* not to take that action.

11. If a sale takes place, always attend the sale, take a witness, and take a tape recorder to record the sale. (If there are any goofs, such as a refusal to recognize bidders, the sale can be set aside.)

12. When your rights of redemption have expired, approach the Real Estate Owned department of the bank and see if they will reinstate you as owner. I have seen sales where the holder of the first wiped out other liens and judgements and then, after the sale, reinstated the old owner who now was able to continue to live in the property with much lower payments and obligations.

13. If you are really desperate you can transfer title to someone you trust (a friend or relative) who is in the armed services. Under the Soldiers and Sailors Relief Act, a creditor cannot proceed with a foreclosure where the owner (or one of the owners) is in the armed services. This can turn a nonjudicial foreclosure into a judicial foreclosure. For this technique to be effective you must notify the creditor of the name of the individual who now has an interest in the property and that they are in the armed services.

Of course, all of these are holding actions. They are the sorts of things to do to protect what you have. Now let's get far more positive. Let's see what can be done to improve your position whether you are fighting to hold on to what you have or already have cash available to take advantage of the exciting opportunities in today's market.

5

Where to Begin

If you keep on doing the same old things, in the same old way, you'll be the same old broke. . . .

Let me pose a hypothetical question to you. Here's the situation.

You drive into your garage one night and the phone is ringing. You get out of the car and race to the phone, hoping to get there before they've hung up. You grab up the phone to find it is one of your best friends. The friend says:

"You know, the most unbelievable thing has happened to me. I have just had an offer from a millionaire whom I met three weeks ago. The offer is open to me and two of my best friends. I've chosen you, and here's the proposal.

"If you can be ready tomorrow night at 8 o'clock, he is going to have his personal Lear jet pick us up at the airport and fly us to Maui, Hawaii. On the island of Maui there will be a chauffeur-driven limousine waiting to pick us up and drive us to his 8000-square-foot house right on the point with the world's most gorgeous ocean view. Out in front is a beautiful sandy beach. A ninety-foot sailboat will be at our disposal. We can live like we never have lived before for three whole weeks, all expenses paid. Can you be ready to go with me tomorrow night at 8 o'clock?"

How about it? Would you be there at 8?

If you think so, think again.

Do you know what percentage of Americans would be on that plane tomorrow night? Government statistics tell us 5 percent. That's right, 95 percent *would not* be there. Ninety-five percent *could not* be there.

The reason is, that they don't have control of their own lives. They have to get up tomorrow morning and go to work. They can't just leave on a three-week vacation.

Yet they could if they had financial freedom. Financial freedom is the ability to do tomorrow morning what you want to do, when you want to do it. Financial freedom is the ability to be ready to go at 8 when your friend calls.

I bring this up now because I want to talk about goals.

No matter how many opportunities exist in the market, we can't take advantage of them unless we have specifically defined goals in real estate. What do we want? Are we going to be satisfied with buying one house and holding it for twenty years? Do we want apartment buildings?

Are we going after a monthly income?

Do we want to acquire vast amounts of wealth?

Our goals will in large measure determine how we take advantage of the market conditions. With one set of goals we may set out looking for distressed property (depending also on where we are in the pile and what stage of the crisis we're in).

With another set of goals we'll begin acquiring homes at full asking price.

What is our goal in real estate?

My feeling is that our goal should be financial freedom. Our goal should not be simply to buy a property, if we can, and hang onto it without a specific intention in mind. Our goal should be to buy specific properties with specific objectives to be achieved in a certain amount of time.

A good goal for us would be to attain financial freedom through real estate in no more than five years.

Is that realistic?

It certainly isn't when compared to other investment areas. Ask yourself some simple questions. Do you know anybody who has ever become a millionaire playing the stock market? Do you know anybody who has ever become a millionaire buying gold, silver, or diamonds? What about someone who's into bonds or commodities? Do you know anyone who became a millionaire investing in savings accounts?

When I was asking these questions once at a seminar, a member of the audience rose and said "Does *anyone* know of a person who ever made money in those fields?" No answers.

Now ask yourself "How many people do I know who would sell their real estate today for what they paid for it?"

I have asked that question of over 25,000 people who attended my seminars. Guess how many have raised their hands. Nine. Guess what kind of property they owned. Swamp land in Florida. Desert in Arizona.

For most of us, real estate is the *safest* investment we know about.

WHERE DO I BEGIN?

The best place to begin in real estate today is the single-family residence. It can be a house, a condo, a duplex or whatever. The point is that we are talking about one of the two basics in life— food and *shelter*.

The safest investment for the 80's is residential income property. The single family house (or condo) offers unbelievable benefits. The 1981 tax law just provided a tool to dissolve negative cash flows. With the accelerated cost recovery system (ARCS) you can write off 12% of the improvement costs in the first year of ownership. On an $80,000 home you deduct the land (non-depreciable) say $20,000. Then the $60,000 in improvements times 12 equals $7,200 first year write off just for depreciation. For someone in the 50% tax bracket that is $3,600 a year or $300 a month that the government is providing to motivate you to invest. As Adam Smith says, the government wants you to buy houses and we should do what the government wants.

If our goal is financial freedom, if we want to achieve it in five years or less, then the best place to start for the average person must be the single-family residence.

Now hold on just a minute. When I was asking questions just a few paragraphs ago about whether you've ever known anyone who lost money in real estate, I didn't give you *my* answer. Yes, I have known people who've lost money in real estate. Regardless of the times, it is the person who invests in an investment that is illiquid (land) or does not have staying power (the ability to handle unexpected payments). It has also been in commercial properties and apartment houses purchased by partnerships with a bad general partner.

But, I have never, ever, met anyone who invested in a single-family house at any time who lost money.

Houses are safe. And I think they offer the average investor the best opportunity for profit. Here are my ten reasons for choosing the single-family home or condominium:

1. In 83 out of the last 85 years, single-family homes have gone up in value. The only years that they did not go up were during the depth of the Great Depression.

That is the record which I believe is unparalleled by any other investment medium. It can't be beaten by gold (it didn't go up in price for over forty years) or silver (it spent several decades declining in price) or diamonds (which sunk in value to almost nothing during the Great Depression) or stocks and bonds (which recently have been in trouble) or anything else I know of.

Think of it. During the last eighty-five years we've seen two great world wars, not to mention the Korean and Viet Nam conflicts. We've had a Great Depression and half a dozen recessions. We've had inflation and deflation. We've had Presidential assassinations. We've had rioting in our cities. We've had a complete revolution in racial relations. We've had a baby boom and a women's liberation movement and even a gay liberation movement. We've seen a trend away from cities to suburban areas, the blossoming of the bedroom community and, most recently, a trend back to the cities. And through it all—through what has

probably been the most difficult century of America's exis-
tence—the price of single-family housing has risen! It's a feat
unparalleled anywhere else.

Anyone who puts faith in the single-family dwelling is not
buying something new and untried. He or she is buying into an
investment with a track record that speaks for itself.

**2. The single family house or condominium is the best
hedge available against inflation.** In every inflation period in this
century, single-family home prices have gone up *faster* than
inflation except for one period—1916 through 1920. At that
time inflation was raging at 17 percent a year and home prices
only averaged a 7 percent increase per year. During all other
periods, homes have outpaced inflation.

It only stands to reason when you think about it. The cost
of building homes is directly related to inflation. When inflation
goes up, so does the price of lumber, sheetrock, cement, bricks,
insulation, pipes, and all the other building materials, not to
mention labor costs. Additionally, land prices accelerate. On top
of all this is the fact that builders borrow money to put up their
houses. During inflationary periods, interest rates go up so the
builders have to pay higher interest charges. These too are added
to the cost of new homes. The result has to be housing prices
going up at a rate far faster than inflation.

While the rate of inflation has been down recently, I don't
know of anyone who believes it is out for the count. We're going
to have some kind of inflation around for a very long time. And
every smart investor is going to look for a way to hedge his or
her money against the dollars that inflation steals away. There
is no better inflation hedge than the single family house, taken
historically, since the start of this century.

3. Scarcity. Back in 1970 a federal-government study
revealed that, to meet the housing needs of the country, we
would have to build over two million housing units per year
every year during the 1970s. We fell short of the goal in every
year but two during that decade. Recently we have been building
at closer to the one million mark.

This comes at a time when we are seeing greater migration into the country and a baby-boom generation looking at housing. This is not to mention the fact that our population is getting older and there are more singles who need housing.

The simple fact of the matter, as I noted in the last chapter, is that there's a definite housing shortage. Single-family homes and condominiums are scarce.

Perhaps the most important factor of this scarcity, however, is that it is highly *visible*. I don't really have to do much to prove that houses are scarce. You already know it. Almost everyone has either themselves or some friend or relative who is trying to find housing and who is having trouble. The visibility of housing scarcity means that lots of potential investors know about it and are making it a point to get into the field. This tends to increase sales volume, to add to the scarcity, and, most important, to make houses liquid. They are the most saleable of all real estate.

4.   The best financing in real estate is available for single-family housing. I don't know how many of you have tried to finance other types of real estate, but I have. I've handled shopping centers and apartments and commercial buildings, and I can tell you from experience that houses are the easiest of any of them to get financed.

I like to think of the comparison here between homes and apartment buildings. Many, many real-estate investors like to think of "moving up" in real estate as moving to apartment buildings.

Nothing could be further from the truth. Consider the financing. On an apartment building, which is strictly an investment type of property, lenders base their loans on the *cash flow*. Lenders figure a suitable return, take a look at how much money is coming in, and then offer a mortgage.

Think about it. It only makes sense. If an apartment building is bringing in $5000 a month, a lender will only lend a mortgage whose size is such that the borrower can pay the mortgage, taxes, insurance and other costs out of the $5000 income.

Yet if you've taken any kind of look at apartment buildings today, you know that almost all of them have negative cash flow. There is no way they can make mortgage payments, taxes, insurance and other costs out of income. They only come out when the owner puts in money each month. (Of course, the owner is at the same time getting most of it back in tax savings.)

Lenders simply won't lend on negative cash flow. That is the reason that, instead of seeing those 80% mortgages on apartment buildings, we're seeing them at 50%. With today's high prices and high interest rates, the financing just isn't there. With homes and condos the financing is not related to cash flow, but to 75% or 80% of appraised value.

Horizontal Apartment Buildings

Yet there's still that desire to get into apartment buildings on the part of some investors. To them it seems like a great way to invest money, to pyramid money in real estate.

The answer is to think of buying houses as buying what Jack Miller, a real-estate lecturer, calls *horizontal apartment buildings*. You can have a four-story apartment building with four units. Or you can have four single-family homes. The apartment house is vertical real estate. The homes are horizontal. The money you make doesn't know or care where it comes from or what you do with it.

The point is that the financing on the four houses is infinitely easier than on the one apartment building.

There's another big reason that houses have such good financing. It's that in most cases the current owners took out their mortgages a few years ago when rates were lower and when they didn't vary according to short-term interest. In many cases it's possible to buy "subject to" the existing financing. You can have a house and get yesterday's great financing as well. Many of those loans have a large portion of the payment now going to principal.

5. The appreciation factor. This is something few people seem to understand. Yet it is vital to calculating profit.

Let's say you put 20 percent down on a house and that house appreciates at the rate of 10% a year. What is the YIELD on your investment?

The answer is, 50 percent.

No, that must be wrong, I can hear several readers saying. How can you get a 50 percent return on a 10% appreciation rate? Can't work out.

But it does! The reason is *leverage.* Remember, the 10% appreciation is on 100 percent of the investment. But you only put 20 percent, or one-fifth, of that investment up in cash. Your 20 percent or one-fifth means that the 10% appreciation is multiplied by five to give you your actual rate of return.

Don't believe me? Hal has gone off the deep end on this? Let's take an example.

$100,000   house appreciates at 10%
 110,000   new house value
$ 10,000   amount of appreciation

50% = $10,000   amount of appreciation
         $20,000   20% of original price you put down

It's all in the leveraging. In a house where you put 20 percent down and the appreciation rate is only 4% percent a year, that still means a 20% percent return on your investment. Think about it. Where else can you do that?

6. Liquidity. The single-family house is the most liquid of all real estate. If you need to get your money out, it is the easiest to sell or to borrow against.

The reason for this has to do with the very nature of single-family housing. We're talking about investing in it, but, for the vast majority of people, it's a matter of living in it.

I don't know what the actual figures are (and I suspect neither does anyone else) as to what percentage of single family houses are owner-occupied and what percentage are owned by investors. My guess is that only about 10 to 15 percent are investor-owned. That means that close to 90 percent have the owners living in them.

For lenders this means that houses represent a totally different situation from other investment property. If you (or a lender taking a property back through foreclosure) have to sell, what is your market? A lender must always consider that.

With investment property—apartment buildings, office buildings, commercial units, virtually all other real estate—the only other purchaser *is another investor!*

That means two critical things.

First, the property has to show it can make a profit either on its day-to-day operation or longterm when the investor sells. This involves management, proper structuring of financing, and many other factors. Lenders are hesitant to become involved when there are so many variables.

Second, if the real-estate market goes down, investors won't want to buy. That means that a potential lender who has to foreclose could be stuck with a property he or she couldn't sell.

But, neither of these two problems exists with single-family houses. As we've seen, almost 90 percent of them are purchased by buyers, not for investment, but *to live in.* The buyer doesn't look to the cash coming out of the property. The buyer looks to the shelter.

Should there be a downturn in the market and investors stop buying, people will still be buying houses! People have to live somewhere and houses are always, always in demand.

Lenders, therefore, have structured their financing to buyer/ occupant needs and they are willing to make loans without regard to cash flow.

If you own a house and you need to get some money out quickly, you can go to a mortgage broker and, assuming you have sufficient equity, almost instantly get a hard-money second. The broker looks to the house only, not to the cash flow.

Try the same thing with an apartment building in which you have a lot of equity but negative cash flow.

7. It's easier to get started in single-family houses or condominiums. They're easier to buy, to manage and to rent.

It's hard to prove this until you've actually tried it and compared it to other forms of real estate. But it's true. The government wants you to own a house. Their policies are geared to getting as many as possible to realize their dream of home ownership. This is where Americans now have their savings—$2.3 trillion!

8. The occupancy rates are far higher for single-family houses than for apartment buildings. Given a choice, most people prefer the privacy of a single-family house over an apartment building. This means that apartments tend to be vacant far more than houses. It also means that the turnover in tenants is far greater in apartment buildings than in houses.

Nationally, when the apartment vacancy rate is about 5 percent, in single family housing it is usually between 1.1 and 1.3 percent. In some house rentals, tenants stay put for years and years. I know of one investor who has a house in which the same tenant has lived for nearly 14 years!

If we go back to the concept of "Haves" and "Have nots" the tenant has the perfect psychology of a "Have not." The perennial tenant thinks only of the money that he or she didn't have to pay in mortgage payments, taxes, insurance and so forth. And in the end, the tenant has nothing to show for 14 years of making rent payments.

In the meantime, the owner has had an enormous equity building up, not to mention appreciation—almost all of which was paid for by the tenant. It's the tenant's choice to be a "Have not," that allows the owner to be a "Have."

9. Fewer problems with rent control. Have you ever heard of an organized rent strike for a single-family house?

Rent strikes and rent controls are sweeping the country. Every apartment building owner fears them. That, in fact, is one of the reasons for the decline in appreciation, in some cases the devaluation, of many apartment buildings.

Not long ago on a flight to New York I visited with Tom Hayden, who has helped organize and led the fight for rent control. I asked him what his goals were. Was he interested in seeing rent controls over every piece of rental real estate in the country?

His answer was no. He said that he wanted rent controls on property that had four units or more. He was not interested in controls on units with less than that. He felt that single-family housing should be excluded—as they did when instituting rent controls in Santa Monica, where he lives.

That doesn't mean, of course, that in all areas of the country there is no rent control on single-family housing. There is. A few areas have exercised control over the single-family unit. But compared to apartment buildings, the figures are in no way related. With the single-family home you have the greatest protection against rent control.

10. Tax benefits. You can purchase the single-family home for maximum tax benefits. I put this advantage last for a big reason. Some people look to the tax benefits *first*. They see what they can save on taxes, and then, with that being their *primary* motive, plunge in.

Don't, don't do it! It is like some do in a restaurant. They look on the right side of the menu until they find the lowest price. Then look to the left to see if they can stomach it!

The property has to make sense economically first. Only if the economics make sense should someone then consider the tax advantages.

Well, okay, Hal, we're with you. Now, just what are the tax advantages?

They are enormous. When you own a single rental house, you can write off enormous expenses. They include the interest and taxes that all homeowners get to deduct. But, in addition, they include items which homeowners don't get to deduct. That means insurance, fees for renting, advertising, gardening, painting, mileage to and from the property and just about any other expense involved in its operation. As a rule of thumb, most investors can deduct an additional $500 per year for operating costs per house.

Then there's depreciation. Let's quickly see how depreciation works.

The depreciation is the amount the government allows you to deduct each year because your house is becoming older and, in theory, less valuable.

We buy a house for $65,000. Figure the land is worth $15,000 (the land cannot be depreciated), which makes the house itself a value of $50,000.

We have $50,000 to depreciate. According to the 1981 tax act, we can depreciate this property in 15 years. Let's do it.

$50,000 divided by 15 equals $3333.

Each year we can deduct $3333 dollars *in addition to* all other expenses. Even without a negative cash flow, we see that our house will probably show a big loss *on paper*.

If our house shows a $3333 tax loss from depreciation and we are in a 33% tax bracket, that means that we save 33 percent of $3000 (or $1000) in taxes *that we would otherwise have to pay to the government*. And as I mentioned earlier, if you elect accelerated depreciation you would have $6,000 first year write-off ($50,000 × 12% = $6,000).

Our investment house acts as a tax shelter for our other income.

Of course, depending on how the property is structured taxwise, its value, and other factors, the savings could be considerably more (or less). In many cases I've seen, an average couple earning $40,000 a year wipe out their *entire* tax liability by owning five houses.

Think of it. You buy the homes and you stop paying taxes.

All right, you've convinced us. Single-family houses are the place to start. But if we're under the pile, how do we buy our first house? Single-family housing prices are soaring.

If we're in the middle of the pile, how do we begin buying single-family houses? All we have is the house we live in.

If we're on top, what do you want us to do?

Yes, all of you can buy single-family houses. Let's begin with the person in the middle, the person who already owns his or her own home, but not much else.

6

Five Years to Financial Freedom in Real Estate

**Money may not be important to you,
but I rank it right up there with oxygen!**
—Ruth Buzzi

I have always believed that if you want to be successful, you must find the successful people and learn from them. Find out what they are doing and why. I studied the superstars of real estate, the most successful people in the field. I felt that if I could learn from them how they achieved their success, I would increase the odds of my being successful.

I want to relate to you one of the stories. Of course, everyone has a story about someone who's made a pile of money in real estate. But this person has done exceptionally well. And what he's done with his money and is doing with it now, I think, makes a strong point for the five-year plan I'm going to discuss here.

I was told about an individual who had a net worth of about $671 million. Yet he started out as a chemist who had little or no money. He started out with zero in assets.

His first investment was an apartment house, which he bought with a partner.

It was successful. They made money. So he and his partner bought a couple of other apartment houses. It wasn't long until

they said "Hey, let's quit work and go out and put together partnerships for investors to buy apartment buildings."

They grew financially, and soon they were controlling thousands and thousands of apartment units. Their net worth grew
and they became financially independent.

I heard about them and telephoned. I said I was going to do
a book (which I'm still working on) called *Real Estate Superstars.* I asked this gentleman's secretary if I could set up an
interview with him.

His secretary said she would check. She called back and said
he'd be happy to do an interview for a project like that. Only it
would be nine to twelve months before I could get an
appointment.

I thought to myself "If he's too busy to talk about where he's
at today and what he's doing, there's probably somebody very
close to him who knows and can give me the same information.
Who is it that every wealthy person goes to before they close a
transaction? (Besides his wife and analyst, of course!)

It's his CPA and attorney. So I made an appointment with
the law firm that handled the man's legal affairs. After a brief
meeting I said "I understand that this person is a client of
yours."

They said yes.

I asked "What in the world is someone like that doing at this
point in time?"

They didn't mind saying.

Guess what the answer was? They said he was selling his
apartment buildings. Selling them and buying *single-family
homes.*

"He's buying them in Las Vegas, Nevada. Right now he has
purchased about 38 that have closed. There are another 15 or 18
in escrow. He's just quietly accumulating anything that comes
on the market."

It wasn't long until I had an appointment with them again,
and I said "Where is he now?"

They said "He is over 300."

I later mentioned that at a seminar, and someone came over
at the break and said, "Hal, I was in Las Vegas over the weekend.

There was an article in the local paper about an individual who has accumulated over 1000 single-family homes in the Las Vegas area."

You're right. It was he.

By the way, this person is not my personal hero. But I think his case is enlightening. I think it illustrates that it makes sense to get involved in single-family homes today. Smart, successful people are making the shift. They are selling their apartment buildings and other real estate investments and putting their money into single-family houses.

WHERE TO BUY

Of course, they're not doing it everywhere. The location is critical. Most of the people are buying these single-family homes in the Sun Belt. The reason is appreciation.

In its June 1980 issue, *Consumer's Digest* said "In most housing areas you can estimate that residences will increase in value about 10 percent each year. Some areas, like California, will go up by 15 percent yearly, while some Northeast areas will be as low as 5 percent."

What the article alluded to was the growth patterns in the United States. They tend to be away from the colder regions and toward the warmer regions. In particular they appear to be toward California, Texas, Florida and the other Sun Belt states.

A recent article in the *San Francisco Examiner* pointed out "The Study for the Center for Real Estate and Urban Economics at the University of California, Berkeley, states that there will be a demand for 21 million (housing) units between now and 1990 in California and that, based on the forecast of economic conditions, house prices will rise at a rate of at least 12% per year to bring the average home price to over $220,000 by 1990."

Of course, both studies could be wrong. But if they're right . . . !

THE FIVE-YEAR PLAN

I am going to begin by assuming that the person starting this plan is somewhere in the middle of the pile. (For those of you under the pile, the plan also works, and I'll explain how you get started in the next chapter.)

The profile of the average couple in the middle of the pile is that they have a joint income of anywhere from $30,000 to $40,000. They have a tax bracket of about 35 percent (based on their income and tax deductions.)

In addition, our average couple also has some assets. They have a home, which is valued at about $100,000.

They have a mortgage on that home which they took out a number of years ago at an interest rate of 8%. The balance due is $20,000 and their payments are $220 per month. They have 20 years of payments to go before they pay it off.

Let's consider what that home mortgage payment really costs. Two hundred dollars of it is interest, which is fully deductible.

$200	interest payment
35%	tax bracket
$ 70	tax savings

When we subtract the $70 in tax savings from the $220 in monthly payments, we see that our couple is actually only paying $150 a month on their home.

It's important to make this last calculation, because without it, we don't know the real costs of housing. It reminds me of what inevitably happens when most people come to a seminar planning session. Somebody will say, "How much did you pay in taxes last year?"

The rejoinder will usually be "I didn't pay any. I got money back!"

Did this person really get money back? Yes. Did they pay taxes? Yes, what they got was a refund check. But they still paid a lot in taxes.

Now that we have our average couple, we are going to get them started in a five-year plan. First, let's decide what their goal is. Their goal is financial freedom. *Your* goal should be to have enough assets built up that in five years the interest on those assets can give you a check each month in the amount needed to permit you to live in the style you desire.

REMEMBER, IF YOU BUY ONE INVESTMENT HOUSE TODAY, YOU'LL BE ABLE TO TAKE OUT OF IT (not necessarily sell it) $25,000 FIVE YEARS FROM TODAY. (That's $2000 per month to live on.)

IF I BUY ONE HOUSE EACH YEAR FOR THE NEXT FIVE YEARS, I'LL BE ABLE TO TAKE OUT $25,000 A YEAR FOR LIFE!

If $25,000 a year is not enough, then you simply have to buy two houses a year. That will give you $50,000 at the end of five years. Three houses will yield $75,000 a year. Four houses will yield $100,000.

No, it's not alchemy and it's not impossible. It's all rather simple.

Let's say you buy a home tomorrow that costs $65,000. Further, let's say that price appreciation is 10 percent per year. What is that home going to be worth five years down the road?

At 10% per year, it's going to be worth $105,000. It will increase by $40,000 in value during those intervening five years.

I'll show you how, without selling, you'll be able to withdraw $25,000 of that $40,000 and have it virtually tax-free to live on!

HARVESTING YOUR INVESTMENT

I like to think of it as *harvesting*. You go into your home orchard and harvest your house. You take $25,000 out through refinancing. Then you wait another five years. During that time the price has appreciated again and you are able to take out another $25,000.

You don't sell the property. There are only two reasons to sell, as we'll see, and neither have to do with getting the $25,000 out. You simply harvest. If you have five houses, you'll be able to harvest each one over each of five years and have a constant stream of fresh cash coming in.

C'mon Hal. You make it sound too easy! How can I, an average person, pull off something like that?

It's really not very hard. Let's take our average couple and see how they could do it.

You'll recall that our average couple had a home worth $100,000 with a mortgage on it for $20,000 at a low interest rate. To get started in real estate, they are going to have to refinance their house.

"Oh," I hear some people say. "Give them big payments from the start with a big refinance mortgage. That's no way out. Who wants to have their own house mortgaged to the hilt?"

No, that's not it at all. They are going to refinance their present house and their *real* monthly payments are going to end up less than they are now!

Here's what they do. They obtain a new 80% mortgage:

$100,000	home value
× 80%	mortgage to value ratio
$ 80,000	new mortgage value
− 20,000	to pay off old first
$ 60,000	in cash

Our couple ends up with an $80,000 mortgage on their home and $60,000 in cash. What is that mortgage costing them?

I'm going to assume that the interest rate is 14%. In that case that mortgage is costing them, in monthly payments, exactly $947. I want you to remember that figure. $947. Because we are going to come back to it and see it whittle down to almost nothing right before our eyes.

Now, what does our couple do with the $60,000 in cash?

The first thing they do is to establish a "peace of mind" fund.

PEACE-OF-MIND FUND

A peace-of-mind fund is a reserve account. In analyses of corporations that fail, one of the main reasons cited is lack of capital. Something unexpected happened and they simply didn't have enough capital to see it through. Psychologist friends of mine tell me that one of the major reasons that marriages fail is lack of money.

So, to prevent failure for this reason, we are going to have a peace-of-mind fund. This is money that we are going to sock away in a high-interest-bearing account—a money market fund, and that we are not going to invest in stocks, gold, real estate or anything. It has one purpose—to give us peace of mind. If something unexpected should happen, it will be there, ready to be used.

Out of our $60,000 in cash, we are going to put $10,000 in our peace-of-mind fund.

$60,000   cash from mortgage residence
− 10,000   peace of mind fund
$50,000   remaining money available

Now, do we start with our $50,000 and go out and buy houses?

Not if we want to succeed. Remember, one of the realities of today's market is that there is going to be negative cash flow on the purchase of homes. We are not going to be able to rent our property out for what our expenses are. Income will not meet costs, at least not at first.

So, we will need some money to meet the needs of our negative cash flow. We'll take 10 percent for that.

$50,000
× 10%
$ 5,000   slush fund for negative cash flow

I should point out that the negative cash flow will not last indefinitely. As I've indicated elsewhere, even a falling real-estate market does not mean a falling rental market. Rentals are at an all-time low in terms of supply. No matter what happens to the real-estate market, up or down, we can expect the rental market to continue upward in price. I don't know of a single economist anywhere who would dispute this. And of course, in our single-family home we are least likely to be burdened by rent control.

My own estimate, which I use on my own property, is that with rent increases, I expect that my negative cash flow should be under control within two years. That means that the slush fund, the $5000, has to last us for two years.

$50,000   remaining cash
− 5,000   slush fund for negative cash flow
$45,000   cash available to spend buying property

Now we've gotten to the bottom line. We have $45,000 to spend on property purchases. What do we do with that money?

We are going to buy properties in the $65,000 price range.

We've got the money to invest and now the question arises, should we put it all into one house? Or should we try initially to buy as many houses as possible?

An answer to this might come from a parable a friend once told me. He said that in olden times there were two men going along a road on horseback. All of a sudden they were blinded by a huge light in the sky. They heard a voice speak to them. The voice said, "Dismount and go over to the side of the road. On the side of the road are pebbles. Place these pebbles in your pockets. Mount your steeds once again and ride on into the gates of the city. Do not look at the pebbles till then. Once you are within the city walls, reach into your pockets and look at the pebbles.

So that's exactly what they did. They dismounted, went over, picked up pebbles, put them in their pockets, got on their horses, rode in. When they got to the gates of the city, just as they had been instructed, they got off of the horses, stood by the side of the road, reached into their pockets and looked at the "pebbles." What they saw made them very happy and, at the same time, very very sad.

The pebbles had turned to gold. That's what made them happy. But they were very, very, sad because they had not picked up more pebbles!

Should we buy one house with our money or two? With the money from this refinancing I believe we can buy *four*! What we do to get started, is go out and buy four homes for $65,000 each, and put an average of $11,000 down (including costs) on each home. Our purchase:

$65,000   home price
  11,000   down payment
$54,000   financing

Now we rent out the property. (I'm assuming our negative cash flow on each property will be roughly $100 per month.)

We've spent the $45,000 we had left over from the refinancing of our own house. What do we have to show for it? We have ownership of four houses, all mortgaged. And we have a negative cash flow, that is, money we have to take out of our pocket to keep the properties going, of $100 per house or $400 per month.

SOLVING THE NEGATIVE CASH FLOW

Our first questions should be, where are we going to get that money to pay our negative?

The answer is that Uncle Sam is going to give us some of it. We don't really have $400 in negative cash flow. If we think about it, that money is all deductible from our taxes. Assuming we're in a 35 percent tax bracket, it works out something like this:

$400   negative
×   35%   tax bracket
$140   tax saving

We normally would be giving $140 a month to Uncle Sam in taxes. But, because of the negative that's money we won't have to pay in. It's money that will go into our own pockets. Which means that we can subtract the $140 from our negative. (We increase the number of allowances on our W-4 form—once we know how much we'll save—and this is subtracted from withholding and added to our monthly payments.)

$400   negative
− 140   cash savings
$260   real negative

Our net negative cash flow is only $260 a month. If we annualize it, we come up with $3120 for the first year, assuming we don't raise rents.

We have $5000 in our slush fund to handle this. Of course we're getting interest on our slush fund and we have the first and last months' rent plus the security deposit and we're planning to raise rents every six months, so that by the end of two years, our slush fund should more than meet the negative cash flow. (In case it doesn't we still have our peace-of-mind fund to fall back upon.)

REDUCING THE PAYMENTS ON OUR OWN HOUSE

Now, we've got out four houses and we've taken care of our negative cash flow. But, what about our own house? Remember, we had payments there of $947 a month. That's up from our old payments of only $220 a month. What about all that extra money?

It doesn't really exist. I'll show you why.

Deducting Interest

Let's start with the $947. That's our new payment. But of that amount, roughly $900 goes to income, $47 goes to principal. Principal return is money back into our pocket. It's money that's actually going to pay off the mortgage and increase the equity in our home.

$947   monthly payment
− 47   equity return (principal reduction)
$900   real cost per month on our own house

This $900 is all interest. And, if we'll remember some basic taxation, interest is deductible. We are now able to deduct all of this interest from our taxes. We are in the 35 percent tax bracket, so our savings here come to $315 per month:

$900   real monthly cost of
               house mortgage
×   35% tax bracket
$315   tax savings

That $315 is money we would otherwise have had to pay the IRS. Now we deduct that from our real monthly cost of our house mortgage:

$900 real monthly cost of house mortgage
− 315 tax savings from interest
$585 new real monthly cost of house mortgage

We've cut our real monthly house payment a whole lot simply because of the tax benefits. But we're not through. In fact, we've barely begun. Now there's depreciation.

DEDUCTING DEPRECIATION

We can't depreciate our own home. But we *can* depreciate our rental property. I'm going to assume that on our rental property $15,000 represents undepreciable land, while $50,000 represents depreciable improvements. We have four houses, so our total depreciation would be $200,000.

(Stay with me on this material. It's all very logical if you think about it for a few moments!)

$50,000 improvements value only
×   4 houses
$200,000 total value of all buildings (minus land)

I'm going to use a simple straight-line depreciation method. As I mentioned earlier, according to the new tax legislation the term for depreciation is 15 years. To find out how much we can depreciate each year, we just divide 15 into our total value of buildings:

$$\$200{,}000 \div 15 = \$13{,}333$$

Our total depreciation is $13,333. But, of course, there are other costs we are able to write off. There's the cost of putting an ad in the paper, our transportation to and from our houses to check them out, our phone costs, etc. I'm going to estimate that it's a flat $500 a year per house.

$$
\begin{array}{rl}
\$500 & \text{other costs per year} \\
\times \quad 4 & \text{number of houses} \\
\hline
\$2000 & \text{other write-offs} \\
\end{array}
$$

$$
\begin{array}{rl}
\$13{,}333 & \text{depreciation} \\
+ \quad 2{,}000 & \text{other write-offs} \\
\hline
\$15{,}333 & \text{total write-off} \\
\end{array}
$$

The total write-off for our four houses comes to a little over $15,333 a year. That's the amount we're able to subtract from our taxes. Now, let's go back to the fact that we're in a 35 percent tax bracket.

$$
\begin{array}{rl}
\$15{,}333 & \text{total write-off from four houses} \\
\times \quad 35\% & \text{tax bracket} \\
\hline
\$ \ 5{,}366 & \text{annual tax savings} \\
\div \quad 12 & \text{to determine monthly tax savings} \\
\hline
\$ \quad 447 & \text{monthly tax savings (obtained by adjusting withholding)} \\
\end{array}
$$

I've carried this one step further. I've given both our annual tax savings and the monthly tax savings. Take a close look at that figure. Assuming a static 35 percent tax bracket, we come up with savings of $447 a month. That's money we'd otherwise end up paying to the government.

Now, let's see what happens when we subtract that money from our real monthly house-payment cost:

$$
\begin{array}{rl}
\$585 & \text{new real monthly house-payment cost} \\
- \ 447 & \text{tax savings} \\
\hline
\$138 & \text{even newer real monthly house-payment cost} \\
\end{array}
$$

We cut the real house payment cost down to $138. And I'm still not finished!

DEDUCTIBLE INTEREST ON BORROWED MONEY

Remember that peace-of-mind account? We stuck $10,000 in a high-paying money-market account. I'm going to assume we are getting 15 percent a year on that money:

$10,000	Peace of Mind fund
× 15%	interest rate
$1500	annual interest paid
÷ 12	divided by 12 months
$125	monthly interest paid

That's another $125 we are making just on the interest on our money each month. Now if we receive $125 interest we must figure our tax due (125 × 35% = $44) or $44. So our net on the peace-of-mind fund is $81. We can also subtract that from our latest real monthly house payments:

$138	even newer real monthly house-payment cost
− 81	net interest on our $10,000 peace-of-mind fund
$ 57	newest real monthly house-payment cost

Think of it. We've bought four houses. We've eliminated the cash flow on all of them. AND we've reduced our monthly payment on our own house to a *real* payment of only $57!

Just in case you think I've pulled some sleight-of-hand along the way, here are the figures again, all put together so you can see them as they develop.

REDUCTION OF RESIDENCE MORTGAGE PAYMENT THROUGH PURCHASE OF FOUR HOMES:

$949	mortgage payment after refinance		
− 47	equity reduction		
$900	real cost per month on our own house	$900	
		tax bracket × 35%	
		tax savings $315	

− 315	
$585	new real monthly cost of mortgage
	tax savings through depreciation and other
− 447	expenses on our four rental houses
$138	Even newer real monthly house cost
− 81	net interest on our peace-of-mind fund
$ 57	Real monthly house-payment cost

There you have it all at once. It should be clear why I say that you can wipe out your entire tax liability and virtually live free in your own home, if you own FIVE rental homes. And this example was using the conservative depreciation method. If we used the accelerated method the figures would show the government paying you to live in your house each month!

Let's get back to our goal.

Our goal was to become financially independent in five years, not to reduce our monthly house payment. Where are we going to be in five years?

We will have four homes, which we purchased at $65,000 apiece. Assuming a modest 10 percent appreciation, we end up with four homes then worth $418,732:

$418,732	value after five years (assuming 10% a year increase)
− 216,000	mortgages
$202,000	equity

We end up with over $200,000 in equity. If we were to have a 15 percent appreciation rate, our equity would be even higher. It would be $520,000.

$520,000	value after five years (assuming 15% a year increase)
− 216,000	mortgages
$304,000	equity

Either way, at 10 percent or at 15 percent appreciation, we end up with a lot of money. What are we going to do with that money?

1.   We can sell with no money down, the buyer purchasing subject to the existing loan. That means we will end up carrying back a mortgage value of $202,000 (figuring the modest 10 percent appreciation). Assuming an also modest 12 percent interest rate, that works out to $24,240 per year. That's $2020 a month in income from our properties. Question: If we sell with nothing down and 12% interest-only note for 5 to 10 years, what capital gain tax is due? Answer—0. If we take nothing down we do not have to pay the tax until we get *principal!* So we can earn money on money we would normally pay the government in taxes!

2.   We can simply sell our properties, pay the capital gains (at this time the top capital gains is 20 percent, so our maximum tax would be about $40,000, leaving us with $160,000) and do what we want. We could just take off, or we could reinvest.

3.   If we decided to reinvest in real estate, we could avoid paying *any* taxes at the time by doing a 1031 tax-deferred exchange. We could roll the houses over for other property through trades.

4.   Or we could "harvest" the money: We could refinance one house.

$105,000	house value
× 80%	loan to value ratio
$84,000	new mortgage to pay off existing mortgage
− 54,000	
$30,000	in cash to us
− 5,000	in slush fund to pay for negative for two years on new mortgage
$25,000	in cash to us to spend

Check those figures closely. There's nothing magical about them. What we've done is *not sell* our investment house, but instead we've *harvested* it. We've taken our money out through

FINANCIAL PLANNING WORKSHEET

Name _____   Date _____

Net worth _____   Tax bracket _____ %

Cash available now _____   Monthly cash flow available _____

ANALYSIS OF BORROWING ON CURRENT RESIDENCE

	Current		**Potential**

Current loan   _____ Current value   _____

Current monthly   New loan
payment   _____   _____

Less principal   (−) _____ Less old loans   (−) _____

Total monthly   Less peace-of-mind
interest payment   _____ fund   (−) _____

Less interest tax   Less slush fund
savings   (−) _____   (−) _____   (−) _____

Current cost   Cash available for
                                _____ investment   _____

New payment   _____

Less equity   (−) _____

Interest payment   _____

(1) Less interest tax savings (tax
     bracket % × interest payment)   (−) _____

(2) Less peace-of-mind income (total
     interest income less tax liability on
     interest earnings)   (−) _____

(3) Less depreciation tax savings   (−) _____

(4) Less negative cash flow write-off
     (negative cash flow × tax bracket
     %)   (−) _____

     Cost of new loan   _____

FIVE YEAR PLAN

		X (Number of homes)	
Purchase price	_____		_____
Cash required	_____	X	_____
Loans	_____	X	_____

	10%	
	Appreciation	Appreciation
1st year	_____	_____
2nd year	_____	_____
3rd year	_____	_____
4th year	_____	_____
5th year	_____	_____
Less loans	(−) _____	(−) _____
Equity	_____	_____

FIFTH YEAR

Refinance		(or)	Sell	
Total value	_____	Total value		_____
Loan potential	_____	Sales price		_____
Less existing loans	_____	Less loans		_____
Cash available	_____	Net		_____
		Annual income potential		_____

refinancing. And we've provided for the new negative this would create by setting aside money in a slush fund.

But, best of all, this $25,000 is tax-free to us! As long as we don't sell, we don't have to pay taxes on it!

Remember. We have obtained the money through *borrowing*. And we don't have to pay taxes immediately on money we borrow!

We've withdrawn $25,000 from our first house. Next year we take out another $25,000 from a second house. The third year we harvest a third house, until after four years we've harvested all four houses. Then, you know what? The first house is ready to be harvested again! Our house orchard grows, tenants keep it well watered, and we enjoy the fruit.

Not bad options, are they?

Five years to financial freedom in real-estate *works*. To help you get started with your own plan, I'm including a worksheet I use at my seminars. It will help you to calculate how much you can borrow on your current residence and what that will lead to in five years.

FIVE YEARS TO "FREE AND CLEAR" IN DiSTRESSED TIMES

There is an alternate "five-year plan" for those who are in the middle or on top of the pile, one that works particularly well during periods of crisis. This incredible plan allows a person to buy a property and to own it free and clear in only five years!

I recently bought a condominium in North Carolina using this method and I think the transaction serves as an excellent means of describing how it works.

The condominium was being offered by a builder and the sales price was $70,000. Here's the deal I offered the builder:

down payment	$30,000	cash
5 year mortgage payable $667 month principal only	40,000	
	$70,000	

What's unusual about this transaction is the mortgage—it's *no interest*! The payments came to $667 per month for five years at which time (because there was no interest) it would be completely paid off.

Why would the builder accept such a transaction?

There were at least two good reasons. The first was that he had dozens of condominiums which he simply couldn't sell. It was a real estate depression. There were simply no buyers to be found. He wanted out. That was his first motivation.

Second, I was offering him nearly half his price in cash— $30,000. He needed cash badly. He was having great difficulty in borrowing it. My cash offer seemed highly appealing. Cash was his second motivation.

Of course, I had to have the $30,000 in cash to begin with. But for a person on top of the pile, that shouldn't be too difficult. And for a person in the middle of the pile, refinancing the home should provide the needed cash.

Offering sellers a big cash down if they're willing to take a big no-interest mortgage only works, however, if the existing financing is right. In the builder's case, he had a "blanket" or single mortgage covering all his condominiums. He was able to get the one I bought released. In essence, he was in a position to offer it without previous financing.

I then leased the property for five years to Kent Hadlock, the realtor who sold me the condo. Kent is going to pay me $650 a month for five years and retain a "sandwich" position for himself by sub-leasing each year and picking up the profit between what he pays me and what he receives. In that area of North Carolina I expect to see 12% to 15% per year appreciation. That means in five or six years the property will be worth $140,000. At that time I could:

1. Realize $900 to $1000 a month in income with no mortgage payments.
2. Sell with nothing down and carry back a 12% first mortgage with annual income of $16,800!
3. Refinance at 80% of value and realize $112,000 tax free!
4. Do a tax deferred exchange with the $140,000 in equity, perhaps into three more transactions just like this one.

In most cases, however, in order to work this free and clear transaction, you have to find a seller who has property free and clear or a very low existing mortgage. The seller can then either pay off the mortgage with the cash you put up, or pay it off out of the monthly payments for the five years. Of the 52 million houses in the U.S., 18 million are owned free and clear, so there are opportunities for you in the free and clear 5 year plan.

"FREE AND CLEAR" IN INVESTMENT PROPERTY

There is an interesting alternative to this free and clear plan which can be done with investment property, particularly apartments. It does, however, require that you be on top of the pile.

Let's assume that we have an apartment building which is offered for sale for one million dollars. The sellers want $200,000 down and they own it free and clear or have a very low mortgage. Here's the deal to be offered to them:

down payment	$200,000	cash
mortgage—principal only for five years	800,000	
	$1,000,000	purchase price

Essentially it is the same deal as the condominium earlier. The buyer here puts up $200,000 in cash. The seller accepts a mortgage with principal-only payments sufficient to amortize it in five years ($1,333 per month). And the buyer ends up with a free and clear building!

The seller's motivations have to be the same—a desperate need to sell and a fast need for cash. Additionally, the building must have either no existing financing or very low mortgages. (Surprisingly, there are a lot of these around.)

There is a variation on this which if played properly can get the buyer into the property without even putting up the $200,000 in cash!

The buyer, before escrow closes, offers the apartment building for sale for nothing down. The buyer goes looking for investors, most likely a small limited partnership looking for a tax sheltered investment.

If our buyer finds a likely partnership, he offers them the following deal:

nothing down	— 0 —
mortgage at normal rate of interest	1,000,000
	$1,000,000 purchase price

Our buyer additionally, however, offers the partnership to accept $200,000 in prepaid interest. This is interest that the partnership can use as a write-off.

(**Note:** the tax laws do not allow an individual or a partnership to write off interest until it comes due. There is no prohibition, however, against paying that interest off in advance and then claiming as it comes due. The partnership could pay, for example, $200,000 in interest on January 1, and then claim a full year's worth of interest on December 31.)

Having secured a partnership to repurchase the property, our buyer now uses the $200,000 in interest money the partnership puts up to make the $200,000 down payment on the original purchase.

Then for the next two years (during which time the partnership makes principal-only payments) our buyer must keep making the payments on the principal-only mortgage to the original seller. But after two years, the limited partnership begins making full payments with interest to our buyer. Our buyer then can use that money to make payments to the original seller. Our buyer, after two years, has no additional money out of pocket.

Of course, if you haven't already seen it, the beauty of this arrangement is that our buyer is making principal-only payments while the limited partnership to whom he sold the property is making *principal plus interest* payments. That means that in five years our buyer will fully have paid off the mortgage to the original seller. But the limited partnership will still have 25 years to run on its mortgage, which will have an unpaid balance of roughly $950,000!

Our buyer has created, almost out of thin air, a huge mortgage payable to himself. It all works because our buyer was able to find a seller who was willing to accept a principal-only mortgage to get out of the property.

7

Getting Started When You're on the Bottom of the Pile

Whatever you want to be worth in five to seven years is the amount you should be in debt today. . . .

It's easy to buy four properties when you have a nearly paid-off house to begin with. (I'm sure that's what a lot of readers are saying.) Sure, you can refinance, get cash out and use that money to get started. But we're not all that well off. Many of us don't have enough equity in our home to refinance. Many of us are renting and don't own a house at all. Many of us are renting and don't have any kind of substantial income. And some of us simply don't want to borrow in today's environment to get started in the five-year program.

Hal, what do we do? If we're on the bottom of the pile, just getting started, how do we begin controlling assets—begin controlling houses?

I'll tell you how, but first a word to those who are either in the middle of the pile or are on top. The information that follows (or some part of it) will help you to increase your profits and your assets. Stay tuned. While some of this may be familiar, I'm sure some of it will be new and helpful.

CREATIVE FINANCING

There are a lot of people who talk creative financing today. But, surprisingly, many people still really don't know what it is. I'd like to give you my definition of *creative financing* by telling a little story that was reported in a small West Coast newspaper.

A dying father called each of his three sons to his bedside. On his deathbed, he requested each of them as a sign of their affection to put one thousand dollars into his coffin after he was gone.

He died shortly thereafter.

The first son, who was an attorney, arrived at the funeral home and looked sadly down at his father's remains. Then, remembering his dying request, he took a big wad of $20 bills out of his pocket and put $1000 into the coffin.

The second son, who was a doctor, arrived, paused a moment over his father, and then took out a giant roll of $1 bills and put a thousand of them in the coffin.

The third son, who happened to be a real-estate broker, arrived in tears. He knelt quietly for several minutes looking into the coffin. Then he took out his checkbook. He carefully wrote a check for $3000, placed the check into the coffin, and withdrew the $2000 in cash.

That is creative thinking!

The point I am trying to make is that too often we overlook the obvious. Day in and day out we are told how things are done, how they have always been done, and we never really think about or question it. We just go on doing as before.

But times change, and once in a while we find that the old methods don't work. That's happened a lot in real estate lately.

I don't know how many of my readers can recall that there was a time in real estate, just a few years ago, when almost nobody used creative financing. In those days the purchase of property was simple and straightforward. The buyer went out and got a new first mortgage from a lender such as a savings and loan. The buyer put either 20 percent down in cash, or 10 percent down with the seller carrying back a 10% second. For lower down payments the buyer went FHA or VA. And that's all there was to it.

There was nothing else that had to be known to buy property, either by the real-estate broker, the buyer or the seller.

But today, it's a different ball game. Today we have buyers, like you, who realize that in order to be a "Have" during the 1980s and beyond, you have to control assets. Assuming you feel that real estate is going to go upward from the present crisis, you want to get into property. But the obstacles that are present to keep you out are enormous.

High prices, incredibly high interest rates, mortgages whose interest rates fluctuate—we've already covered them all. It's as if the whole world of real estate is conspiring to keep you out just when you want to get in.

But you can get in! Even if you have no assets, even if you have almost no money, you can get in and do well in real estate, if you think creatively.

I know that some readers aren't going to believe this. Some are going to say, "C'mon, Hal, people just can't get into property at all in this environment."

I'll be the first one to admit that I don't know all the answers. But I'll also be the first one to insist that a creative solution does exist for almost everyone's problem.

Let me tell you why I believe this. It's a true story and it happened to me. It's the reason that I became so convinced that creative financing could work for almost anyone.

One day I got a phone call. It was from a young man who had come down to the Los Angeles area, where I live, from Oregon.

This young man called me up and said, "I have been referred to you as the best possible person to work with in Southern California. I want you to help me buy a house.

"I'm coming down from Oregon to go to school at California State college at Northridge, where I'm going to complete my studies to become a marriage counselor. I'll be in your area for one year. Rather than rent for that year, I want to buy. I'm convinced that with the profit I'll make by buying, holding for one

year and then selling, I'll have enough money to set up my own
marriage counseling practice back in Oregon."

He said he really didn't care where the house was. "It can
be in an outlying area. I don't care if it's an hour or an hour-and-
a-half drive from the city. It can be in one of the older and run-
down areas of the city. I'm not concerned about its location. And
I'll pay between $70,000 and $90,000.

"My situation is this. My wife does not work. We have two
children under the age of six. I'm going to work tomorrow at a
new job at the Safeway warehouse loading trucks, and I'll be able
to afford payments of $550 per month including taxes, insur-
ance, principal and interest. And I think I can borrow $3000 for
a down payment."

Remember, this happened in Southern California, where the
median-priced home was close to $100,000 at that time.

What do you think my reaction was? What do you think his
chances of qualifying for *any* kind of a mortgage were, what
with high interest rates and high prices?

My first reaction was "Forget it." But, I believe in not dis-
couraging people who think they can accomplish things, so I
said "If I can come up with something, I'll let you know."

And I totally dismissed him. I didn't give him thirty seconds
of thought. To my mind he had about as much chance of buying
a house in Southern California as he had of landing on the moon
by the end of the week.

The next day the phone rang. Guess who was on the line?

You're right. He said "Hal, at breakfast this morning I told
my wife that I just know you're going to find us a house."

I said "OK, that's great" and hung up.

He called me the next morning and said, "Hal, yesterday at
lunch I told my boss that I just know you're going to find me
a house."

Four days in a row he called. The fourth day he said "Hal,
you're the key to my future happiness."

I didn't know this kid four days ago, and now I am the key
to his future happiness!

By that fourth day can you imagine what was happening to me? I'm saying to myself, "Is there *any way* to find this kid a property?"

I got to thinking, and I remembered a fellow from church who had told me a story of going down to the courthouse steps and buying property at a trustee's sale for $42,000. He then spent about $10,000 fixing up the house. He painted it, pulled out the weeds (which were waist-high), redid the kitchen and all the other necessary things.

He sold the property for $78,000. It went into escrow, and 90 days later, the deal fell through. It fell out of escrow.

He sold it again for $75,500 and it went into escrow. Ninety days later it fell out again.

He sold it a third time. He went into escrow at $72,000 and you guessed it, 120 days later it fell out of escrow.

This fellow was a speculator. He bought the house with the explicit intent of fixing it up and selling for a profit. He didn't live in the house and he didn't rent it because it had been in escrow all the time, presumably sold for nearly a year.

Guess what's happened to the weeds during that time? And the paint job? The original bid he got for painting that house was $3000. But some fellows were on their way through town from Juarez, Mexico, and their bid to paint the house was $900 plus all the beer they could drink. It cost him $1800! After nearly a year, that paint looked as though it had been through a war. It looked worse than when he bought the house!

You can guess how this fellow felt about the house by this time. He's got no deal. In order to sell it again, he's got to repaint it, do the weeds, do the yard, and go through the whole emotional thing all over again.

So I called him and said "Listen, how would you feel about an offer in which you would receive $70,000, $3000 down, on a contract of sale (a contract to purchase) all due and payable in 12 months with total payments of $550 per month?"

The $550 was less than interest-only, but there is nothing in the rule book that says you have to make even the interest payments on a mortgage. (The interest alone at 15% would be $875 per month.) I was asking the seller to carry back the mortgage at less than the interest-only payment with only $3000 down.)

The seller told me he'd have to discuss it with his wife and think it over.

The next day he called back. He said "My wife hates that house, my son hates that house, I hate that house. They can have the house if you can put it together."

Sounds pretty good, eh?

But I believe in giving people options. So now I called a real-estate broker I know. This broker handled a lot of tax-deferred exchanges, and on one of them he had taken back a house in lieu of his commission. There hadn't been enough cash in the sale to give him his commission, so he got ownership of a house.

This broker, quite frankly, was a bit of a braggart. He liked to brag how much he made and how he always got his price.

Well, this house he had taken back was a bit overpriced. It was $90,000. And all the other brokers in the area office were waiting to see how he'd come out on it. They wanted to see if he'd get the $90,000 out or if he'd have to take less.

His ego was at stake here and he'd rather let that house sit on the market for six months or a year until the market values caught up, then admit he couldn't get the $90,000.

I called him and offered him the same deal—$3000 down, contract of sale, and $550 a month. You know what? He took it too!

I called up the young man and told him that I had, not one house for him to look at, but two!

He picked the first house. He bought exactly according to the terms I had specified. He lived in it for twelve months, repainted it, fixed it up, put it on the market and sold it for $98,000.

He had achieved his goal. He got enough out of the property to go back to Oregon at the end of one year and start up his marriage-counseling practice. As he was leaving, he called me to say "Hal, if my marriage-counseling practice doesn't work out, I'm coming back here to buy houses and fix them up, because it is so EASY to make money in the real-estate business!"

This experience taught me that I had not really been practicing creative thinking. I didn't really know what was possible until I was forced into being truly creative.

The key for you is that you must realize *it is possible to do what seems miraculous in real-estate financing.* Creative financing has had some abuses in many areas of the country. Some people have taken advantage of unsuspecting sellers. The key is to provide the benefits the sellers desire (eliminating negative cash flow, managements headaches) and to do it on a win-win basis.

I feel very strongly that we need some legislation that would make it a criminal offense to buy real estate, put money in your pocket from over-financing, and then let the property go through foreclosure. Right now people are taking money out of properties through over-financing and they have no liabilities—in many states they just walk away. There is nothing wrong with 110% financing, provided the seller is secured and understands the transaction.

BUYING FOR NOTHING DOWN

Our first assumptions are the following:

1. We have no money to put down on the property.
2. We have *some income* that we can use to cover negative cash flow.
3. We are not going to live in the property ourselves; it is strictly for investment.

Can we buy a piece of property? Is it hard to do? Where do we start?

It's *not* hard to do. It's easy. In fact, as part of one of the seminars I do, I offer an optional evening exercise in which the members of the seminar actually go out that very night and buy a property with nothing down.

But, to get started, let's consider what you have to do to buy a property for nothing down, given the conditions at the beginning of this section (some income for negative, not owner-occupied.)

Solution 1

The first thing you need to do to buy a nothing-down property is get a copy of the local paper and start looking for *fisbos*. Fisbos are really FSBO, which is an acronym for For Sale By Owner. (Some say that this really should be FSBG—For Sale By Greedy.)

The reason we begin with the FSBO is because we can find out firsthand what their needs are (and it takes less cash). When we come in with nothing down, there is always the problem of cash. The seller always has his or her own needs. Throw in a real-estate commission and those needs are amplified. Without a commission to pay, the cash needs are reduced.

Once we've identified the fisbos in the paper, and there are usually a great many, we begin calling them. We first ask the basic questions such as where is the property located, what condition is it in, how many bedrooms and bathrooms it has, and so forth.

In a later chapter we'll go into selecting the right type of investment house, but for now let's assume the property is in the right part of town, suitable for our investment needs and in the condition we want. Now we immediately ask two key questions. These questions will tell us very quickly if we can purchase this house for nothing down.

1. The first question is "What is the amount of the existing first mortgage?"

We are looking primarily for properties on which there is only one mortgage, and hopefully that mortgage is *low*. Of course, if we should find a property the owner owns free and clear, all the better. A property where there is already a second, third, or other mortgages will not do here.

2. Assuring the owner says that the property has an existing first that is low, we now ask "What is the minimum amount of cash you need to close the transaction?"

This tells us the cash requirements for the deal. Now we do the numbers.

The way we are going to buy this property is quite simple. We are going to purchase the property "subject to" the existing first mortgage. This is, we are going to take over the existing financing.

Then we are going to go out and get a hard-money second from a mortgage banker. We will buy that second and it will give us cash.

Last, we are going to ask the seller to take back a third trust deed (or mortgage) for the balance of the purchase price. This all becomes simple when put into an actual case. I'm going to take a situation that really did happen in a seminar within the past year. A member of the group called up an owner and these were the figures.

```
59,550   asking price
20,000   existing first mortgage
20,000   minimum cash required by owner
```

The price was rounded up to $60,000 (we will pay their price if we can name our terms) and there was a first on the property of $20,000. The owner, in order to sell, wanted only $20,000 in cash.

Now we have to do what I call *the Rule of 75*.

The Rule of 75 states this: When we add the existing financing to the cash the owner wants, if both these figures come out to less than 75 percent of the asking price, we can do a no-down deal on the property.

```
$20,000   existing first mortgage
 20,000   minimum cash required by owner
$40,000   balance
```

What percentage of the asking price is this figure?

$$\$60,000 \div \$40,000 = 66\%$$

Since the figure is less than 75 percent, we can do the deal.

Hold on there, Hal, where did you get that Rule of 75 and what does it mean?

A fair question. As I said earlier, we're going to buy this property, in part by getting a hard-money second. That means we're going to get a second mortgage from a mortgage broker. He's going to advance us the cash. How much cash do we need?

We need enough to pay the owner the minimum amount of cash he needs to close the deal. In this case that's $20,000.

But no mortgage broker will lend more than 75 to 80 percent of the value of the property. (Remember, mortgage brokers look to the property as their security. They have to have that buffer of 20 to 25 percent to be sure the money they lend is secure.)

Therefore, to see if we can generate a big enough hard-money second to pay off the owner's needs, we simply add what the owner needs to what he owes. If that combined figure is 75 percent or less of the property's value, we know that we can get a big enough second to pay the owner. We can proceed with the deal.

OK, so we're going to take over an existing first of $20,000. We're going to get a hard-money second for approximately another $20,000. That still leaves about $20,000 to complete the deal. Where are we going to get that?

The answer is that the seller is going to lend it to us through a third mortgage on the property.

OK, Hal, that's it. Why would any seller want to give you a big third mortgage? That's a really inferior position.

The reason, quite simply, is because it will be to the seller's advantage. We're not going to hold up anyone. We're not going to browbeat them. We're simply going to show them why it's to their advantage to sell to us no-money-down.

Let's get back to our example. We've learned the seller wants $59,500, and that he owes only $20,000 on the house. Now it's time for us to read his body language.

On the phone?

You think you can't read body language on the phone. Just read on.

The woman in our seminar who found the property now makes 3 statements and asks the owner one question in this exact order and in this manner:

1. I'm going to buy a house this evening. (statement one)
2. Based on the facts you've given me, I'm going to select your house as one of four to see. (statement two)
3. Are you in a position to enter into a transaction tonight? (question)

Assuming the seller is alive and breathing, the answer to the question will undoubtedly be yes.

4. I will be by sometime between 6 and 11 o'clock tonight, so don't go to bed until I get there. (statement four)

It's right here that body language comes into play. Here's where you read the seller.

Nobody likes to have people come to look through a house at 11 p.m. It's inconvenient. In some areas it might even be dangerous.

If this seller says he and his wife are going to go to bed at 9 tonight, and if we want to come by, we can come by before 9 or wait until tomorrow, we don't have a motivated seller. This is a seller who's out there fishing for a buyer with a hook in the water, but no bait. If a fish happens to come by and chomp down on that hook, great. If not, well it's not a big loss.

We are looking for a motivated seller.

The woman who contacted our seller replies "No, it has to be tonight and it has to be sometime between 6 and 11."

If the seller instead says "Couldn't you make it some other time? My husband hasn't taken me out for dinner in nine months, and he's taking me out tonight."

"Sorry, it has to be tonight."

"Well, selling that house is more important to me than dinner, so we will be here."

Did you see the body language? That's a motivated seller. If she's willing to give up a dinner after nine months of not going out just on the chance a looker might buy, she is highly motivated to sell.

Now, we've found a house we can buy and a seller who's motivated. We go through the same procedure over again until we actually do have four houses to look at this evening.

In this particular situation where the house was priced at $59,500, there were nineteen people in the exercise, including realtors, CPAs and attorneys. Normally we break up into groups of four or five, but this time the group decided to go through the whole procedure together. Can you imagine our group of 19 people showing up at sellers' houses!

We were intent on going to all four. When we got to the first one, we slowly marched in. We filled up the dining room, the living room, and a portion of the hall. The seller was flabbergasted.

But he was good-humored—and guess what occupation he was in? He was a real-estate salesman!

The first thing we did was ask him why he was selling the house. We knew he was highly motivated from what his wife had said, but until then we didn't know why.

The seller/salesman told us that six years earlier he had borrowed against the house we were in, where he had lived for years. With the money, he went out and bought two other homes. After a time he borrowed against those and went out and bought two more. Now he had a total of thirty homes.

He said "Anytime we need cash, we peel off one of the homes like $5 bills in a wad. The home I'm trying to sell isn't even the one your're standing in. It's about two miles down the road!"

He then said that the reason he needed to sell now was that the real-estate business had turned sour. In the past he'd been making lots of deals and that had given him the cash to handle his negative cash flow. But lately he hadn't made any deals. So he needed money to keep his properties out of foreclosure. He was selling one and using the money to keep the others.

(Of course, we weren't affected by his being negative about real-estate sales. We had read the signals and were assuming the market was going to turn up.)

We now disclosed our own objective—to buy with nothing down. We told him we wanted to do exactly what he had done. We wanted to buy one house now and one house each year from now on until we could achieve financial freedom. We also wanted a hedge against inflation and the tax benefits that houses offer.

So we made him an offer.

I should explain what I mean by "we." What we do in these seminar exercises is ultimately form a limited partnership. Those who participate are the limited partners. One member, usually someone who lives in the area and can handle management, becomes the general partner. He or she receives an extra share of the partnership free for that service.

The first thing we told him was that we were going to *increase* his price. Instead of the $59,500 he was asking, we were going to pay him $60,000.

We did this for two reasons. The first is that it simply was a lot easier to work with an even number like $60,000. And in explaining a sophisticated deal like this, you don't want to get hung up on the numbers.

Second, it impressed the dickens out of him that we didn't hammer his price down. We were actually going to pay him more than he was asking. (In effect, we were saying "We won't hammer your price, if you'll work with us on terms.")

The figures on the deal looked like this:

$60,000	purchase price
$20,000	existing first bought "subject to"
25,000	hard-money second in which the *seller* would pay the points
15,000	tax-deferred third from the seller, for 5 years and 10% interest
$60,000	

Look again at those figures and what they mean. If there are some things here you don't understand, don't feel left out. Lots of people don't understand them.

Let's take them one at a time. First of all, the first mortgage. Buying "subject to" means that we aren't *assuming* the mortgage, but are simply buying it and agreeing to make the payments.

The reason we are going this route is because many mortgages have "due on" clauses, which means that if the seller sells the property he has to pay off the mortgage. In many states, we can't assume the mortgage but we can take it over "subject to." The way around this is to buy with a lease/option, and in a later chapter I'll spell out exactly how this is done.

Next, let's take a look at the $25,000 hard-money second. This is money we are going to borrow through a mortgage broker. The broker (it later turned out) wanted 10 points (or 10 percent) of the loan as his fee!

$25,000	hard-money second
2,500	points to mortgage broker
$22,500	cash left to seller

You can bet the seller was tickled pink by this deal. He was getting $2500 more in cash that he figured his minimum needs were. He was saving the commission and points on an FHA loan that he would have been willing to pay.

Finally, there is that $15,000 third. Note that I said it was *tax-deferred*. Now what does that mean?

If this is a new term to you, it is one you should consider using.

Let me explain. On this property we're going to have to make payments on the first and the second, not to mention taxes and insurance. If we also have to make payments on a third, our negative cash flow is going to be substantial. So we are going to write this third mortgage in such a way that it is a *single-payment note*. It's all due and payable in one lump sum five years from now.

But what seller would accept that kind of a third?

The answer is that most sellers would, if the advantages are pointed out to them. And the advantages come from the tax angle. Remember, our seller is going to be faced with a capital-gains tax liability when he sells this house. He's going to have to give up some of his profits to Uncle.

But if we can show him how he won't have to give up *any* of the money to Uncle, he's going to be interested.

One way is to keep him from receiving any cash. Under a tax-deferred sale, you only pay taxes on the money you actually receive in the year you receive it. To make this point come home clearly, we call the third mortgage a "tax-deferred" third. Since he won't be receiving any money on it for five years (except interest, which will accrue), he won't have any immediate tax liability. He won't have to pay taxes for five years, not even for interest! Interest is taxable on second mortgages when received. His net worth goes up each year, but he won't be taxed until he receives it—which for many people will be when they are in a lower tax bracket. (At the end of five years he might roll over the mortgage or string it out with payments for ten more years, reducing his taxes considerably.)

Seen from the viewpoint of tax deferral, the third mortgage suddenly becomes a terrific opportunity for the seller.

(Note: We have the seller take out the second mortgage too, prior to sale. This becomes borrowed money on which he again doesn't have to pay taxes as long as his liability under the mortgage is not relieved.)

Our seller ended up with *no immediate taxes to pay* on the sale. It was a big plus he hadn't even counted on.

The only hitch seemed to be the points to be paid on the second—$2500. We wanted to get in with no money down, so we asked the seller to pay this $2500.

We explained to him that if he sold FHA or VA (which he had been willing to do) he would have had to pay far more points. FHA and VA were then charging nearly 8 points, and that on the total loan. It could have been $4000 or more. And he was saving the commission. He would have had to pay at least a seller's commission to any agent who sold the property.

Finally, we repeated what he had mentioned earlier. The property had been on the market for some time with no offers.

Did he want to sell? Will a candy bar make you fat?

This actual case, I believe, illustrates how buying with no cash down really works. At first blush you might have said he'd be crazy to sell. But upon closer examination and a thorough airing of benefits to the seller, we see that it's to his advantage to sell this way.

Our seller agreed. We had him explain the entire deal back to us, just to be sure that he understood and he did.

Then he knocked us off our chairs with a proposal of his own. He said, "I've got thirty properties. I like the deal you're doing so well, I'd like to package it. I'd like to do the same thing with four more properties. We'll make it five at once. How does that sound?"

A CPA in the group said, "We'll do it, if you manage all five free." He agreed, and the deal was made.

I'm not so sure how the management angle will work, since the seller wasn't getting paid for it. But other than that, the seminar grads got themselves a house with no money down, tax benefits in terms of depreciation write-off, and an inflation hedge (since we locked in a price). Since we believe in a big appreciation in the future, all we had to do now was wait.

(Actually, in this deal our seller wasn't as hard as he could have been. He could have insisted on part of that appreciation we were anticipating getting. He could have demanded that we "index" the interest rate on the third. Instead of the 10 percent he agreed upon, he could have said that the interest rate would be tied to the Consumer Price Index. As it goes, so goes the interest rate.)

We had our first property(s). With no money down and with only the ability to maintain a negative cash flow, we were on our way to five. Since I always assume that we can raise rents to eliminate the negative in about two years, we can buy again, this same way, in two years. If our income increases, we can probably buy this way in one year.

We can continue until we become financially free.

Of course, not everyone has the advantage of a strong enough income to support a no-down property purchased in this fashion. Some people want to get into the market with both no cash to put down and no income to support negative. *This too is possible.*

Solution 2

So you want to buy your first house with no cash and no income to support negative cash flow.

One method of buying without cash or negative that almost no one takes advantage of is buying through government programs.

Of course there's the FHA program in which the buyer can put down as little as 3 percent and the GI program where there's no down at all to the buyer. But both these programs require Mr. and Mrs. Buyer to qualify for the mortgages. They have to have strong incomes in order to meet the payments. And they have to live in the properties.

I'm talking about a different kind of government program. Recently I was flying to San Diego and I happened to be sitting next to a banker. He represented one of the largest banks on the West Coast. We started talking and I asked him about government loan programs. Was there any way a person could get into them with no money down AND with no income to handle negative?

He smiled at me and said there certainly was. There were many programs. His bank at that time happened to be administering one in San Diego. It worked in the following way.

The federal government gave San Diego a lump sum of money to use in rehabilitating older areas of the city. His bank had gone to San Diego and said "You're going to have to spend a lot of money administering this program. By the time you set up an agency to handle it, pay salaries, and do the bureaucratic paper work, you will have spent a large portion of the $5 million given to you.

"We have an alternative. Just stick the entire amount in our bank without interest and we'll administer the whole program for you for free!" He said the city jumped at the chance and now his bank was handling the program. That's how he knew so much about it.

The way it worked was that certain areas had been designated as suitable for rehabilitation. A person wanting to rehabilitate could go in, buy the property from the owner at ridiculously low prices (since the area was currently run down) and the government, through the bank, would offer all the financing needed to completely refurbish the house.

The kicker was that the government would lend this money out *long-term* at *3.5% interest!*

That's Depression days interest! I asked him again because I thought I hadn't heard correctly.

Yes, that was right, 3.5%. Not only that, but the mortgage that the bank made on the government money was *assumable!* The buyer could resell later and have someone else take it over at the old 3.5% rate.

Think about it for a minute. A buyer goes into the area and purchases for nothing down, as in our last example. Then he or she obtains a government loan at 3.5% to fix up the property. Once it's fixed up, the buyer sells to someone else, again for nothing down, taking back a big fat second or third mortgage. And the spread is all profit!

Let's take an example.

Purchase price	$37,000	(Remember it's run down)
Government loan	20,000	(long-term at 3.5%)
Total investment	$57,000	
Resale price	87,000	(Now it's completely fixed up)
Third mortgage	$30,000	(You carry this back)

Of course, the house is still in a blighted area when it comes time for you to resell. That's the reason that you sell "nothing down" to a new buyer. The motivation for the new buyer is *no cash.* If the turnaround between the time you buy, fix up, and sell is short enough, it should be possible to do it on the "float."

To use some of the interest on the loan money to help offset the payments. Also, if you do the work, some of the loan money from the government should go to you and that also helps offset the payments. The negative can almost be eliminated.

Finally, I asked the banker "Isn't this program for owner-occupants only? I mean, doesn't this only work if you intend to live in the property?"

"That's the way it may have been intended," he said. "But we can't discriminate. We can't hinder a person who wants to come in, fix it up and then sell for a profit. Our goal is to refurbish the neighborhood and an investor could do it just as well, maybe better, than an owner-occupant."

There it was. An opportunity for someone who wanted to use a little elbow grease to get in on the ground floor. It's not for everyone. But for the right person, it was a really great deal.

There are even more incredible deals offered in most of the older cities of the East Coast, including New York, Chicago and Detroit. There for $1 you can buy a house!

That's right. I'm not joking. The government will sell an abandoned house to anybody for one dollar with the only condition being that the new owner must go in there and fix it up. And the government will provide low-interest loans for the fix-up.

These houses are not in the best of areas and it takes a certain kind of person to do it. But, to say there's no opportunity in housing with deals like this out there would be very wrong.

Solution 3

Here we're going to take a little different tack. We're going to assume that our buyer has a few bucks to put into the property. But he doesn't have any income to support any negative. He can't handle a dollar of negative.

Our buyer believes that prices are going to go up and that the market is going to bounce back from the present crisis. He wants to take advantage of it by getting into houses now when the prices are still relatively low.

Yet he can't buy because any house he looks at will have negative cash flow. What is he or she to do?

The answer here is to use the *option*.

The option is a particularly helpful tool in a crisis situation. It works quite simply. Instead of buying the property, you simply buy an "option to buy." The option states that at your decision, up to a specific time in the future, you can purchase the property at a price set today.

Think about that for a moment. The price is set today. But, you don't have to buy until some time in the future. What are you doing? You're locking in today's price without actually buying! You're getting a seller to commit to sell as much as three years in the future, at today's prices.

Why would any seller do that? For the seller it can't make any sense, can it?

It sure can in a crisis situation IF that seller happens to think the market is going to collapse. If he thinks his house is going to be worth *less* tomorrow, he's going to be very willing to give you an option on today's price for 4 or 5 percent of that price.

The fee for the option could be anything from a few hundred dollars to $10,000 or more. It could be a car, a boat or some other personal property. Options are wide open. If you have some cash and you want to lock in today's prices, they are a good way to go.

A variation on this is to *have the seller give you an option!* Here the seller *pays you!* This case is for the buyer who has no cash to put down, no income to satisfy negative, but has some other assets that the seller can tie up.

The way it works is like this. A *seller* offers 10 percent on an option to buy. It usually breaks down to 6 percent going to the broker who handles it and 4 percent going to the potential buyer.

It differs from the first option we described in this fashion. In the first option, the decision on whether or not actually to buy was the buyer's. In this option, the decision is the sellers! The seller has a period of time, say up to three years, in which to exercise this option. At any time during this period, he or she can say "Hey, the prices of real estate have fallen. So now I insist you buy from me at the price we originally agreed upon." And you, the buyer now, have to purchase. (Of course, the buyer has received anywhere from 4 to 10 percent of the purchase price already.)

What are the benefits here?

For the seller they are obvious. Our seller feels that the market is going to collapse. So he wants to lock in today's prices. He does this for 10 percent.

For the buyer, the benefits are equally great. Right off the bat for doing *nothing*, the buyer gets between 4 and 10 percent of the purchase price, cash on the barrelhead. And because this buyer feels that the market is going to go up, not collapse, he or she is not worried about buying. The buyer believes that, if the seller exercises the option, prices will be so much higher at that time that our buyer will be able to buy quickly and easily and resell at a profit.

The rub comes if the buyer should be wrong and the seller right. If prices should collapse and the seller exercise his option, the buyer must purchase at the originally agreed price.

It's a risky game. But, for a buyer who feels sure of what the market is going to do, it has a lot of potential.

Sellers will only usually go along with this kind of option if the buyer can demonstrate assets that can be tied up to guarantee the buyer will follow through and make the purchase. What the assets are and how the buyer is tied up has to be a contractual matter between each buyer and seller.

These options are closely akin to "puts" and "calls" in the stock market and are very seldom used, but the entire area of options is going to grow dramatically in the future.

There are two remaining methods by which someone under the pile can get started (or someone in the middle or top can expand) without much cash or without much negative. These are the *lease/option and equity sharing*. They are so big and so important that each is going to be covered in its own chapter.

8

The Lease/Option: Getting in with Nothing

The meek shall inherit the earth—but not its mineral rights.
—J. Paul Getty

Keep the old financing, gain the benefits of appreciation, don't put up any money, don't worry about big negative cash flows. Interested?

It's possible with lease/options. If you're on the bottom of the pile, they're terrific. They're a fantastic way to get going.

If you're in the middle or on top, they have benefits for you too, not the least of which is the *second category* of lease/option, which allows you to take over 95 percent of existing mortgages regardless of whether they have a clause prohibiting assumption! (We'll discuss this second category at the end of the chapter.)

The lease/option is little known and seldom used, because most real-estate agents do not get paid a commission until you exercise the option, perhaps years later. They tend to discourage its use.

But if you do not need a tax write-off, and if you want to control as much real estate as possible with as little negative cash flow as possible, it is an excellent investment method.

BENEFITS OF THE LEASE/OPTION

1. Little or no down payment
2. You can sublease quickly
3. Little or no negative cash flow

Lease/options have been around for years. I'm sure that you have heard the term *lease* and the term *option*. *A lease is simply an agreement to rent.* It's a formalized agreement in writing spelling out the monthly rent and for how long the term will be.

An option is simply a contract to purchase at some time in the future, often at a stated price, at the decision (the option) of one of the parties. In this case, it's at the option of the buyer.

Put them together and you have a lease or agreement to rent *combined with* an agreement to buy. You agree to lease and the seller signs an agreement to let you buy in the future. You have to honor the lease. But the decision of whether or not to purchase is yours. It's at your option.

A lease/option is an opportunity. It is a way to control property and to gain financial independence. But, it is not for everyone. How do you know if it's for you?

We all bring with us certain qualities that we can use in making our fortune or in accomplishing anything in life. I've distinguished three of these. They are:

1. Time
2. Energy
3. Money

When we get started in real estate, each of us has a certain amount of each of these qualities. The person who is under the pile usually has a good deal of time, but often has very little money. Graphically, he or she might look like this:

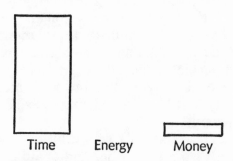

Of course the quality I didn't consider was energy. What I mean by energy is *willingness to work*. Each of us is different. If our energy level is very low *and* we're under the pile—quite frankly it's going to be tough. We may have little money and a lot of time, but without energy what are we going to do with that great asset, time? The answer is nothing, and we're going to remain under the pile.

On the other hand, if we have energy, then we can move upward. If we have energy, graphically we might look like this:

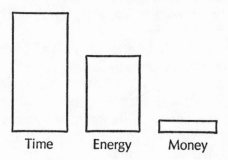

In order to succeed in real-estate investing, the person with no assets must have two out of the three. Usually the person under the pile has time and energy, but not money.

On the other hand, more mature individuals have money but lack time or energy, or both. In the next chapter we'll see how to take advantage of the benefits of money and energy but no time.

But for now, let's stick with the person on the bottom of the pile. He or she has time and energy, but no money to speak of.

How is our individual going to get started acquiring houses on the road to financial independence?

Of course, he or she might use some of the methods outlined in the last chapter. But here we're going to explore a new alternative, the lease/option.

Our individual is going to gain control of a property by offering to lease it from the owner and obtaining an option to buy. The lease will give us control of the monthly amount we have to pay the owner. The option will lock in today's price.

If you're having trouble understanding this, don't worry. It should become clear in just a few moments. Let's take an actual example.

This is a man who I will call Charles. Charles was a mechanic. He never finished high school. He had no savings. He came from a minority ethnic background. Most people would say the cards were stacked against Charles. But he assessed himself and, although he found he had no money, he discovered he *did* have both time and energy.

Charles began controlling property through the lease/option method. Here's how he did it.

Charles went to the local newspaper and looked in the classified ads for "houses for rent, unfurnished."

I had told him that 1 out of 10 people who listed their house in the column would eventually agree to a lease/option with him, if he handled it correctly. In other words, they would agree to a three- to five-year lease locking up a specific monthly payment, and they would agree to a three- to five-year option locking up today's price.

Charles had an additional problem. He didn't own the house he was living in. He was renting. So his first lease/option was going to be a house for him to live in.

Charles had to understand that this first house was not going to be the house of his dreams. This was not going to be a Beverly Hills mansion on a five-acre estate. He was going to have to start at the bottom and work up. This was his chance to get his leg up on the first rung of the ladder. Climbing to the top of the ladder would come later.

Charles decided what he could afford to pay per month for rent, then he went down the colunn of "houses for rent, unfurnished" and began calling the owners.

When the owner got on the line, he asked the usual questions that any prospective tenant would ask. How big is the house? Do you allow pets? What about children? What kind of a neighborhood is it in? And so forth.

Once he had established that the house was suitable for him, Charles hit the owner with two questions. One was a soft question, but the second was a hard one. Here's what he said, word for word.

(Soft question) "I'm looking for a home that I can rent now and buy later. How would you feel about that?"

Right away Charles learned what the thinking of the owner was. Some owners don't ever want to think about selling their property. If that's the case, they'll tell you right out. No, they're not interested in selling later.

They are in the minority. Most owners will say "Yes, certainly we'll consider selling later." Anyone who's an investor is always looking for an easy way to liquidize his real-estate assets.

Once past the soft question, Charles now would ask the hard one.

(Hard question) "If I were to take all of the management headaches of this property off your hands and give you a three- to five-year lease, would you reduce the rent by $100 a month and give me an option to purchase?"

Now why would anyone do that? Why would even 1 in 10 owners agree to lower the rent under a lease and give Charles an option to buy?

As an owner of property, I did. Let me interrupt Charles' story here for a moment and tell you why.

I had a rental house in a nice section of the city and rented it to an attorney. She had just gone through a divorce and was starting her career all over again.

She stayed in the house a little over two years, then moved out. She said to me "Let me rent it for you. I'll get nice people in and I won't have to worry about you coming through night and day to show the property while I'm still living here."

Naturally I agreed.

Eventually she came up with a nice older couple. They happened to be refugees from the war in Viet Nam. She said she had investigated them thoroughly and they would be able to make the rent payments and they were fine people.

Great, I said and signed a rental agreement with them.

Within three weeks after they moved in there were four families living in that house. It only had three bedrooms. But into those three bedrooms were crammed *twenty-one people!*

I drove by, and I couldn't believe it. There were two cars parked on the front lawn and, without authority, they had selected an intense eggyolk yellow and painted the front of the house. Apparently they decided (as I did) that it looked terrible, because they stopped painting, leaving the sides and back the old color!

I thought that, rather than go into eviction proceedings, I would just raise the rent. So I sent a young man over to raise the rent. He said "Mr. Morris asked me to deliver you this notice that he is going to raise your rent."

Perhaps they still didn't speak very good English, for they told him "Good! We have been having trouble raising the rent by ourselves!" Then they stopped paying rent altogether.

I had no alternative but to start eviction proceedings. But before I had gotten very far they told me that it was against the law to evict a Vietnamese refugee.

Do you have any idea how hard it is to find out if such a law exists? Who do you turn to? The State Penal Code makes no mention of it. But then, you wouldn't expect it to. It might come under some federal jurisdiction. But which one: Justice, Housing, maybe Immigration?

If there were such a law and I evicted them, I might be subject to severe penalties. So, until I could find out, my hands were tied. (Later I learned there is no such law.)

What could I do? One thing was to try to find a new tenant as soon as these would leave.

What if right at this time Charles had called and hit me with first the soft question? Would I consider renting it out now and selling later? You bet I would.

Then what about the hard question? Would I give him a lease/option and lower the rent $100 a month? No, I wouldn't lower the rent. Why should I? But a lease with an option to buy that house in its present state? You bet.

Charles's hard question had really been the "shuffle." He never truly expected me to lower the rent $100 per month. It was just something that I could focus my mind on. Something on which I could take a hard position. But once I had refused him the $100-a-month reduction, giving him the lease/option seemed reasonable enough.

(I would continue to get the tax benefits I needed without the management headaches. At that time I was not aware of equity sharing, or I would have used an equity-sharing agreement to solve my problems and meet the buyer's goals.)

Charles moved into his first house, paying only the first and last months' rent on the lease. Normally a person has to give a seller some consideration (money) for an option. But a lease is considered sufficient consideration for an option, so Charles didn't pay anything extra for the option.

Now let's look at the benefits.

Charles immediately took over a house, got rid of the present tenants, who were giving the owner trouble, and moved in. He was paying a rental price he could afford and he knew two basic things:

1. The rental rate *couldn't* be increased over the next three years because he had signed an agreement to that effect with the owner (the lease). That meant his house payments were locked in.
2. He had an option to buy the property at any time he wanted during the next three years at a price that had been set *today*. He had locked in today's prices.

Consider Charles's benefits closely. He's gained control of the property. He will now receive all the appreciation. Inflation and other factors will make the value of the house go up over the next three years (remember, our assumption under this scenario is that the real estate is going to turn upward), and he'll get all of the profit.

Charles actually did this. And then, after a while, he realized that he could do it with other houses as well. After all, if the owner agreed to let him *sublet* (to re-rent to someone else), he could take over as many houses as he could find willing owners.

It worked like this. Charles made this same phone call, found the same kind of owner, sick of management headaches, and made the same offer, only getting the owner to agree to let him sublet.

Then Charles went out and found a tenant, sometimes for the same rent, sometimes for a few dollars more. He put the tenant in the property. The tenant paid Charles, and Charles paid the owner. But Charles controlled the asset. He had the rent payment locked in and the price locked in.

After six months, when he raised rents, he (not the owner) got the difference between the old rental and the new. And when Charles sold, he (not the owner) got the profits from appreciation.

Charles started two years ago. Right now he has 18 different properties and he is actually getting a *positive* cash flow of nearly $1500 a month from them!

He is using his energy and his time to become a property manager, but he's a manager who controls the property like an owner.

I should point out something about Charles. When he meets the owners of the properties, they never fail to be impressed by two things. The first is his integrity. If Charles says he's going to do something, he does it. And the second is his management ability. Charles performs. If a tenant doesn't make a rent payment to him, Charles makes up the difference and is sure the owner is paid. (Then, of course, he gets a new tenant!)

There is one last benefit to the owner under this arrangement—which Charles brings up when the management headache isn't enough to convince the owner to make a move. It's the tax benefits. The owner retains the depreciation on the property. The owner can continue to depreciate the property as a rental, and often that means a bigger savings than if the owner had sold the property on a small cash down with a big second and then put that cash in the bank. The money from the depreciation can be bigger than the money from the interest on the cash.

There is only one area where Charles sometimes has real trouble, and that is establishing today's price. Sometimes owners say to him "Why should we lock in today's price? Tomorrow prices will be higher?"

In this case Charles sometimes agrees to an option to buy at a price *higher* than today's market will bear. Even if the price is 5 or 10 percent higher, Charles is still going to come out, because he doesn't have to exercise his option until three to five years down the road. By that time the property (assuming our boom scenario) should be at least 30 percent higher in value.

In today's market the lease/option opens up all kinds of possibilities, not only for the person under the pile, but also for all investors. And it doesn't even have to be someone with a management headache. I have seen individuals who were happy to give a lease/option because they had been transferred by their company, had moved and bought a new home, had the old one vacant, and were making two payments. Such a person would often be tickled pink to get out of the second payment and the whole headache under a lease/option.

TAKING ADVANTAGE

I was describing this lease/option approach in one of my seminars once when an interesting thing happened.

We were doing what I described in the last chapter. We were going to four houses, but instead of a low down on purchase, we were proposing a lease/option to each owner. We got to the last house at 11:30 p.m. and were met by a big bear of a guy. I remember exactly what he said: "I thought you were joking on the phone." There were five of us who went in, and it turned out that the house he advertised was a rental property. He piled us all into his station wagon, drove us to it, woke up the tenants and walked us through.

We told him we liked the property, and would consider an offer of a three- to five-year lease/option, with the option at his asking price today. Then we explained we had seen three other properties, and we were now going to an all-night coffee shop to discuss them. We would make a decision within an hour. We told him not to go to sleep because we'd call him one way or another within the hour.

When we got to the coffee shop I noticed one girl in the group who was silent. The others were working out the figures, trying to decide, but she didn't seem to be taking part.

I asked her if anything was wrong.

She said yes, there was. She said she thought that what we were doing was not right. She happened to be a real-estate broker and she said she knew the market. The price we were fixing on the house was low even at today's market. Further, she knew that the house could be rented for at least $25 more than the current owner was charging his tenants. We could increase the rent almost immediately. She said it just wasn't fair to the owner.

I explained that the owner hadn't just fallen off the turnip truck. He had purchased the property at a foreclosure sale. We had given him full disclosure. We had told him we would only buy from him if we were going to make a profit. We told him to save us all a lot of time if he had any trouble with our making a profit. She agreed, but obviously wasn't convinced.

The group decided to buy the house, so we went back. After some more negotiating we signed the deal at 3 o'clock in the morning.

As soon as it was signed, he sat back in the chair and gave such a huge sigh of relief that we got worried! What did he know about this property that made him so relieved to be rid of it?

We asked him, and he explained, "I found out less than 90 days ago that I have a serious heart condition. I don't know how much longer I can live. I might go on for a year or two, or it might be tomorrow. I've been trying to buy more life insurance but, in my condition, no one will sell me any.

"I need the peace of mind of knowing that if I die tomorrow my wife won't have the hassle of handling tenants or trying to sell the property. I don't think she could do it and I was worried that it would make her sick.

"But I just know that you folks can handle it. When you came in you told me you would only deal with me if you could make a profit. Your coming to me and making this offer was an answer to prayer, because you are my insurance policy. I know that my appreciation ends when I sign this. But I also know that all the appreciation I have gotten up to this point will be protected for my wife by you. And I'm still getting the depreciation tax benefits. This is the best deal I could ever ask for!"

We have no idea why people sell. So many of us imagine why people will or should say no that we never ask.

In reality, people have their own reasons and they usually act in their own best interests. As long as we explain fully, make full disclosure, so that the person understands and winds up with the benefits he or she needs, we are promoting a win-win situation.

PROCEDURE FOR HANDLING THE LEASE/OPTION

In order to protect ourselves as buyers (and also to protect the seller), there are certain procedural things we should do when creating a lease/option. A typical lease/option form that I use is included in this chapter. It covers most of the basic material that has to be covered.

My own suggestion is that, if you're going to go into the area seriously, you contact an attorney and have him or her draw one up for you that is suitable for your area, perhaps based on my model. (Each little area of the country has slightly different laws, so you shouldn't use the enclosed form until an attorney tells you it conforms to your area.)

Before closing the transaction, you should be sure that you have covered all of these five areas:

1. The contract between buyer and seller should spell out all of the financing including interest rate, terms, the payment, and so forth. In addition, the lease term and the amount the lessee (tenant) will pay to lessor (owner) should also be spelled out.

2. The lease needs to be properly notarized and recorded in either the county or township recorder's office. This gives constructive notice to all concerned that the buyer has an interest in the property. It also helps prevent the seller from reselling to someone else.

3. The option agreement should also be properly notarized and recorded for the reasons just cited.

4. The purchase price for the option should be precisely indicated. This is critical if you are the buyer. The whole point behind the lease/option is to lock into today's price. If the purchase price isn't spelled out, you haven't accomplished your goal.

(On the other hand, when I *sell* under a lease/option, I don't want the purchase price spelled out. As a seller I want the price to be the current price at the time of sale, some three to five years down the road. What I do as seller is to specify that the price will be based on an FHA appraisal to be made at the time the option is exercised.)

5. If title insurance is available in your state, get it. This insures that the seller has legal title to the property and that there aren't any hidden encumbrances (mortgages or liens). In states where legal opinions are used in place of title insurance, get one.

LEASE/OPTION AGREEMENT

THIS AGREEMENT made this _____ day of _____, 19_____,

between _____

_____, called LESSOR,

and _____

_____ , called LESSEE.

WITNESSETH:
   1. SUBJECT PROPERTY: LESSOR hereby leases to LESSEE that real property

commonly known as _____
and which is more particularly described as:

   2. TERM: The term of this lease shall be for a period of _____

commencing on the _____ day of _____, 19_____, and ending on the _____ day of _____, 19_____.

3. RENTAL: Lessee shall pay Lessor as rental for subject premises the sum of $_____ per month, commencing on the _____ day of _____, 19_____, and continuing on the _____ day of each succeeding month during the term hereof. In addition, Lessee shall pay all taxes, assessments and bonds of said real property including the existing ones as well as those hereafter imposed.

4. PAYMENT OF RENTALS: The parties designate _____ _____ , hereinafter called _____, as collection agent, and shall mutually instruct collection agent among other things to:

(a) Collect the monthly rental payments from Lessee together with _____ monthly charge which shall be the expense of Lessee and shall pay therefrom:

(1) Payments on existing loans .... $_____

(2) Balance to Lessor .... $_____

(3) Collection charge .... $_____

(b) Pay as required from funds provided by Lessee monthly for taxes, assessments, insurance, etc., if any.

5. POSSESSION: Possession shall be delivered to Lessee on _____ _____.

6. ENCUMBRANCES: The only outstanding encumbrances against said real property are:

Lender	Approximate Balance	Monthly Payment (Including Impounds)	Maturity Date	Interest Rate
_____	_____	_____	_____	_____
_____	_____	_____	_____	_____
_____	_____	_____	_____	_____

_____ Real estate taxes and assessments for 19_____ to 19_____. Conditions, covenants, restrictions, easements, and right of way of record.

The parties agree that neither will cause or permit any lien to attach to or exist on or against the subject property which shall or may be superior to the right of either party or to encumber the property in any manner without having attained the written consent of the other.

7. OPTION TO PURCHASE: Lessor grants Lessee, subject to the provisions of Paragraphs 8 and 9, the right to purchase the subject real property at any time prior

to _____, 19_____, upon the following terms and conditions:

(a) Lessee has paid to Lessor the sum of $_____ as and for OPTION CONSIDERATION for the right to purchase granted Lessee herein.

(b) The option price shall be in an amount equal to $_____

with interest thereon at the rate of _____% per annum from date endorsed on that portion of the purchase price which is in excess of the OPTION CONSIDERATION. Said interest shall be computed and considered as received by Lessor as a portion of each monthly rental payment.

(c) Lessee shall receive a credit in paying said option purchase price for:
(1) The total amount of OPTION CONSIDERATION
(2) That portion of each monthly rental payment paid Lessor in excess of said interest amount.

(d) Lessor shall execute and deliver to _____ all documents required to

transfer title to subject real property and shall instruct _____ to record said docu-

ments when Lessee timely delivers to _____ the total purchase price.

(e) Taxes are being prorated between the parties as of the date of this agree-

ment. All excess of tax deposits made by Lessee to the _____ account shall be the property of Lessee.

(f) The parties shall pay the following costs of transfer of title:

(1) LESSOR—Stamps on Deed, unless prepaid

(2) LESSEE—Recording of Deed

8. CONDITION OF TITLE: Upon exercise of the Option, the conveyance to be made by Optionor to Optionee shall be expressly subject to the following:

(a) All taxes and special assessments levied after the date for taking possession pursuant to this Agreement.
(b) All conditions, covenants and restrictions of record as of date of possession set forth herein.
(c) All easements and rights of way of record as of date of possession.
(d) All encumbrances of record set forth in Paragraph 6 herein.

9. ACCELERATION OF PAYMENT: The parties are aware that Lessee, in the event he exercises his option herein, takes subject to and with the knowledge and understanding that, the recorded Deeds of Trust of the Encumbrances set forth in Paragraph 6 are, or may be, subject to conditions which shall permit the lender, obligee or beneficiary of a Deed of Trust upon the sale, transfer, hypothecation or assignment by Lessor of said real property or any interest therein, to accelerate the "due date" of the obligation so that the entire amount of principal and interest are immediately due and payable in their entirety.

10. ASSUMPTION, ACCOUNT TRANSFER FEES AND REFINANCING EXPENSES: Upon exercising his option, Lessee shall be responsible for and shall pay:

(a) All assumption fees imposed by the secured lienholders set forth in Paragraph 6, if Lessee elects to formally assume such loans of record.

(b) Account transfer and other related costs of said lienholders if Lessee does not formally assume said encumbrances.

(c) Any charges, prepayment penalties or expenses imposed by the terms of the underlying Deeds of Trust and promissory notes of the lienholders set forth in Paragraph 6 in the event Lessee elects to refinance or to pay off any of said encumbrances.

11. INSURANCE: Lessee shall provide, at Lessee's expense:

(a) Fire insurance, on existing buildings or any buildings thereafter placed on the leased premises, in amounts equal to the total option price set forth herein.

(b) Public liability insurance with limits of $100,000.00 for injury or death of one person, and $300,000.00 for injury or death of more than one person, for the benefit of Lessee, making Lessor an additional insured thereunder, and under the terms of which the parties of whatsoever nature, arising out of or in connection with the use of or operations on the leased premises.

(c) Lessee shall deliver to Lessor within 10 days after possession either policies or certificates of insurance and in the event Lessee fails to timely provide said insurance coverage and evidence of insuredness, then Lessor shall have the option to secure said insurance coverages at the cost and expense of Lessee or to declare this lease null, void and of no further effect.

12. REPAIRS: Lessee accepts the premises as being in good condition and repair. Lessee, at Lessee's sole cost and without obligation to Lessor, shall keep and maintain the premises, and every part thereof, in good and satisfactory repair and condition, reasonable wear and tear excepted. Lessee waives Sections 1941 and 1942 of the California Civil Code. Lessee shall indemnify and hold Lessor harmless from any and all mechanics liens or claims of lien and all attorney fees, costs and expenses which may accrue, grow out of, or be incurred by reason of or on account of such lien or claim of lien.

13. DEPRECIATION AND INTEREST: In the event the property covered by this Agreement is sub-leased or rented by the Leseee herein, said Lessee shall be allowed to claim depreciation for tax purposes and the Lessor agrees not to claim depreciation and any portions of the payments made on the loans of record which is applicable as interest may be claimed by Lessee. As long as Lessee is not in default, Lessor shall not claim any portion of the depreciation or interest.

14. LOSS: Any loss to the real property or personal property contained therein for any reason whatsoever, including condemnation by any governmental agency, fire, flood, earthquake, or whatever, shall be apportioned between the parties as their interests are pursuant to this Agreement.

15. LATE CHARGES: Lessee acknowledges that late payment of rent will cause Lessor to incur costs not contemplated by this lease the exact amount of which is extremely difficult to ascertain. If any installment of rent is more than 10 days past due, Lessee shall pay Lessor a late charge equal to 5% of such overdue amount. The parties agree that such late charge represents a fair and reasonable estimate of the costs of Lessor incurred for extra accounting charges and late charges imposed by lenders of record.

16. DEFAULT: The occurrence of any of the following shall constitute a material default and breach of lease by Lessee.

(a) Any failure by Lessee to pay the rental or to make any other payment required by Lessee where such failure continues for 30 days after written notice thereof by Lessor to Lessee.

(b) Any failure by Lessee to perform any other provisions of this lease to be performed by Lessee where such failure continues 30 days after written notice thereof by Lessor.

17. REMEDIES UPON DEFAULT: In the event of any such default by Lessee, then in addition to any other remedies available to Lessor at law or in equity, Lessor shall have the option to terminate this lease and all rights hereunder by giving written notice of intention to terminate.

18. HOLDING OVER: Any holding over after the expiration of the term of the lease in the event Lessee's option to purchase is not exercised or upon the exercise of Lessor's option to terminate the lease pursuant to the Default provisions of Paragraphs 16 and 17, shall be construed to be a tenancy from month to month at a monthly rental equal to 1% of the option price set forth in Paragraph 7.

The parties have bargained for and agree that said monthly sum of 1% of the option price is a fair and reasonable monthly rental for the subject premises and a sum which would have been reasonably used as a lease rental amount during the term thereof except for the negotiated anticipation of the parties that Lessee would have exercised the option to purchase prior to termination.

19. Whenever in this lease it is provided or required that notice and/or demand be given or served by either party on the other, such notice and/or demand shall be deemed to have been duly given if it is in writing, forwarded by certified mail, and addressed as follows:

LESSOR: _____   **LESSEE:** _____

_____   _____

_____   _____

20. WAIVER: The waiver by Lessor of any provision of this Agreement shall not constitute a waiver of any other provision of this Agreement or any future waiver of the same provision.

21. MEMORANDUM OF LEASE: The parties agree to execute a memorandum of this lease which may be recorded at the direction of the Lessee.

22. ATTORNEY'S FEES: Should either party hereto find it necessary to enforce any of the provisions of this Agreement against the other, the prevailing party shall be entitled to reasonable attorney's fees and all costs and expenses in connection therewith.

23. GENDER, TENSE AND PLURALITY OF WORDS: All words used in this Agreement, including the words Lessor and Lessee, and Optionor and Optionee, shall be construed to include the plural as well as the singular number; words used herein in the present tense shall include the future as well as the present; and words used in the masculine gender shall include the feminine and neuter.

24. TIME: Time is the essence of this lease and the options given thereunder.

IT IS FULLY UNDERSTOOD BY THE PARTIES HERETO, THAT EXECUTION OF THIS AGREEMENT CAN, AND LIKELY WILL, CREATE OR CHANGE EXISTING LEGAL RIGHTS OR OBLIGATIONS RELATIVE TO SUCH THINGS AS, BUT NOT NECESSARILY LIMITED TO, DEPRECIATION ALLOWANCES, PROPERTY TAXES AND INTEREST DEDUCTIONS. THEREFORE, EACH PARTY HERETO SHOULD SEEK THE ADVICE OF LEGAL COUNSEL BEFORE EXECUTION OF THIS DOCUMENT.

IN WITNESS WHEREOF, the parties hereto have caused this instrument to be executed as of the day and year first above written.

LESSOR   **LESSEE**

_____   _____

_____   _____

_____   _____

LEASE/OPTION VS. THE "DUE ON SALE" CLAUSE

There's a second category of lease/options. This is a use of the method that can benefit either the buyer or the *seller* in the middle or top of the pile.

The best financing that's available today is the financing of yesterday. As I pointed out earlier, there are billions of dollars of old fixed-rate low-interest loans on property around the country. The best way to buy is to take over one of these old loans. If you can get an old fixed-rate mortgage at 10% interest, you're doing a whole lot better than going out and trying to get a new mortgage at 17%.

An old mortgage at 10%, when combined with a second at around 18%, will yield a combined interest rate of 13% or 14% (depending on the numbers involved)—which is still far better than trying to get a new loan.

There is, however, a big problem in getting one of those old fixed-rate mortgages. The lender usually doesn't want you to do it.

That old lender is sitting there like a spider in its web, just waiting and hoping. You know what that lender's hoping for? He's hoping someone will trip into his web and he can gobble them up.

"Gobble them up" means getting rid of that low-interest-rate loan he's currently got out at 9% or 10% or whatever, and rolling it over into a new 16% or 17% mortgage.

Those old low-interest-rate mortgages are killing the lenders. They are having to pay interest to their depositors at a higher rate than that at which they lent the money out!

But, don't feel too sorry for them. They're big boys, and they got into the problem all by themselves, and they can get out by themselves. Think about your own situation. You don't want to fall into their web and get caught with a mortgage that they can suddenly pull out from under you and jack up the interest rate.

How can they do that?

The answer is the "due on sale" clause.

This is a clause inserted in almost every mortgage that says something like, "This mortgage will become *immediately* due and payable on the sale or transfer of the property."

That's the spider web. If the owner sells the property, the lender has the right to call in the mortgage, which comes down to the lender's demanding a higher interest rate.

But the courts have come to the aid of buyers and sellers. First in California, and then in nearly a dozen other states, the courts have acted on the "due on" clause. They have ruled that it is enforceable *only if* the lender can prove one of two things:

1. Risk of default
2. Impairment of security in the mortgage

If the owner transfers the property without risk or impairment, they cannot enforce the "due on" clause. They *must* let the new buyer purchase "subject to" the old mortgages.

What does *assume* mean?

1. The buyer must qualify for the loan.
2. The lender can raise the interest rate.
3. The lender may charge points for a new loan.

Under a "subject to" none of these apply. For example, the new buyer's name does not go on the loan.

BUT, and it's a big but, state and federal law have come into conflict here. While the state courts have often upheld that the "due on" clause is unenforceable, the federal courts have held that federal law supercedes state law. This means the state ruling does not apply to federal lenders. Since federal law supercedes state law, a "due on" clause written into the mortgage issued by a federally chartered S & L or bank *is enforceable* (as of this writing).

This is still being wrangled in the courts. But for our purposes, it is important to understand that many loans issued by federally chartered S & L's and banks (which are among the biggest in many states) are enforceable. That means that you really can't assume them. It means that normally the buyer can't get the advantages of the older existing low-interest-rate mortgage on the seller's property.

But, there are ways around this by using the lease/option.

It is possible for 90 to 95 percent of old mortgages to be kept on the books through the lease/option. When you're looking for a home, you can go through the multiple listing book of the broker you're with. In 90 to 95 percent of the cases you *can* take over that non-assumable loan using the lease/option plan!

The lease/option is really a panacea for the "due on" clause. It allows buyers to hang onto those great old fixed-rate low-interest mortgages.

(It should be noted that in many states the agreement of sale, contract for sale, contract for deed, etc., is used to accomplish the same results as the lease/option.)

How is it done?

The answer is so simple it's almost unbelievable. Instead of buying the house in the normal fashion, the buyer executes a lease/option such as we've just described. However, rather than nothing down, the buyer may give the seller a substantial portion of the down payment and that becomes the consideration for the option.

We've already gone through the procedure and the contract for the lease/option. The only real question that remains is, how does it work?

It works because *no transfer of title* has taken place. Remember, under the lease/option the title to the property remains with the seller until the buyer exercises the option.

How can there be a calling in of the mortgage by the lender when there's been no title transfer? The lender can't exercise the "due on" clause because *no sale has taken place.*

In California, where I've seen these lease/options in practice, over 2000 of them have been done without a single federal lender being able to call in the mortgage. They do work!

There might, however, be some questions regarding them. Here are typical questions and answers that arise in this second category of the lease/option.

Question: The lease option is for three to five years. What happens after that?

Answer: In category one we said that we made the lease/option for three to five years to lock in the price of property until appreciation had taken place. In category two the term may be as long as we like. If the low-interest mortgage has 27 years to run, we can make the lease/option for 27 years! There's no legal limitation on the term.

Question: As a buyer, won't I lose the tax advantages by going through a lease/option?

Answer: No!

I've spent a lot of money and hours of time with attorneys to get a legal opinion on this. It turns out that the buyer under a lease/option *can* deduct the amount he pays that goes for interest and taxes on the property. That's right, the *buyer* can deduct it instead of the seller!

The pioneers in the lease/purchase (to avoid "due on sale") are Rose-Marie Sines-Morrisey of Huntington Escrow Service, Inc., in Fountain Valley, California, and Roger Saevig, a top real estate attorney in Tustin, California. They provided me with the insights into how to do a lease/option so the "buyer" gets the depreciation.

The IRS, in its Revenue Ruling 55-540, has a test in which the *intention* of the parties entering into the lease/option agreement is spelled out. This test determines who gets the tax benefits. Check with your C.P.A. or tax attorney for the particulars.

Sums paid by the lessee/optionee for interest and for real property taxes are deductible by him. The reason is that the transaction is basically a sale rather than a true lease. The lease/option agreement has been used, in these transactions, to legally circumvent and avoid the clause in existing notes and trust deeds making the remaining principal balance due and payable in full in the event of a sale of the property.

The position of the Internal Revenue Service on the validity of such deductions by the lessee/optionee is expressed in Revenue Ruling 55-540 in which the test is said to be the intention of the parties in entering into the lease/option agreement. If the parties intended to make a sale even though they used the device of the lease/option agreement, that intent will prevail and the lessee/optionee will have the same deductions available that he would have as if he had received a grant deed to the property.

While "intent" is often a difficult fact to prove, the tax courts have used several factors in deciding the intent of the parties. These include:

(1) *Where there is a substantial amount paid for the option and a relatively small amount to be paid to exercise the option and receive the deed.* EXAMPLE: Property price $40,000.00; first trust deed $30,000.00; down payment on option $8,000.00; balance to pay to exercise option and receive fee title $2,000.00. The courts feel that no prudent person would pay $8,000.00 merely to lease a $40,000.00 property and have held that the transaction is actually a sale for tax purposes.

(2) *Where the option price plus the rental or option payment are equal to the property value plus interest.* EXAMPLE: Property value $40,000.00; first trust

deed $30,000.00; option price $10,000.00, payable $2,000.00 down and
$8,000.00 balance payable $80.00 per month including 8% interest. A revenue
ruling plus several court decisions say that such an arrangement is a sale on credit
even though dressed up as a lease.

(3) *Application of option of option or lease payments to the lessee's equity.*
EXAMPLE: Property value $40,000.00; first trust deed $30,000.00; option
price $10,000.00, payable $5,000.00 down and $50.00 per month including
interest at 8%; lessee to make the payments on the firet trust deed and all
amounts paid by the lessee other than interest are deducted from the remaining
balance. The Tax Court ruled that this lease was indicative of a sale.

(4) *Designating part of the lease payment as interest.* In all of the examples
set forth above, interest is clearly and separately identified. If designated as
interest, it's a sale for tax purposes said the Tax Court.

(5) *A combination of factors.* A combination of all or some of the factors
listed above may make it clear that a sale was intended rather than a lease
according to the Internal Revenue Service and the Tax Court.

If any of the parties to your escrows or their brokers are so inclined or if
their attorneys are interested in the source of the five factors listed above,
the following citations are grouped following the number of the paragraph
discussing the particular factor:

(1) *Quartzite Stone Company* 30 **Tax** Court 511; *Oesterreich vs.
Commissioner* 226 R2d 798.

(2) Revenue Ruling 55-540, Sec. 4.05 and cases collected thereunder.

(3) *Bowen* 12 Tax Court 446.

(4) *Judson Mills* 11 Tax Court 25.

(5) Revenue Ruling 55-542; *M&W Gear Co.* 54 Tax Court 385.*

*This material is taken from a letter written by Roger Saevig to Rose Marie
Sines-Morrisey on July 22, 1974, and is quoted by permission.

Question: Should you try a lease/option first?

Answer: Using a lease/option to avoid the lender's calling in
the loan is a *last resort.* As a buyer, you normally start out trying
to assume the old mortgage. If that is not possible, negotiate
with the lender. Only when you cannot reach agreement should
you resort to the lease/option technique.

This has an interesting sidelight that sometimes comes into
play. It has to do with your position of power.

When dealing with a lender, most people feel powerless.
After all, the lender has all that money and muscle working for
it. There is that magnificent building with the fake marble
facade. There is a complete legal department. What it says, most

people take as close to a Commandment. (In one study of believability, banks rated higher than the church!)

But the power of the lender really depends on the power we give it. If we decide in our own minds that the lender is allpowerful, then very often it is.

For example, the lender, a federally chartered S & L, may be adamant about refusing to allow us as a buyer to take over the existing low-interest-rate mortgage. The lender may say "No, under no circumstances will we allow an assumption."

We're powerless, right?

Wrong.

We now can explain to the lender exactly what we're going to do. We are going to use a lease/option device. We are going to purchase the property "subject to" the mortgage. (Remember this means the original owner's name remains on it.) And since there will be no actual transfer, there's not a thing the lender can do about it.

Now how powerless are we? If the lender believes we are in earnest, it poses a problem for him. If we go through with it, the lender will still have an old low-interest-rate mortgage on the books. But now, the lender's position will be weaker. The old mortgage will be in the name of a borrower who has gone, left the house and maybe even the county. The lender has no leverage in trying to get that borrower to keep current on payments or even to keep the property out of foreclosure.

The lender would prefer to have our name, the new buyer, on the mortgage so we have some liability for its payment. In such cases, where the true nature of the situation has been carefully explained to the lender, I've seen lender's abruptly turn about face. Suddenly they've agreed. Yes, they will agree to let us assume! Or, they will negotiate a new loan at below-market rates.

Question: How do you make payments to the lender? If they come from a new person, won't the lender suspect a sale and accelerate (call in) the mortgage?

Answer: First of all, the lender can't call in the mortgage because there's been no sale. Second, to avoid any problems with the lender, it is possible to set up a collection account with a private collection company or a friendly bank. The bank receives your money each month and then mails a check to the lender. The old owner (mortgagor or beneficiary) instructs the lender to accept the payment in this fashion.

Under a long-term lease/option:

1. A property can be bought or sold.
2. The deed and fire-insurance policy remain in the seller's name so the lender has no way to contend that legal ownership has changed. (The insurance is paid by buyer with an assignment of proceeds.)
3. Today some S & L's are including a three-year lease provision in their mortgages calling for a "due on" if the property is leased for more than three years. Smart investors are avoiding this problem by writing two-year, eleven-month leases, with options for additional leases.
4. The buyer can get the tax benefits (write off interest, taxes *and* depreciation). The seller is considered to have conducted an installment sale. As far as the IRS is concerned, if it walks like a duck, talks like a duck, looks like a duck and smells like a duck, it *is* a duck (or in this case, a sale!).
6. The buyer may assign his or her interest or receive a deed by paying off the option balance.
7. Protection is afforded to the buyer by recording the option agreements.

Finally, there is the matter of who will handle a lease/option if you want to do one?

In California, Huntington Escrow is set up to do this. If you do a lease/option, you can pay a $100 fee that goes toward paying for an attorney to represent you if any future problems should arise. The attorney will represent you at no additional cost. There are similar arrangements with escrows being currently set up in Minnesota, Indiana and other states. The lease/option is a marvelous tool, even if you only use it as a negotiating weapon with a lender.

The lease/option is as old as the hills. Yet, in today's market is is one of the newest and most exciting creative-finance tools. In the first category it allows a buyer at the bottom of the pile to get started in real estate with no money down and no ability to handle negative cash flow.

In the second category it allows a buyer in the middle to top of the pile to *legally* circumvent the "due on" clause found in most mortgages.

It is one of those great achievements in real estate—and it really works!

9

Equity Sharing:
An Answer for the 1980s

Lack of money is no longer a valid excuse. . . .

Equity sharing is a very unusual breed of cat. It is a device that allows a person who is under the pile to work with a person who is on top of the pile, to their mutual benefit.

Equity sharing is a win/win situation. If you are on top of the pile, you win with equity sharing. If you're on the bottom, you also win. And it's specifically geared to work during times of high interest rates and high-priced properties. You might say it's a win/win/win method! And that's the reason it is an answer for the eighties.

HOW IT WORKS

How does this wonderful method work? Equity sharing is not a new concept. It comes out of the tradition that, for centuries, saw parents helping their children to get started in home ownership. The kids couldn't afford to buy a home of their own. So the parents chipped in from their reserves—either for some of the down payment, or to help the kids with some of the income needed to make the monthly payments.

The key word is *sharing*. The parents and the kids shared in the cost of acquiring the house.

Today the concept of equity sharing has developed a little further. Instead of just sharing the cost, there is a sharing of the appreciation and of the ownership benefits as well. Two parties, who most likely are totally unrelated, share in the purchase of a property and subsequently share in the profits from ownership.

The occupant co-owner selects a home. An *investor* comes in and puts up the money for the down payment. The *occupant* lives in the house, maintains it, and makes the payments on principal, interest and insurance. For the occupant this comes under the category of "kiss your landlord goodbye! "

Each party then will share in the appreciation of the property, based upon a mutually agreed upon formula. The parties may also share in the tax benefits of ownership.

Let's look at the benefits of equity sharing for the occupant:

1. You get into the property either with no down or with much less down than you'd otherwise have to pay.
2. You get the benefits of ownership, including tax write-offs.
3. You share in the appreciation of the property.

If you're the investor, look at it this way—what are all the reasons NOT to get involved in real estate:

1. Negative cash flow
2. Finding tenants
3. Evicting tenants
4. Collecting rent
5. Arguing about rent
6. Fixing broken plumbing and making other repairs
7. Worrying about making the payments during periods of vacancy
8. Taking care of regular maintenance such as painting
9. Cannot get loans on non-owner-occupied property

I'm sure that if you've ever owned property you can come up with many more. My point is, what if you could own property and do away with ALL of the headaches I've just named? What if you never had to worry about tenants, or vacancies, or repairs, or maintenance, or negative cash flows?

That's the main benefit to the investor of equity sharing— peace of mind. To list them they are:

1. *Peace of mind*
2. Tax write-offs
3. A share of the appreciation

I think this will become clearer if we take an actual example. This case happened about a year ago in Southern California.

A couple, we'll call them the Shepards, came to Southern California from Minnesota. The minute they arrived in the Southland they went into culture shock. They couldn't believe the price of houses. They had been living in a nice two-story house in an excellent area of Minneapolis. In addition they had a large basement which provided them with a huge recreation room. They had nearly 3000 square feet of living area back there. They sold their home for $130,000.

But, in Los Angeles, it was a shockingly different story. They looked in a similar area, which happened to be Pacific Palisades. The cheapest home they could find in the entire area cost $240,000. It was a tiny two-bedroom crackerbox of less than 1000 equare feet that they wouldn't consider living in.

Now it was decision time. The Shepards realized that their lifestyle was threatened. To get a home that was roughly comparable to the one they left in Minnesota meant they would have to go so far away from Los Angeles that it would be an hour to an hour-and-a-half commute one way!

OR, they could accept a considerably smaller home somewhat closer in. Either way, it appeared they couldn't have their cake and eat it too. They couldn't get the house they wanted, where they wanted it.

Or could they?

It turned out they could. They ultimately did buy a grand house in the Pacific Palisades area. And they did it through equity sharing.

Here's how.

Our couple from Minnesota took the equity from the sale of their old house (which was nearly $100,000) and found an investor who put up an equal amount of equity. With the two equities combined, the Shepards had enough to buy a much larger house in the area they wanted and afford the payments on it.

Of course, they had to give up something. They gave up half the future appreciation to the investor. When they sold five years down the road, they would have to split the appreciation fifty-fifty.

But in the meantime their benefits were enormous. They now had a home they wanted, where they felt it should be. They were able to live the lifestyle they chose. And for them, the best part of it was that their neighbors never knew they only owned half their home! They were still controlling the same number of real-estate dollars, plus the quality of lifestyle fit their needs.

The moral of this story is that sharing equity provides benefits that are otherwise unaffordable.

Let's look at it from that investor's viewpoint. Why would he put up so much cash in the property?

There were many reasons. The first was that he believed the current crisis in real estate was ending and that property values were going to take off soon. He further believed that the Pacific Palisades area was one that would show rapid appreciation. (In the next chapter, we'll go into how to pick good areas.)

The second major benefit for the investor was that he didn't have to worry about managing the property. He would never, ever have to be concerned about collecting rent or fixing a leaky faucet or cleaning out a plugged toilet. No one would call him up in the middle of the night to say that the water heater had sprung a leak and flooded the kitchen. Because there were "owners" in the house, they would take care of all those problems.

Third, he would not have to worry about negative cash flow. The occupants were making the payments. All the investor had to put up was the initial half of the down payment (in this case). The occupants took care of the monthly payments. There was no negative.

Finally, the investor shared in the tax write-offs. The investor got to write off the taxes and interest on the mortgage.

For the investor, the promise of a tremendous yield plus no headaches made this an excellent opportunity.

The bottom line of equity sharing is that it is a win/win situation. Both parties get strong benefits.

Of course, I'm sure certain readers are wondering how this works out for them, particularly if they are on the bottom of the pile. How do they benefit when they don't have any money to put down? In the example, our couple from Minnesota had a substantial equity. What if our buyer has no equity at all, or no cash to put down?

Equity sharing still works. In some ways it works even better!

At the end of one of my seminars, three young men came up to me and said they were interested in equity sharing. They wanted to do it. But could they do it, since at that time they had no assets at all? They said their goal was to be successful as quickly as possible. Was there a way equity sharing could work for them?

I asked them only one question. Did they have some income that was in excess of their expenses?

They answered yes. They were all salesmen, and roommates. They weren't married and they had good incomes. (One worked for IBM and the other two for Xerox.) They did have some excess income over expenses. They didn't, however, have any cash for a down payment.

I told them yes, it certainly was possible, and that very night with the help of a broker who was also at the seminar we set the wheels in motion to put together a transaction for them.

Here's how it worked. The broker knew of an investor who wanted to get involved in real estate in a passive way. This

investor had a sum of money to invest, but she didn't want any
of the headaches that we often find with property. She didn't
want to worry about repairs. She didn't want to ever hear about
management. And she didn't want to get into a situation that
had negative cash flow.

Our three young men were brought together with this
investor, with the understanding that they would be "playing
the role" of an occupant. They wouldn't occupy the property
itself. But they would fulfill all the functions of an occupant.
They would handle all management, repairs and any negative
cash flow. In exchange, the investor would put up the down
payment.

The woman was fully aware of all aspects of the deal. She
met the young men and liked the idea.

The property they found was an $85,000 house. Here's how
the money for the purchase went:

$15,000   down with the investor
  70,000   mortgage
$85,000   purchase price

The payments on the house were $850 a month, including
mortgage and taxes. Our three young men paid this each month.
Almost immediately they rented the property out for $650 a
month.

$850   expenses
 650   rent
$200   negative

The $200 a month negative they chipped in from their own
pockets.

The term of the agreement was for five years. At the end of
five years they would sell the property. First, the woman who
put up the $15,000 would get her money back. Then our three
investors would split the remainder with her.

What did they stand to gain after five years?

I usually find that in economically sound deals, the negative
cash flow will disappear after two years when the rent is raised

to cover it (and the equity return on the mortgage increases).
Now let's calculate their out-of-pocket expenses, plus the money
they will receive back:

$$
\begin{array}{rl}
\$200 & \text{per month negative} \\
\times \quad 24 & \text{months} \\
\hline
\$4800 & \text{total investment}
\end{array}
$$

(Note: Our three investors will not have to pay $200 a month
each month. By the end of the first year, their negative should
only be about $100 per month and declining. But, we haven't
included other purchase costs such as closing, so to balance
things out and make them simple, I'm just going to assume that
their investment is roughly $5000 in cash in the property over
five years.)

Now, what is their return?

First, because it's a rental they have annual tax write-offs,
which they split with their investor. These include three items:
negative cash flow, depreciation, and other costs. Let's take each
separately.

Negative Cash Flow

The property is showing a *loss*, not a profit, during the first two
years. We'll assume this amount is $2500. So the first write-off
is $2500.

Depreciation

According to the new tax laws of 1981, real estate can be depreciated over a term of 15 years. In addition you can take accelerated depreciation of 175% declining balance.

This is not really as difficult as it sounds and the calculation
is fairly easy. Here's how it's made.

First we determine the value of the improvements. (We can
only depreciate buildings, not land.)

$$
\begin{array}{rl}
\$85,000 & \text{value} \\
-\ 25,000 & \text{land value} \\
\hline
\$60,000 & \text{building cost}
\end{array}
$$

Our building cost $60,000. Now we divide this by the term of the depreciation period—15 years.

$$\$60,000 \div 15 = \$4000$$

The first year the depreciation, on a "straight-line" or 100-percent basis, would be $4000. But, we are allowed to depreciate it by a 175% rate. So for additional write-off we can take 12% of the improvements during the 12 months of ownership.

$60,000	value of improvements
× 12%	accelerated first 12-month write-off
$ 7,200	

The first year's depreciation write-off would be $7,200.

Of course, since so much would be written off the first year, the second year's write-off would be less. Over five years we can figure an average of about $6000 a year or a total write-off of $30,000. (If you have problems understanding how a declining balance works, don't worry about it. Just have your accountant figure it out for you. It won't cost much and you'll be sure you get it right.)

Finally, there is the write-off that comes from incidental items such as transportation to and from the property, phone calls, advertisements and so forth. I just assume $500 per year for this. For five years it would be $2500.

Total write-offs:

Negative cash flow	$ 2,500
Depreciation	30,000
Incidental expense	2,500
	$35,000

Total write-offs after five years equals $35,000.

Of course, our friends have to split this with their investor. Their share is half, or $17,500.

Since our friends are in the 35% tax bracket, what are their savings in taxes over the five-year period?

$$\begin{array}{r} \$17,500 \\ \times \quad\quad 35\% \\ \hline \$\ 6,125 \end{array}$$

Their tax savings are $6125.

What was the total cash they put up? Go back a few pages and see if you can find that figure.

The reason I went through with this long example was to show the actual, true benefits to the investor with no cash from an equity-sharing venture. By the way, their total investment in cash was $5000:

$$\begin{array}{rl} \$5,000 & \text{cash invested over 5 years} \\ & \quad \text{(for negative cash flow and closing cost)} \\ \underline{\$6,250} & \text{tax savings} \\ -\ \$1,250 & \text{total investment} \end{array}$$

That's right. Their total investment was a MINUS $1250!

By the time the five-year period was up and they went to sell the property, they had already made $1250 on it plus got back every penny they put in. Now, what was their ultimate profit?

I'm going to assume the property appreciated at the rate of 10 percent a year. That means that at the end of five years it was worth $134,000. Here's how the figures go for the profit:

$$\begin{array}{rl} \$134,000 & \text{value at sale time} \\ -\quad 8,000 & \text{commission for sale and closing costs} \\ \hline \$126,000 & \text{net sales price} \\ -\ 15,000 & \text{goes to the investor (her original down} \\ \hline \$111,000 & \quad \text{payment)} \\ -\ 68,000 & \text{pay off mortgage(s)} \\ \hline \$43,000 & \text{net profit} \\ \div\quad\quad 2 & \text{split between investor and three guys} \\ \hline \$21,500 \end{array}$$

Our three guys end up with a $21,500 profit. (Of course, there's capital gains to pay on this profit and capital gains plus ordinary income taxes on the accelerated portion of the depreciation taken earlier.)

The point should be obvious and I hope worth the time spent going through this example. They've made a lot of money on essentially no investment at all. How would you calculate this return—$21,500 on a minus $1250 investment?

Equity sharing does work both for the individual who wants to upgrade a lifestyle, as was the case of the Shepards from Minnesota, and for the investor. In fact, it's possible to make a list of the specific benefits to both the occupant and the investor of equity sharing.

Let's look once again at the benefits of equity sharing.

BENEFITS OF EQUITY SHARING

For the occupant:

1. Little or no down payment
2. Easier to qualify
3. One-half ownership at start
4. Option to buy out investor is possible
5. Lower monthly payments (because the investor has put up a down payment which lowers the mortgage amount)
6. Yearly tax write-offs

For the investor:

1. No negative cash flow
2. No repairs or maintenance
3. No management problems
4. Tremendous yield. (Besides the tax write-offs, our investor in the last example more than doubled her money!)
5. Yearly tax write-off
6. Safety, security and *peace* of *mind* (No worry about eviction, vacancy, rent control, or a loan turned down because non-owner occupied)

And that's equity sharing.

I'm sure that, after this presentation, you have many questions. The reason I'm sure is that in my seminars people always have lots of questions. So what I've done is to list the most commonly asked questions about equity sharing.

QUESTIONS AND ANSWERS ON EQUITY SHARING

1. What is the difference between a SAM (Shared Appreciation Mortgage) and equity sharing? There's a lot of confusion because people use these terms interchangeably. People will say "Oh yes, you mean a SAM" when I talk about equity sharing.

No, these are *two different things.* Equity sharing plans are not mortgages. They are investments. There is no guaranteed return of principle or profit. The bottom line is that the SAM is a real-estate loan in which the lender, in consideration for lowering the rate of interest charged the buyer, shares a portion of the profit realized from the appreciated profit from the house when sold.

The equity sharing plan is one in which two parties join together in an ownership venture.

The SAMs were created for two reasons. The first was to get the home buyer in with a lower monthly payment. But, the second was to allow the lenders to keep up with the rate of inflation. I sometimes think the lender's viewpoint is that "Inflation is a fate worse than debt!"

2. Can a seller participate in equity sharing? Sure. Many sellers love to do it. For one reason or another, they may be forced to sell now. But if they think they can sell AND get some of the property's future appreciation, they'll jump at the chance.

Consider it from the viewpoint of a seller of a $100,000 house. That seller may owe half (or $50,000) and need $30,000 in cash.

Suppose a buyer comes in and says "I'll get a new mortgage (either a new first or a hard-money second) and you'll get the cash from that. But, instead of my giving you a $20,000 down payment, we'll share the equity.

$80,000	mortgages (new first or hard-money second)
− 50,000	existing first
$30,000	cash to seller
$20,000	remaining down payment which the seller now
	leaves in for half the future appreciation

The seller is getting $30,000 in cash out of this deal. At the same time she's going to keep $20,000 of her equity in the property. But she'll be removed from all negative cash flow worries and from management and repair headaches. Plus, she'll share in some of the tax write-offs. And at the end of five years (or whenever) she'll share in half the appreciation.

You're doggone right that many sellers will jump at this plan!

Another way that sellers can participate is when the seller carries back the mortgage. Here we're not talking about splitting the equity, but a straightforward sale. In today's market the seller might be expected to carry back a mortgage at 16% or 18% or higher.

But the buyer may say whoa. Instead of your getting all that interest, why not charge me only 8% or 9%? In return, when I sell the property at the end of five years, you can have 10 or 20 percent of the appreciation.

It's important to understand that the equity does *not* have to be shared fifty-fifty. Any combination that fits buyer and sellers needs and demands can be used.

3. How are the funds handled for both the occupant and the investor? It's relatively simple. There is an escrow and an appraisal to determine the property's value. The investor who comes in with money on a property knows the price is fair because of the appraisal. The investor writes an initial check to open escrow and puts up the remaining funds upon the close of escrow.

Title insurance is issued along with a title report to both occupant and investor.

From there on, the occupant handles the responsibility of the monthly payments.

There is the matter of the initial closing costs. In most cases the *occupant* will come up with the initial closing costs. In cases where there is no new first mortgage to a lender, these costs are usually low, and almost always they are less than $3000 (depending, of course, on the price of the property).

4.   Is being a co-owner a sound investment? This question, I think, relates to the potential yield from the property. This has to do with the property, its location, and the outlook for investment in that particular marketplace. (We'll go into choosing a property in the next chapter.) Equity sharing is the kind of investment that you go into when you're bullish on real estate. If you've looked at the signals I gave back in Chapter 2 and you've decided that the market's going to crash—don't get into equity sharing.

But, if you're convinced that the market's going to go up then, yes, it can be a sound investment.

I like to remember what Will Rogers used to say about property and inflation. "Invest in inflation. It's the only thing I know of that always goes up!"

Equity sharing can be one of the soundest investments you can make. It can be one of the safest and best investments you could make during the 1980s *and* you can help some first-time buyer who could not have bought without your help.

5.   What protection do I receive as an investor? The answer is that, as an investor, you go on the deed. You will have recorded in your name a 50-percent interest in the property. Title will actually be taken as "tenants in common," so that you will have an undivided 50 percent interest.

At a later date you can sell that interest. You can will it. If you die it goes into your estate. The bottom line is that you are protected. You have all the safeguards that would normally be provided in a "prudent-man" investment in property.

6.   Has this type of ownership been successfully used? Does it have a good track record? For hundreds of years parents have been doing this exact same thing to help their children get into property. In essence, it's institutionalizing the concept of the parents helping children, only now we're doing it between unrelated parties for purely economic reasons.

7. What happens when the property is sold? It depends on your initial agreement between occupant and investor. There are four basic approaches.

Approach 1. There is a pure fifty-fifty split. This is what I call the "KISS" formula. That stands for "Keep It Simple, Stupid!"

This is the shortest, easiest agreement to construct. It is usually for five years. At the end of that time either the occupant refinances and buys out the investor (for an appraised value determined by an FHA appraiser) OR the occupant and investor put the property on the market, sell it for the best price possible, and then (after closing costs) split the profits fifty-fifty.

There are at least three other approaches that require different types of forms and agreements.

Approach 2. This is the "co-owner" approach. Under this approach there is specified preferential return to the investor. If the investor says, for example, "I should be earning interest on this money I'm putting into the property," the agreement can provide that the investor will receive a specific credit of 7 percent per year, or 8 percent per year, or whatever. At the time of sale (or refinance), this amount would be subtracted from the profits *before* they were split.

The investor would get his original investment, plus his 7 or 8 percent per year, and then the profits would be split fifty-fifty.

Approach 3. This is the "tenant's approach." Here the occupant says to the investor "Wait a minute, here. My payments are going to be a thousand dollars a month. I could go out and rent this same property for only $650 a month. I'm not sure this is such a good deal for me. I'm going to have to make up a $350 a month negative for a long time."

Under this approach the contract is written so that the payment will remain at over a thousand a month. But one-third or $333 will be a credit toward your return when the property is sold.

This approach is particularly useful when the investor says "Hey, I want all the depreciation" and the occupant says "Whoa, I could rent the house next door for a whole lot less than this will cost." Under this arrangement, each party gets the very benefits they want.

Approach 4. This is the conservative "investor's approach." This is usually a three-year agreement where the investor receives the first 5, 6, or 7 percent per year of appreciation. (Of course it could be 4 percent or whatever is agreed upon.)

Everything over that goes to the occupant.

How does this benefit the investor?

It assures him of the first appreciation and a specific return (assuming prices go up). Here the investor doesn't have to worry about tight years when appreciation might only be 7 percent. In that case, the investor would get it all.

Since the investor normally would only put 20 percent down, that means he or she would more than *double* the investment in just three years!

I live in Southern California, in an area where appreciation over the last five years has averaged 13 percent a year. In that case the occupant would get the amount over 7 percent or 16 percent a year. The occupant would come out fine.

The point to understand about this approach is that the majority of the risk is switched from a fifty-fifty kind of thing to the back of the occupant. In some cases both occupant and investor may agree it's fair. After all, the investor is putting up $20,000.

As we saw from the example of the three guys, if things go well, at the end of the investment period the occupant investment can be zero. In fact, the occupant will already have made money back.

In this approach, if both investor and occupant agree, there is an equitable split of the risk as determined by the money put up.

In most areas of the country today there are brokers who know how to use this new approach to investing and have the forms necessary to do it. If you don't know of a broker who can handle this kind of transaction, write a note to the address printed at the end of the next paragraph, and I'll send you the name of someone in your area who does this kind of work.

My knowledge of brokers comes from the fact that I tour the country giving seminars in which I train brokers to use these techniques. Should there be no broker in your area capable of handling equity sharing, you can obtain the four forms plus four hours of tapes that explain how to use them for the same price I charge to brokers. Telephone (213) 577-7444 or write to this address: 100 S. Los Robles Ave., Pasadena, CA 91101.

8. What is my position as an investor in terms of approving the occupant? As the investor, you will receive a financial statement from the occupant. In addition, if there's a conventional loan, it will require the approval of the lender. That gives you some assurance of stability as far as the payments are concerned. Usually lenders carefully screen borrowers. You can be fairly assured, at least from the lender's viewpoint, that the occupant is a good risk.

9. What if a dispute arises? This is an important question. I have inserted in the forms I use a clause that calls for "binding arbitration" by both parties . . . and then investor and occupant use whatever arbitration association they want. I use the American Arbitration Association. They do an excellent job, and it avoids the hassle of having to run to an attorney. Both parties agree to agree.

For example, let's say there's supposed to be a 50/50 profit split at the end of the fifth year.

At the end of this time our occupant has fallen in love with the property and doesn't want to sell. He wants to refinance and buy out the investor.

So the occupant goes to refinance. He gets an appraisal on the property and some refinance money lined up.

But then the investor looks at it and says "Wait a minute! That's a very conservative appraisal. It's a lowball appraisal on the part of the most conservative lender in this area. I'm not going to agree to have my interests sold for 50 percent of that figure."

At this point both investor and occupant go before the arbitrators. Each party presents its own appraisal and the arbitrator can call for a third, independent appraisal.

Then the arbitrator decides on the basis of all three. And because we've agreed to agree, that's the end of the issue.

10.   Can I become an investor on more than one property using equity sharing? Or, if at a later date I would like to be an occupant under an equity-sharing program, is that possible? The answers are yes/yes. There is no limit to the number of equity-sharing programs in which you can be an investor. And even if you are an investor in one program, there's no reason to believe you can't be an occupant in another.

11.   What about visually inspecting the property? You should visually inspect the property if at all possible. But there will be some investors out of the area. The investor may be in New York and want to buy property in California, Texas or Arizona.

In this case an appraisal should be provided to the investor (including color photographs) so he or she can have a feel for what the property looks like.

12.   What about closing costs? These are paid for by the occupant.

13.   What are the potential risks? The potential risks are that the investor could lose the capital he has invested. The occupant could come in, make payments that exceed the amount for which he could have rented a similar property, and wind up having no appreciation.

If you feel that the market is not going to go up, then you should stay out of this kind of investment. The most honest answer to the question is that the risks are *total*. You could lose 100 percent of everything you put in this investment.

14. What's the difference between an equity-sharing investment and a trust-deed investment? It's simple. In a trust deed you're probably going to be receiving a fixed high return in today's market, so you get a high monthly payment plus the ultimate return of your capital. But, you do not get a hedge against inflation. Also you do not have any tax benefits.

Trust deeds can be an excellent tool, used at the right time. They are an important part of the five-year plan to financial freedom.

On the other side of the coin, in equity-sharing you pick up some tax benefits. In addition, you have the potential of enormous yield. You could receive 50 percent or more return per year, depending on appreciation.

15. Can existing loans be assumed? It depends on the laws of the state in which you live. In California, for example, all state-charted mortgages can be assumed.

For federally chartered S & L's, it is possible to do a lease/ option and then turn around and do an equity/sharing. But to do this is pretty sophisticated and it's rare that both an occupant and an investor have the know-how that allows both to understand and handle this kind of deal.

16. What about the different types of new loans? Can they be used under equity sharing? Yes. As long as it's an assumable loan, or you can purchase "subject to," or the lender will approve, there's no reason at all you can't use the equity-sharing approach with any loan.

17. Will there be a credit check of the occupant? Definitely, yes. The transaction should not be completed without a credit check of the occupant, if for no other reason than to protect the investor.

Many investors, however, complain that they don't have an account with TRW and cannot order up a credit report.

In that case you should have a friendly banker or a friend at a credit union, who for a $4 fee can call up a credit report on the occupant. (I've said it before, but it bears repeating. You should take your banker out to lunch at least once a year! It establishes a relationship that will pay off in the future, besides imparting to you an enormous amount of information.)

18. What if I want to sell my interest? You can sell it, but you shouldn't go in expecting to.

There is no guarantee of any liquidity in this particular investment. You could give it away or sell it IF you are able to find someone who will buy.

It's somewhat similar to the position of someone who owns a trust deed. If you wait for the entire term of the mortgage, you should get all your money out. But, if you sell early, you'll have to take a discount. The same thing occurs here.

19. Can the investor or the occupant borrow against the property? Yes. You can provide in the original agreement for some borrowing on the property.

For example, I know of a couple of investors who are getting involved in equity sharing. And they aren't concerned with cashing out in three or five years. They are looking for long-term investment.

So they are saying "We will not lock you in, or put a sword over your head after five years. In return, we want to have the right that, when the property goes up, we can refinance and get our original investment back."

An agreement to this effect has worked for investors and occupants.

20. Do I have to pay a broker's fee if I use an agent? The answer is yes. If you, an investor, have a broker go out and find you a property and an occupant, you have to pay a fee. That fee can be handled in one of three ways: (1) the seller can pay it; (2) the buyer (occupant) can pay it; (3) the investor can pay it.

One of the three must reach down in his or her pocket and come up with the fee if you use an agent.

21. What is the minimum time that must elapse before an occupant can come in and buy out the investor? The answer is one year and one day. The reason for that is to provide a capital gain for the investor. Any time after that, the occupant could buy out the investor.

22. What happens if the occupant is transferred and can't continue as the occupant? If one year and one day have elapsed, the property can be sold. The occupant could rent the property, but the original occupant/co-owner remains obligated under the agreement. The investor/co-owner could refuse to accept a rental that was below expenses, and the occupant/co-owner might have to make up any negative.

23. Is equity sharing limited to single-family housing? Not at all. You can do office buildings, strip centers, commercial buildings. You name it and it can be done.

24. Can a limited partnership be used? Definitely. An "A-B" partnership can be used where one individual picks up the tax benefits while the other picks up the cash flow or the capital gain. There are tremendous possibilities here.

I think it should be clear that equity sharing is an exciting concept and an exciting program that you can use to get your foot up on the first rung of the real-estate ladder. And, for the person in the middle or the top of the pile, it's a great way to be a passive investor.

THE EQUITY SHARING FORM

Here is an equity-sharing *specimen* form for a fifty-fifty sharing of property. *Do not use this document as you find it in this book.* Before you actually become involved in a transaction, take this document to an attorney in your particular area. Wherever you happen to be, you will find little intricacies that differ from other areas. While this form may save you thousands of dollars (in legal fees you might otherwise have to pay to come up with something from scratch), you *must have* a legal authority review the document to make sure it's applicable for you, where you are.

DO NOT USE THIS DOCUMENT UNTIL YOU HAVE TAKEN IT TO AN ATTORNEY AND GOTTEN A LEGAL OPINION ON IT FOR YOUR AREA!

CO-TENANCY AGREEMENT

THIS AGREEMENT entered into this _____ day of _____

19___, by and between _____

hereafter referred to as Investor, and _____

_____ hereafter referred to as Co-Owner.

WHEREAS, Investor is purchasing the property located at _____

_____ , (the "property") and more particularly described in Exhibit "A" attached hereto and incorporated herein by this reference.

WHEREAS, Investor wishes to sell an undivided one-half interest in such property to Co-Owner as tenants in common.

WHEREAS, the parties desire to provide for the financing, management and disposition of such property.

IT IS, THEREFORE, agreed as follows:

1.   TERM OF AGREEMENT

The term of the agreement shall be for a period of _____months, unless modified in a writing signed by both parties.

2.   VALUE OF PROPERTY

The value of said property is agreed to be _____

_____($_____).

3.   INVESTOR'S CONTRIBUTION

The Investor shall contribute cash in the amount of _____

_____($_____).

hereinafter referred to as "Investor's contribution," such contribution changing from time to time as otherwise provided in this Agreement.

4. CO-OWNER'S CONTRIBUTION

The Co-Owner shall contribute cash in the amount of _____

_____($_____).
hereinafter referred to as "Co-Owner's contribution," such contribution changing
from time to time as otherwise provided in this Agreement.

5. CONSIDERATIONS FOR CO-OWNER PURCHASE OF A ONE-HALF INTEREST

(a) Co-Owner agrees to pay to the Investor, for the term of this agreement

monthly payments of _____

_____ ($_____) which shall be based on
the actual amount of payments due on all note(s) encumbering the property along

with 1/12th of the annual taxes, insurance, and _____ .
Such monthly payment shall be automatically adjusted to reflect changes in taxes,
insurance, or other costs referred to above during the term of this agreement. Payments shall be due on the first day of every month and shall be delinquent if not
received by Investor or his designee by the fifth day of each month.

(b) The monthly payment shall be credited as follows:
1) One-half of the payment shall be deemed to be a purchase payment
to Investor for Co-Owner's one-half interest in the property, and
2) The remaining one-half payment shall be a lease payment to Investor
for the one-half interest retained by him in the property.

Any partial or late payments shall be applied first to late charges under paragraph
11 (c), secondly to rent, and any remainder to monthly payments. The Investor, or
his designee, shall make all monthly payments to all beneficiaries and for taxes and
insurance and other costs as referred to above, upon receipt of the monthly payment
from Co-Owner.

(c) Co-Owner shall execute a Deed of Trust (the "Deed of Trust") in favor of
Investor in the form attached hereto as Exhibit "B" for the purpose of securing:
1) Payment to Investor of the purchase payment set forth in paragraph
5 (a) above; and
2) The faithful performance by Co-Owner of his obligations as set forth
in this agreement.

The Deed of Trust shall name _____

_____ as Trustee.

(d) Co-Owner agrees to maintain said property at his sole expense and shall
not make any improvements without prior written consent of Investor.

(e) Co-Owner shall not dispose of any real or personal property located in or
upon the property without prior written consent of Investor.

(f) Upon execution of this agreement, Co-Owner shall pay for a one-year
Homeowners Fire Insurance Policy naming Investor as Co-Insured, which coverage

shall not be less than _____

_____ ($_____)
In the event of a total loss, insurance proceeds shall be distributed as follows;

1) First in payment to Co-Owner and Investor of their respective contributions; and
2) Second, in payment of loss of Co-Owners personal property located on the property; and
3) Remainder of proceeds in payment to Co-Owner and Investor in proportion to their interests in the property.

(g) The parties shall purchase a Home Warranty Policy upon execution of this agreement. The cost of such policy shall be borne equally by the parties. The parties shall maintain this Home Warranty Policy during the term of this agreement.

6. LEASE OF PROPERTY BY CO-OWNER

(a) The parties shall execute a lease agreement in the form attached as Exhibit "C" (the "lease"), whereby Co-Owner shall be entitled to exclusive possession of the property during the term of this agreement.

(b) Notwithstanding the foregoing the lease shall terminate upon the earliest of the following to occur:
1) Sale of the property;
2) Purchase of Investor's interest in the property by Co-Owner;
3) Purchase of Co-Owner's interest in the property by Investor; or
4) Mutual consent of the parties.

7. TITLE TO PROPERTY

The parties shall hold title to the property as tenants in common, each as to an undivided one-half interest.

8. ENCUMBRANCES AND LIENS

The parties acknowledge that the property is currently encumbered as set forth in Exhibit "D", and the parties further acknowledge that they have each made an independent determination that the information contained therein is true and correct.

9. ENCUMBRANCES AND ASSIGNMENTS BY CO-OWNER

Co-Owner shall not sell, transfer, assign or encumber his interest in the property, this agreement, or the lease of the property without the prior written consent of the Investor, which may not be unreasonably withheld.

10. DEFAULT BY CO-OWNER

The occurrence of any of the following shall constitute a default by Co-Owner;

(a) Failure to make any payment under paragraph 5 when due, if the failure continues for five (5) days after written notice has been given to Co-Owner;

(b) Abandonment of the premises by Co-Owner; or

(c) Failure to perform any other provision of this agreement or the lease if the failure to perform is not cured within five (5) days after written notice has been given by Investor. The notice shall state that Co-Owner must cure the default within the applicable period of time or quit the premises. No such notice shall be deemed a forfeiture or a termination of this agreement unless Investor so elects in the notice.

11. INVESTOR'S REMEDIES IN CASE OF DEFAULT

(a) Investor shall have the following remedies if Co-Owner commits default;

(i) If Co-Owner commits any default under paragraph 10 hereof, Investor may terminate the lease referred to in paragraph 6 and regain possession of the property in the manner provided by the laws of unlawful detainer in the State of California in effect at the date of such default. Co-Owner agrees that the right to possession of the property shall terminate by such default, notwithstanding the ownership interest in the property. At Investor's option, Investor may continue the lease in effect

for so long as Investor does not terminate Co-Owner's right to possession by written notice, and Investor may enforce all of the rights and
remedies under this agreement, including the right to recover rent as
it becomes due. Investor's right hereunder shall be in addition to those
provided by the lease hereto.

(ii) If Co-Owner fails to make any payment within five (5) days after notice
of default as set forth in paragraph 10 above or defaults on any of the
obligations under this agreement, the entire amount of Investor's contribution and purchase payments required by paragraph 5 shall become
immediately due and payable to Investor.

(iii) Co-Owner acknowledges that if any monthly payment due from Co-
Owner is not received by Investor when due, Investor will incur costs,
the exact amount of which is extremely difficult and impractical to fix.
Therefore, Co-Owner shall pay to Investor an additional sum equal to
ten (10) percent of the overdue rent and purchase payments as a late
charge. The parties agree that this late charge represents a fair and
reasonable estimate of the costs that Investor will incur by reason of
late payment by Co-Owner. Acceptance of any late charge shall not
constitute a waiver of Co-Owner's default with respect to the overdue
amount, or prevent Investor from exercising any of the other rights and
remedies available to him.

(b)   Each of the remedies of Investor shall be construed as cumulative and no
one of them as exclusive of the other or as exclusive of any remedy provided by law
or equity.

12. DEFAULT BY INVESTOR

Upon execution of this agreement, a Request for Notice of Default shall be given
to all lenders on behalf of the Co-Owner. If the Investor fails to make any payments
of the property when due, it shall be default. If Investor does not cure the default
within five (5) days after written notice has been given by Co-Owner, Co-Owner
may thereafter, at his option;

(a)   Make all payments directly to the holder(s) of the Note(s);
(b)   Pay premiums on insurance covering the property; and
(c)   Pay taxes and assessments due on such property.

Any sums paid by Co-Owner shall be due immediately from the Investor, and if not
paid shall bear interest at the rate of ten (10) percent per annum until paid.

13. OPTIONS TO PURCHASE OR SELL

Each party shall have the right to purchase the interest of the other party in such
premises on the following terms and conditions;

(a)   At any time during the first twelve (12) months after execution of the
agreement, Co-Owner may purchase Investor's interest in the property for the

sum of _____

_____($_____.)

(b)   At any time during the thirteenth (13th) through the twenty-fourth (24th)
month after execution of agreement, Co-Owner may purchase Investor's interest in

the property for the sum of _____

_____($_____.)

(c)   Should agreement term extend beyond twenty-four (24) months buyout

figures for years _____
are computed and stated in exhibit "E" attached hereto.

(d)   If Co-Owner should elect not to purchase Investor's one-half interest prior
to the end of the ____ year as set forth above, Investor shall have the option to
purchase Co-Owner's one-half interest for the same amount as stated in paragraph
13 (b) or (c), as the case may be, less the Investor's contribution. This option shall
expire unless exercised in writing at least sixty (60) days prior to the date of termination of this agreement as set forth in paragraph 1 above.

(e)   Upon the sale of the property, the proceeds shall be distributed as follows;
   (1)   Cost of Sale as shown in Exhibit "E" attached hereto;
   (2)   Payment to Investor and Co-Owner of their respective contributions;
          and
   (3)   The remainder of the proceeds shall be divided equally between
          Investor and Co-Owner.

(f)   All options stated in paragraph 13 shall be in writing and given to the
respective party at least sixty (60) days prior to the expiration of said option.

14. NOTICES
Any and all notices and other communications required by this agreement shall be
in writing and shall be deemed duly served and given when personally delivered
to any of the parties to whom it is directed, or in lieu of such personal service,
when deposited in the United States mail, first class postage prepaid, addressed to

Investor at _____

_____

or Co-Owner at the property address or such other address that the Co-Owner may
give to the Investor.

15. ATTORNEY'S FEES
In the event any legal action is brought by either party to enforce the terms hereof
or relating to the property, the prevailing party shall be entitled to all costs incurred
in connection with such action, including reasonable attorney's fees as determined
by the Court.

16. ARBITRATION
Any controversy or claim arising out of or relating to this agreement, or the breach
thereof, shall be settled by arbitration in accordance with the rules or the American
Arbitration Association, and judgement upon the award rendered by the arbitrator(s)
may be entered in any court having jurisdiction thereof.

17. FINANCIAL DISCLOSURE STATEMENT
PARTIES ACKNOWLEDGE RECEIPT OF THE FINANCIAL DISCLOSURE STATE-
MENT ATTACHED HERETO AS EXHIBIT "E". THE PARTIES FURTHER ACKNOWL-
EDGE THAT THEY HAVE MADE AN INDEPENDENT DETERMINATION THAT THE
INFORMATION CONTAINED THEREIN IS TRUE AND CORRECT. THE PARTIES
AGREE TO INDEMNIFY AND HOLD REALTORS, ITS AGENTS AND EMPLOYEES,
HARMLESS FROM ANY AND ALL LIABILITY ARISING DIRECTLY OR INDIRECTLY
FROM THE USE OF OR RELIANCE UPON INFORMATION CONTAINED IN THE
FINANCIAL DISCLOSURE STATEMENT.

_____	_____
INVESTOR	DATE
_____	_____
INVESTOR	DATE
_____	_____
CO-OWNER	DATE
_____	_____
CO-OWNER	DATE

STATE OF _____

COUNTY OF _____

On, _____, before me, the undersigned, a Notary Public in and for said County and State, personally appeared _____

_____

known to me to be the person(s) whose name(s) is (are) subscribed to the within instrument and acknowledged that _____

_____

executed the same.

_____
(Notary signature line)

10

How to Profit from Distressed Properties

The millionaires of the late eighties will be those who bought distressed properties in the early eighties. . . .

There are more foreclosures and delinquencies today than at any time in the last 33 years. You can buy foreclosure properties. Houses are available for just the delinquent payments. Land, apartments, commercial properties are available with no down payment, no credit check, no refinancing charge, in all areas of the country and in all price ranges. No real-estate license is required.

It works particularly well during a crisis, when so much distressed property is available.

I have had the privilege of interviewing the superstars of real estate, but one investor sticks in my mind when the topic turns to foreclosures.

Today Henry is a multimillionaire. He was formerly a used-car salesman, but in a matter of just a few years he transformed himself into a wealthy man by buying and selling distressed property for profit.

Henry's technique for buying distressed property was hard to beat. (I know, because in at least two instances, Henry beat

a friend of mine out of deals that he thought were sewed up!)
What Henry did was to hire someone to go every day to the
county recorder's office. Her task was to find out which properties had recorded a notice of default on them. (That meant
they were in foreclosure.)

When she found out, she would do two things. The first
thing she would do was address a prewritten card to the property
owners. The card would say, among other things:

"As you may know or will soon be notified (Henry's cards
often reached the property owners *before* notification came from
the lender), your property is in foreclosure. I'm an investor
looking for tax benefits. I will be happy to purchase your property from you before your credit rating is ruined and the sheriff
throws you out onto the street. For more information call...."

You can be sure Henry's card scared a lot of people into
calling him!

The second thing Henry's assistant did was to prepare a list
of all the properties in foreclosure. Henry would scan the list
and choose those properties of interest to him. Then he would
go to each property, knock on the door and introduce himself.
Frequently he would buy the property from the owner for just
$100 cash above the mortgage.

(The way he beat my friend out was this: Twice my friend
arrived on the scene ahead of Henry and offered the $100. When
Henry arrived a day later, he also offered $100. The people signed
and Henry immediately had his sales agreement notarized and
recorded. The recording of the document gave Henry's sale
priority over my friend's, even though the other deal had been
signed first. Not only that—the seller kept my friend's hundred
dollars!)

Henry presented a solution to these sellers' problem. They
were losing their property anyway. At least with Henry they
were able to salvage their credit. By buying up property in this
fashion, then fixing it up, renting it out, and eventually selling
at a profit, Henry was able to make his fortune. He did this
during the strong market of the past three or four years, when
there were very few foreclosures and lots of people looking for
them.

Today, opportunities in distressed property are going to abound.

As real-estate prices begin falling, people who had been barely holding onto their property, counting on a big future appreciation to save them, will suddenly let go. Where there were one or two foreclosures in an area a day, soon there will be dozens. It hardly needs pointing out that those people who made their fortunes during the Great Depression, did so by buying up distressed property. They bought at foreclosure prices, rented for a while, and then, when prices moved upward, sold for huge profits.

I should point out that, even if there were to be no crisis at all, the opportunities in distressed property would still be there. This was brought home to me just the other day.

For my seminars, I get materials copied at one particular copy shop. Each time I would go in, the woman behind the counter would say "Hal, I want to talk to you about property. I've been reading some of these things you have copied and I have things I want to speak with you about."

But, quite frankly, I never seemed to have the time. Either I was late in getting the material ready for the seminar, or I was rushing to consult on financing or something else. I just never had time for her.

Finally, one day just a few weeks ago, she buttonholed me and said "Hal, you really have to see what I've got."

So I agreed to talk with her, and I was amazed. She had gone out and bought property that the state had taken back for failure to pay taxes. (Each state will claim real estate if the taxes are not paid on it for a period of years. The time in California, for example, is five years.)

She said that she had little chance of picking up houses or other developed property. That was because there were lots of other, richer bidders vying for it. But she had good results with land. Almost no one bid on lots which the state had taken for unpaid taxes. "I guess everybody figures that if someone didn't pay the taxes on it, it must be a rotten hunk of land."

But she went out and looked at the property. In some cases the owners had gotten divorced and simply "split." In other cases there were deaths with no relatives to claim or even handle the estate. The reasons for the unpaid taxes were endless. But, her point was that some of the property was terrific.

She had purchased for $8000 two acres in the Lancaster-Palmdale area near where the city of Los Angeles plans to build a super airport. She soon found out that an industrial park was planned next door. Within a year she had an offer of $2 per square *foot* (over $160,000) for those two acres.

She had bought three lake-view lots near the water at Lake Arrowhead, a resort area about a hundred miles outside of Los Angeles. She bought all three lots for $12,000. Good lake-view lots were selling for upwards of $40,000 apiece!

Her list of properties went on and on. She had one lot in Riverside near an off-ramp from the freeway. It looked like it might be sold to a commercial developer.

In each case she had simply gone out and looked at the land, then made a bid. In many cases she had gotten it, and she was rapidly getting rich from her actions.

My friend at the copy store was doing this, not during a real-estate crash period, but during a period of rapid price appreciation. The bottom line is that she, like Henry, did it during good times. So can you. If the market crashes, the opportunities in distressed property will be enormous. But even if it doesn't crash, the opportunities will still be there for those creative and energetic enough to find them.

If I've convinced you to consider distressed property, then your next question must surely be, how do I find it? Here's the answer to that.

FORECLOSURES

In a foreclosure, the trustee (if it's a trust-deed lender) or the mortgagee (usually through the court, if it's a mortgage) notifies the borrower that he or she is in default. That means that payments haven't been made (usually) for a few months. The borrower then has a stated period of time (anywhere from a few days to many months) to make good all the back payments and reinstate the mortgage.

If the borrower can't bring the mortgage back to current status, the lender then goes through a specific legal procedure called a *foreclosure sale*. Essentially what happens is that the property is offered for sale to the highest bidder.

There are two opportunities to buy property that is in foreclosure. The first is the way Henry did it, direct from the owner when the notice of default is recorded.

The second is at the foreclosure sale.

All foreclosure sales must be advertised. That is, legal notice must be given. In most cities and counties there are "legal" newspapers. These are publications of general circulation that the courts have determined have sufficient distribution to give proper notice to the public. Usually they are very small, obscure journals. You may have to consult with a broker or an attorney to find the one in your locale.

Additionally, most areas have information services that weekly list all property that is in foreclosure and going for sale. By paying a fee, you can have the list sent to you each week. (In our earlier example, Henry hired someone to do this for him. That way he often got the information a full week ahead of everyone else!)

In the past, when properties were sold at a foreclosure sale there was often heavy bidding by a large number of people. Even though the loan might be only for, say, $100,000, the bidders would bid the price up well beyond that, perhaps to $125,000 or higher.

But in today's lackluster market there are few, if any, bidders. Often it is possible to pick up the property for just the loan value. I just saw an oceanfront condo in Southern California sell for $120,000 (the exact amount of the first) at a foreclosure sale.

(Note: The lender almost always bids the amount of the mortgage. That is the money that has already been loaned on the property and is usually the minimum bid. The lender takes it back for this price, holds it for a time and tries to resell to recoup the full money loaned. Rarely will a lender allow the property to be sold to someone else for less than the loan amount.)

The negative with foreclosure sales is that, in order to be a successful bidder, you have to have all cash (preferably a cashier's check). The positive is that you can often get property for 25 percent (or more) off the market price. (But don't be fooled by this reduction. Sometimes it is better to pay full price for a property if you can get good longterm financing!)

A word of caution. Stay away from foreclosure sales in states where the borrower has a "judicial right of redemption." That means that the borrower can come back any time up to several years later and redeem the property by paying you your costs plus an interest charge. You would lose the time and effort you spent, not to mention the hoped-for appreciation.

But, I hear a reader in North Carolina asking, "How do I do it? How do I get started?"

Here's how I did it.

I would send a letter in the form of a postcard to people whose property was in foreclosure. Lots of these people were simply having a *temporary* setback. They were behind four or five months payments, and because of a temporary illness or a short-term situation where they were out of work, they couldn't get the money together to make up the back payments.

My idea was to offer to make up the back payments and, if warranted, give additional money to them for their equity. In exchange, they would agree to sell the property and *lease it back.* This way I end up with the property and with what could be an excellent tenant. Here is how my postcard read:

> I can readily understand how an individual can suffer a temporary financial setback by the loss of a job, illness or some other unforeseen circumstance. Not being able to make the payments on your house and the prospect of losing that house is a traumatic experience. The greatest heartbreak comes from having to move out of a home you love. THAT DOES NOT HAVE TO BE YOUR SITUATION. I am an individual investor who will give you cash for your house *and* lease it back to you. YOU CAN CONTINUE TO ENJOY YOUR HOME WITHOUT LOSS OF CREDIT OR REPUTATION. I will also give you cash if you want to move. I will perform in 24 hours or less. *PLEASE CALL ME NOW. I CAN HELP!!*

Hal Morris

PROPERTY INFORMATION SHEET

Address _____

Homeowner _____ Phone (Res.) _____ (Off.) _____

Date purchased _____ $ down _____ Price _____FHA ____ VA ____ Conv ____

Loans

1st TD _____ Phone _____ Original loan amt. _____

Loan # _____

Balloon? _____ Princ. bal. _____ Interest _____% Payments/mo _____

Arrears _____

Date Notice of default filed _____ Confirmed _____

2nd TD _____ Phone _____ Original loan amt. _____

Loan # _____

Balloon? _____ Princ. bal. _____ Interest _____% Payments/mo _____

Arrears _____

Date Notice of default filed _____ Confirmed _____

Property Condition

bedrms._____ bathrms. _____ sq. foot. _____ lot size _____ # stories _____

frame/stucco _____ age _____

built-ins _____ den/family rm _____ pool _____ formal dng. rm. _____ garage

cars _____ attached _____

condition and age of neighborhood _____

improvements needed _____

Value now (seller's estimate) $_____ reason for increase _____

value of houses in that area $ _____ to $ _____

Taxes impounded? _____ amt. $ ____ amt. unpaid _____

Other Liens: _____

_____

Have you ever had a suit filed against you? _____

Have you ever filed for Bankruptcy? _____

_____

Owner of Property (as on Grant Deed) _____

Legal desc. Lot _____ Block _____ Tract _____

_____

_____ County _____

Is house listed now? _____least amt. H.O. will accept for house $ _____

Sell & move _____ Sell & lease back _____ w/purchase opt. __

APPT TO INSPECT & SIGN PURCHASE OPTION: Date _____

Time _____

Seller to have: Grant Deed, Both Trustors, Fire Ins., Title Policies, Termite Report,

Loan Cards for appt.   INTERVIEWER _____

_____

Comparables: obtained from _____ at _____ by _____

1. address _____ sales price $_____

   Comments _____

   Br. _____ Ba. _____   _____ ± $_____

obtained from _____ at _____ _____

2. Address _____ sales price $_____

   comments _____

   Br. _____ Ba. _____   _____ ± $_____

obtained from _____ at _____ by _____

3. Address _____ sales price $_____

    Comments _____

    Br. _____ Ba. _____   _____ ± $_____

Value by Market Approach $_____

Sales Price of Property	$_____		
minus Loan Balances/Arrears	$_____		
minus cash to seller	$_____		
minus remodeling (estimates attached)	$_____	Fair Market Value	$_____
minus closing costs	$_____		− _____
TOTAL CASH OUTLAY	$_____	Expected Gross Profit	_____
		Sales Costs	_____
		Net Profits	_____

DATA SHEET

Address: _____City: _____ Zip _____

0. Vacant? _____ How Long _____ (Check the date on the gas & electric meters)

1. Any other money owed against house _____
    (other than first or second)

    How much, to whom: _____

    _____

2. Is the house listed with a real estate broker: _____ Exclusively: _____

    Who: _____ Agent _____ Phone _____

    Address _____ City _____

3. How old is the house _____ (check toilet tank top or electric meter start card) (and ask homeowner)

4. What is the condition of

Location	Great	Pass	Needs Improvement (how)
Yards			
Porch(s)			
Front Room			
Kitchen			
Bathroom(s)			
Bedroom(s)			
Hall(s)			
Other room (specify)			
House Exterior			
Roof			
Pool & Filter			

(Note the condition of paint, rugs, flooring, electrical fixtures, heating/cooling equip., incomplete construction or house destruction. In the kitchen note what appliances are present and their condition.)

5.   What other improvements will be necessary: _____

      _____

6.   What is the least amount the homeowner will take for the property: _____
      General Appearance of House is (rate on a scale of 1 to 10)
      What does the neighborhood look like? (rate on a scale of 1 to 10)

The response was usually quite good. When someone called, I would go through all the usual basics regarding amount of mortgage, amount in arrears, the owner's best estimate of market value. But the key question that I would ask was *What is the absolute lowest price you would sell this house for* if *I were to permit you to continue living here and we could solve your problem in 48 hours?*

By comparing their answer with the amount owed and the market value, I could quickly see if we could do a deal. Most of the time the purchase price would be the amount needed to solve the current problem plus a little extra cash or credit on future rent. Let's say rent would normally be $400 a month. I would reduce it to $300 rather than give them $1,200 additional cash for their equity.

I should point out that in doing this there are the Good Guys and there are the Bad Guys. I'm referring here to the sellers, not the buyers.

The sellers who are the Bad Guys know about, and sometimes take advantage of, something called the "Unruh law" in California and that also exists in several other states. The law, simply put, says that if someone buys your house in the fashion just described and *does not personally move in*, you have the right to reclaim the property anytime during the next three years by giving them back their money plus 10 percent!

The Bad Guys saw this as a way to get 100 percent financing. They would buy a house that was heavily mortgaged, then allow it to go into foreclosure. Some investor who didn't know the law would come along and buy them out during the foreclosure period. Then the investor would rent it out for three years, watching his or her appreciation grow. Suddenly, before the three years were up, the original owner would come back, arrange a new mortgage for the original amount plus 10 percent and get the property back. That original owner had 100 percent financing plus no management headaches for three years!

Another way to get started with foreclosed property (and perhaps the best way) is through developing relationships with banks or savings and loan associations.

Banks and S & L's always have REO departments (Real Estate Owned). These departments handle property taken back through foreclosure sales.

During good times, these departments are normally very small. But, when times get tough they swell up with properties. Your branch-manager friend, or someone else you know at the lender's office, can get you on the list to be notified of properties that are headed for REO. Sometimes you can be put on the list simply by writing directly to the lender and requesting it.

PREPAID INTEREST

There's an interesting sidelight to working with foreclosed property. Sometimes you can buy it using *prepaid interest*.

If you ask any accountant or attorney about writing off prepaid interest from your taxes, I'm sure they'll say that it simply does not exist. They'll tell you it went out with the tax-reform acts of the last ten years.

Not true! It does exist. The tax law says that you can't deduct any interest before it's due on a mortgage, but it doesn't say that you can't prepay. It's a slight, but important, distinction. And It can work benefits to the buyer of foreclosed property.

An individual, we'll call her Linda, owned a nice home situated in the Santa Monica hills. The problem was that Linda was in over her head. She had a first mortgage, a second, and even a third. For a while things worked out well. She was importing novelty items to the United States. Business was good and her home was her office. When clients came to town, they met at her home and conducted purchases and sales there. Her impressive home was as essential to her business as the fine offices of a bank are to that company's business. Linda needed her fine home.

But times turn bad. She lost money, went into debt and couldn't pay her bills. Worse for her, she couldn't make the mortgage payments. She owed on all three mortgages!

To protect its interest, the holder of the third mortgage put her into foreclosure.

Then, surprisingly, things got better. Linda's business picked up. She had cash flow. But, it was too late for the third. Her house was going to be sold "on the courthouse steps." To prevent that she had to come up with $25,000. But with her bad credit she couldn't do it.

Linda's day was saved by an investor. He came in and offered to bail her out. The problem, however, was price. Linda wanted $175,000 on her house. But, the investor figured it would be a lot better deal at $150,000, the value of the remaining mortgages (the first and second).

So the investor offered her this deal. He would give her $25,000 in cash. This would allow a payoff of the third and bring the house out of foreclosure.

However, that $25,000 would not be called a "cash down." It would be called "prepaid interest" on a special new mortgage he was giving her for $150,000. (The new mortgage would "wrap" around the existing first and second, which would remain in place. The buyer would pay to the wraparound, and the wraparound would pay the first and second. This is also sometimes called an All Inclusive Trust Deed—AITD).

There were two elements here. The existing mortgages and the new wrap. The *buyer* would pay on the $150,000 wrap. The seller (Linda) would take that money and pay on the existing first and second.

BUT, the new wrap was to be *interest only* and the buyer had prepaid 18 months' interest (or $25,000). That meant that the buyer had *no payments* due on the wrap for 18 months!

What are the benefits to the buyer here?

1. There are no payments on the house for a year and a half.
2. The prepaid interest can be written off for income-tax purposes *as it comes due.* In other words, if the buyer bought the house on January 1, by December 31 of that same year one years' worth of interest would be due (two-thirds of $25,000, or $16,666.) The investor could write that off the first year. He could then write off the remaining $8333 the second year.

(**Note:** He's paid the interest in advance, but only writing it off taxes as it normally would come due.)

The benefits to the seller are two-fold.

1. She gets out of the foreclosure and saves whatever credit she may have left.
2. She continues to live in the house. One of the conditions the buyer had that we haven't yet mentioned is that the seller would permit her to continue to live in the house and pay rent. For the seller this meant that no one, including neighbors and clients, had to know that she was in financial trouble. From the outside, her house looked as always, and she was continuing in the old ways.

For the buyer, this last meant that the seller (Linda) would be paying in enough money each month *in rent* to continue making the payments on the existing first and second mortgage.

I hope that didn't go by too fast. The rent pays for the existing first and second. The prepaid interest was for the wraparound, and that $25,000 cash went to pay off the old third mortgage. If your head's swimming, read it through again.

There's one additional benefit to the buyer using this prepaid interest technique. He got Linda's house for $25,000 less!

The seller saw the deal as $175,000 to her. A $150,000 wrap plus $25,000 in cash. What did she care if that $25,000 was called interest. (One reason she might care is that she would have to declare it as *ordinary income* for tax purposes that year.)

But, for the buyer, that $25,000 went toward paying mortgage interest that would have had to be paid over the next 18 months anyhow. For the buyer that $25,000 wasn't part of the down payment or the cost of the house—it was 18 months of monthly payments. Therefore, the house cost the buyer $25,000 less (or $150,000). The buyer, to his thinking, got the house at a better price because of prepaid interest, and the seller continued to live in a house she loved.

TAX LIEN SALES

Remember the woman from the copy shop? She was the one who made all that money, not by working with foreclosed property, but by working with property that had been taken back by the state for unpaid taxes.

You can do what she did. The way to do it is to contact your county tax assessor. Each year the roll is published of properties with unpaid taxes. Those properties are, technically, sold to the state. (What does that mean? First there is a tax lien on them. Then, after a certain number of years, the state actually takes title and sells the property to the highest bidder. In some states the properties are not automatically auctioned off, but must be if some resident writes in requesting it be sold at auction.

The time of such sales, the condition of purchase, the location of properties and other terms are readily available at the county assessor's office.

Be sure you don't think, as most people do, that only junk properties are sold to the state. As the woman in the copy shop found out, all kinds of properties get thrown in. In some cases people get divorced and simply drift out of the area.

In one situation I saw, the wife left her husband and ran off to another state with another man. The husband lost his job and got involved with drugs. The last anyone heard he was somewhere in a Mexican jail on charges of drug smuggling. The house they owned was free and clear and, with nobody to pay taxes, the state took it over. The last I saw it had 18 months to go before it went up for a tax sale. The chances of an owner's coming back and claiming it before then were very remote. And it was an excellent house.

People die, get involved in drugs, get put into mental institutions and a thousand other things. The bottom line is that lots of good property gets abandoned. It often ends up going to the state for back taxes. And when the state sells it, there is the opportunity for an investor to buy good property, inexpensively.

SHERIFF'S SALES

These are sales that occur all over the country all of the time.

Usually they occur when someone wins a lawsuit against another party. The winner gets a judgment and a *writ of execution*. If the loser has real estate, that writ entitles the winner to sell it to recoup money.

As an investor, you have the right to go in and buy the writ of execution on a piece of property from someone who has a judgment. To avoid the hassle and the problems of selling the property, the winner of the lawsuit will frequently sell their rights at a discount.

Then the investor can execute the writ and take over the property. Two benefits are often at play here. One is the discount offered to the person who had the judgment. The other is the opportunity to get the property for less than market price. You can also purchase properties at the actual sale, but most states have rights of redemption so that the debtor has 1 year or longer to reinstate by making a payment for the amount of sale plus interest.

IRS-SEIZED PROPERTY

The Internal Revenue Service may levy and sell any property belonging to any taxpayer if he or she refuses (or is unable) to pay a tax bill within 10 days of demand.

Most people don't realize the full powers of the IRS.

That branch of government doesn't have to go through civil court action. It doesn't need a writ of execution or a sheriff's sale or anything else. All on its own it can step in and seize the property of someone who, it believes, owes taxes and then sell the property to regain the taxes due.

There is, however, a procedure the IRS must follow. And this procedure is an opportunity for many investors. The property seized may often be bought at far below market values. Sometimes it is an excellent parcel of real estate. A word of caution, however. The IRS will *not* guarantee title to the property. This is in part because the property is subject to any liens (including mortgages) already existing on it. A friend in a title company can be a big help here.

Here's the IRS procedure:

The IRS will offer to put you on a mailing list of all IRS-seized properties. The list contains eight items:

1. Name and address of taxpayer
2. Notice whether it will be a public auction or sealed bid
3. Time and place of sale
4. Description of property
5. Terms of payment (whether all cash or 10% down and 90% within 60 days)
6. Minimum bid (if disclosed)
7. Time and place of inspection
8. Name, address and phone number of revenue officer holding the sale

In those cases where there is a minimum bid (find this out initially), and that bid isn't met or there are no bidders, the property is sold to the U.S. government. While the government owns it, the original owner has a two-year "right of redemption." (The government can, however, dispose of the property through a subsequent sale and the right of redemption would expire.)

If you want to bid on an IRS-seized property, use IRS form 2222. You will need a cashier's check payable to the IRS and you could mail it to the proper office and revenue officer. (You may withdraw a bid from a sealed-bid public auction any time prior to its being opened.)

ADVERSE POSSESSION

There is another way to get distressed property. It is seldom used today, but it is such an important method that it can't be overlooked. It's called *adverse possession*.

This method of acquiring property dates back to the days of English commonlaw. Basically it states that if you "act" as the owner for a specific period of time, you can become the owner.

In today's world it works in a remarkably similar fashion. In most states there are seven criteria for gaining title by adverse possession. You must "take over" the property in such a way that your possession is:

1. Actual (you're really on it)
2. Adverse (against the real owner's interest)
3. Open (for everyone to see)
4. Continuous (not just for a month or two, here and there)
5. Exclusive (you don't let anyone else onto the land)
6. For a set period of time (usually seven years)
7. You must pay the taxes.

"Hal, are you saying that if I do that to a piece of property that belongs to somebody else, after seven years it belongs to me?"

Yes, it *can*. But you have to be careful.

In one instance with which I'm familiar, a person owned a residential lot. Next door was a lot with grass three feet high that the owner never cut. Our investor checked out the county tax assessor and found that the taxes weren't paid. So he paid them.

Next he put a fence around the property—his possession was actual. He put up a sign which said No Trespassing. His possession was adverse, open, and exclusive. He kept the fence up, the sign up, and paid the taxes regularly. In addition, to be sure there could be no mistake, twice a year he and his family actually went out to the lot and chopped down the weeds themselves.

It's been six years now and he's hoping the owner won't come by the property for another year. After that time he'll file a "quiet title" action to gain title to the lot.

In another instance, a couple noticed an old house in a fairly nice area of the city that was run down and vacant. Newspapers lay on the front lawn. Junk mail was never picked up. They checked, and the taxes weren't paid.

So this enterprising couple paid the taxes, fixed up the property and rented it out. They, after all, had nothing to lose. The
rental income in excess of taxes was theirs. And if the previous
owner doesn't show up for seven years, the house could end up
being theirs too!

BANKRUPTCY

For a time during the 1970s, there were relatively few bankruptcy sales of real estate. But, with the economic troubles of
the last few years, bankruptcies have soared. And with them
have come the sale of properties through the bankruptcy laws.

All bankruptcies are controlled by the Federal Bankruptcy
Act. One purpose of it is to see to it that real estate is sold off
at a reasonably good price and that the money is used to help
pay back the creditors of the bankrupt.

"Hal, those are junk properties. Everybody knows that before
a guy goes into bankruptcy, he either sells his good property or
puts it in his wife's name!"

It would seem to be the case, if common sense is our guide,
that a reasonable person wouldn't let a good piece of property
fall into bankruptcy. Fortunately for investors, that just isn't
the case.

Consider the Los Angeles gold dealer. A few years ago, when
the price of gold was high, he too was riding high. He bought a
mansion in Beverly Hills. He paid close to $3 million for it.

When the price of gold collapsed, so did our dealer. During
a 12-month period he went from a multimillionaire to a bankrupt. As part of his effort to save his company, he threw his Beverly Hills mansion in.

Now, we have this gorgeous house as part of the bankruptcy.
It's going to be put on the auction block to help pay off creditors.
Is it a bad piece of property? Hardly. It's a beautiful one. It was
purposely put into other assets in an attempt to save a business.

Similar cases happen all the time. Or it could just be that
the person going bankrupt is so involved in keeping his or her

life and business together that he allows a good piece of property to slip away.

The bottom line is that there are good properties available through bankruptcies.

To buy through a bankruptcy, there are really three methods:

1. Make the purchase through a sealed bid
2. Buy at an oral auction conducted by the court
3. Arrange a "negotiated" sale

Note that in a bankruptcy there are really *two* "sellers." One is the court-appointed trustee who is overseeing the property. The other is the court itself.

Often the trustee will negotiate a sale. To do this he or she must advertise the property for sale. I have seen this done in some obscure little journal that almost no one reads or even knows about.

The result is that only those who know about the sale—which may include some friends of the trustee—actually have a chance to make a bid. (To be fair, the court must approve all negotiated sales, so the trustee cannot simply slip the property to a friend.)

The courts only appoint certain individuals as trustees and it is possible to get on the trustee's list for mailings of properties simply by writing a letter of request.

RANKING DISTRESSED PROPERTY

If I were to rank the chances of making profit in distressed properties from those offering greatest opportunities to those offering least, I would list them like this:

1. Tax-lien sales
2. Foreclosure sales
3. Bankruptcy, IRS-seized property and other sales

Overall, it definitely does make sense to try to buy distressed property. The profit to be made is great.

But it can make even more sense to go in and try to deal with a distressed seller BEFORE the property actually gets sold at auction. By doing that you increase your opportunities to get good terms. Once the property goes to sale, it usually requires all cash to make the deal.

11

How to Make
the First Move

Some people feel the rain; others just get wet.
—Song by Roger Miller

It's not going to happen by itself. The first thing I suggest you do is find a mentor.

In this chapter I'm going to show you how it's done. But, if it still seems too hard to do, the best solution is to find somebody who's doing it and learn from them.

A good number of years ago, when I was a stockbroker, I was invited to go with several clients to see the first Ali-Frazier fight.

When I drove up to our meeting place, I saw that one of the clients was driving a new Maserati. Another had a Rolls Royce. Still another was in a Lamborghini. It told me they were all into money, lots of it. And what's more, they were all working in real estate.

Here I was doing stock deals and making dimes and they were doing real estate deals and making dollars. Right then I saw that they had a better answer than I did.

On the way to the fight, I suggested that I invest some of my money with them. When they did their next deal, I could add some of my funds. Why should they, they wanted to know. They were doing just fine and they had their own money. Why share profits with me?

So I tried a different tack. I asked myself what would motivate them. I said "When you come across a deal where you need extra money, count me in and I'll give you one-half of my profit."

Within 45 days they called me up. I stuck $30,000 into a deal they were hatching. It closed in three months and they turned a $47,000 profit. I gave them half of my share.

I had made some money. But more important, I had learned what they were doing and how they were doing it. I saw it happen right in front of my eyes. I saw how it could be done.

After I did a couple more deals with them on the same basis, I was able to go out and do it on my own.

I think the lesson here is fairly obvious. If after reading this chapter you still feel you need some help, find someone you would like to emulate. Find a *financially successful* person.

Then take the person to lunch. Someone once said that poor people should take rich people to lunch. The poor person pays for lunch, but gets the price of the meal back many times over in knowledge.

Once you've found your mentor, tell that person you want to learn from him or her. Let the person feel good about sharing knowledge and success with you! If that's not enough, offer to chip in half your profits on the first few deals. Do whatever it takes to get your mentor to show you the ropes.

FINDING YOUR FIRST PROPERTY

If you haven't invested in real estate before (I'm not talking about buying your own residence—I mean buying a rental), and you wanted to get in because you feel the market's going to boom), there are key things you should look for. Old-time investors know them by heart. But if you're new to the trade, you will want to underline these bits of information, as they can save you a lot of headaches later on.

The first thing we need to do is to take a look at the market we happen to be in. I don't care whether you're in Podunk or Miami Beach or San Francisco or Houston, markets everywhere can be described as diamond-shaped.

There are three elements to the diamond. At the top is the luxury market. In Southern California that would be Beverly Hills or Malibu or San Marino or some similar area.

At the bottom of the diamond is what I call the welfare market. In terms of homes, it's at the bottom of the pile. The people who live in these homes tend to be either on welfare or are having trouble finding work to support themselves.

Both of these markets, the top and the bottom, are relatively small. That's why I have them at top and bottom where the diamond comes to a point.

In the middle, the broadest area of the diamond, is what I call the working-class market. This is the largest market and also the one that makes the most sense for the investor.

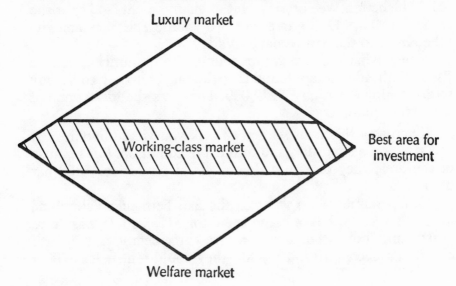

The working-class market comprises the bread-and-butter rentals. Here you are providing one of the two essentials of life, food and *shelter*. As far as I'm concerned, this is the best market for someone who wants to get started on the five-year program to financial independence. I identify it by drawing a line across the diamond.

If you get too far down below the line, you end up in the welfare market. These are the people who come and go on jobs. Rent is hard to collect and rental increases are hard to come by. Most people can easily understand this concept.

But a harder concept to understand is why I suggest not going to the luxury market on top. Aren't those homes better built, bigger, in choice locations, and so forth, I've heard people argue.

The answer is yes. But there is another factor involved. Let me give an example from a seminar I conducted in Santa Monica, California, not long ago. The assignment for this particular class involved buying a home for nothing down, as described in the lease/option chapter. A lot of the people in the seminar lived and worked in Pacific Palisades, which is a luxury area. They wanted to look for a home in that area.

I was suggesting that a working-class area, such as certain parts of the San Fernando Valley about twenty miles away, would be better. We got into a bit of an argument, so I split the group into two. One group went to Pacific Palisades and the other went to the San Fernando Valley.

Here's what the two groups found. Group number one (the Pacific Palisades group) found that the property they could buy with nothing down cost $229,000. That was the lowest end of the luxury market.

If you saw this house, I don't think you would live in it. It was tiny, on a small lot, and in terrible condition. But because of the area, they determined they could rent it for $800 per month.

Group number two went to the San Fernando Valley and found they could buy a home there for $115,000. It wasn't an outstanding home, but it was a nice three-bedroom, two-bath home in a decent area. They felt they could rent it for $700 a month.

Now let's look at the negative cash flow.

Group number one's property in Pacific Palisades cost $229,000. The total monthly payments came to $2600 per month. Subtracting a rental of $800, we come up with a negative cash flow of $1800 per month:

```
  $2600   monthly costs
−    800   rental income
  $1800   monthly negative on Pacific Palisades home
```

Group number two's property in the San Fernando Valley, because the owner was willing to carry back some paper, had a monthly cost of $900. Against a rental income of $700, this yielded a negative of $200 per month.

```
   $900   monthly costs
−   700   rental income
   $200   monthly negative in San Fernando Valley
```

A monthly negative of $1800 in Pacific Palisades against a monthly negative of $200 in the San Fernando Valley. Both houses were nothing down, but look at the difference in negative cash flows!

I think you get the point. The bottom line is that rental rates don't necessarily go up as fast as prices when we move from a working-class area to a luxury area. You reach a level where the price of a home has no impact on the rent you can charge.

For a person who wants to get started without a big negative cash flow, the working-class area is the place to begin.

All right, we've defined the area. Now what do we look for in a house?

1. The most important thing is to find a house that you would be willing to live in. That doesn't mean live in today, based on your current lifestyle. It could mean that you would live in it if you and your spouse were 23, just out of college, and starting up the economic ladder.

If my wife and I were starting out again, I know there are portions of any city where working-class houses are located in nice tracts close to luxury areas where I wouldn't mind living. I'm sure you can find similar areas.

2.   Follow the Graffiti Rule of Thumb. You want an attractive area where there is no graffiti and where there are no jacked-up cars for at least four blocks in all directions.

You will be surprised at how close to a nice-looking area some bad areas are. Sometimes you can drive just a block or two and suddenly you're into a really tough area. You wouldn't want to live so close to a tough area and neither will tenants. So don't buy there.

3.   You want a house in a stable area. An area achieves stability by having a broad cross section of the population. You want young and old, single and married all living there.

An unstable area is one in which only one segment of the population is congregated. This sometimes happens when there are too many apartment buildings cramped close together and all are filled with young single adults. Or it can happen where there are too many tiny, older houses, all filled with seniors.

Either way, the ideal area will be one with a mix that will give you the option of renting to a variety of tenants.

4.   This is an ideal to shoot for. You want to have the only rental home in the area. We probably can't achieve it very often. But, we can try.

Pretty hard to come by, eh? Besides, how do you know how many houses in the area are rentals?

Easy. Just drive up and down the street. Count the number of houses with dead lawns in front. Those are the rentals! It's just a rule of thumb, but it works most of the time. If you're the only rental, it's lots easier to find tenants who will stay.

5.   If possible, you want skilled craftsmen to be able to rent your property. You want carpenters, plumbers, people who are good with their hands. The reason is selfish and obvious. These people tend to fix things themselves before they call you.

Another reason is that these people tend to make good money today. They can make $25,000 to $30,000 a year. They can afford rent in the $700 to $900 range.

Those are my five rules for selecting a suitable rental property. They aren't unique to me. I've learned them from others, I've used them, and I'm happy to pass them on to you. They won't guarantee success, but they'll go a long way toward eliminating failure.

What we've just discussed is how to find a rental house to buy. But there's a whole other side of the coin. In the previous two chapters we've talked about finding properties on which we could come in with nothing down, either through lease/option or equity sharing. How do we find these properties? How do we find the right kind of sellers?

FINDING THE RIGHT SELLER

I advocate a method of finding sellers called *farming*.

Farming is a tried-and-true method that real-estate agents use to get listings. They pick an area of town and call that area their farm, then go out and begin farming. They go door-to-door, calling on owners, telling them they're in the area, and generally getting well known.

The idea is that after a time—after coming by every few months or so—the owners will get to know you. Then, when the owner wants to list the property, they will be inclined to call this agent first.

The same practice works with investors. You too can farm an area. You can simply go up to people in the area you've chosen and tell them "I'm an investor. I'm going to buy properties in this area. If you want to sell, deal direct and save the commission, give me a call. I will pay fair market value based on an FHA appraisal if you will sell ~a terms I can live with!"

You'll be surprised how much interest this generates. When you tell people you're not going to hammer them on price, they immediately get interested. Most people are hung up on price anyway, so right away they like what you're saying. Coming by like this every three or four months should soon generate more potential sellers for you than you can handle.

An important point to realize here is that most people, most investors, don't have time or energy to do this. But, if you do take the time and expend the energy, people start thinking of you as a friend. They like the idea of avoiding the commission and they like your enterprising technique. This is the kind of seller to whom you can propose an "80-20" deal.

"How would you like to get 80 percent of the value (not necessarily in a *new* loan, possibly in an owner-carried second) of your house in cash and still retain half of the future appreciation?"

50%	Existing first
30%	Hard-money second to cash out seller
20%	Seller co-owner for 50% future appreciation
100%	No down to buyer

Develop a "Brag" Book

As you already know, I give seminars all over the country, with the result that lots of people come up to me afterward, wanting to talk privately about their own situations. New investors also write to me, wanting to get together. I have learned that it is impossible to get together and counsel individually with people, even though I would enjoy doing so.

Well, one day a few years back I got a letter that said "I have enclosed a booklet with my background and affiliations." This intrigued me. Why would anyone send me a booklet about their background?

My curiosity was aroused, so I opened the booklet. It was my first introduction to a "brag" book.

On the first page was a letter from former California Governor Pat Brown saying what a great guy this person was.

On page two was a letter from the president of Lockheed that said the same thing.

Page three was a letter from a banker. Another banker's letter was on the fourth page, and a letter from a CPA was on the fifth.

There were letters from famous movie stars, wealthy business people, and even one from a four-star general!

You know what I was thinking as I was reading this book? I was thinking, who *is* this guy? And I was thinking that I couldn't afford *not* to meet with him!

We did eventually get together, but that's another story. For now, just think what an unbelievable tool a brag book is in dealing with sellers.

You've been farming an area, and now a couple invites you to come over and talk serious selling. As you sit down with them, you casually mention that you'd like them to know you better. Then you haul out your brag book and let them browse through. (You might even have a copy you could leave with them.) You think they're not going to be impressed?

How do you make up a brag book? Where do you get the letters?

It's easy! You may not be able to get a former governor in there (though if you've contributed to a political campaign, maybe you can!). But everyone knows someone at the bank where they do business. You can get a letter from an assistant manager on the bank's letterhead. How about your CPA and your attorney? How about your pastor and your doctor? When you do business with someone, it's no big thing to ask them to just write a letter to you saying they think you've got good character, and are a nice person.

It doesn't matter if the letters are fourteen years old! The brag book provides somthing that's hard to get any other way—*credibility*.

Be Creative

I hope to sell a million of these books. If I do that it means that you're not the only person out there who knows what I'm writing. (Even if I don't sell a million, there are lots of people from my seminars who are already using these techniques.)

That means that there's competition. You always have to come to grips with the competition and beat it in your particular area.

How do you beat the competition? By being creative.

Let me give you an example of what one real-estate agent did when farming his particular area for potential listers.

This agent's area happened to be Beverly Hills. Now, Beverly Hills is a tough nut to crack. People don't exactly stand out on their front lawns and talk to anyone who comes by. If you knock on a door without being solicited, you may find that before the door opens, a security guard is hauling you off.

How was this agent going to farm Beverly Hills?

Well, it turned out that there happened to be a garbage strike just about that time. The garbage collectors were refusing to pick up the trash and it was accumulating in people's driveways.

Everyone saw this as a problem except our agent. He saw it as an opportunity.

He rented a garbage truck! Then he hired someone to drive it and pick up the garbage. He went door-to-door in Beverly Hills and, at no charge, collected people's garbage.

While his hired man was cleaning out the trash cans, he went to the door of the house (where by now most people were standing in amazement) and introduced himself. He got acquainted and left his card.

You think people didn't remember him? He gave them a benefit first. He *gave* them something they needed, and he didn't ask anything in return.

From that time on he was never short of listings in the area and he made a lot of money. People figured if he was creative and clever enough to pull off the garbage stunt, he was smart enough to sell their house.

You can do the same thing, although it doesn't have to be in garbage. Give potential sellers a reason to believe that you're a person who cares about them and they'll call you. Develop a relationship. Find out what people need, and fill that need.

SELLING THE SELLER

Farming, the brag book, and being creative all lead up to developing a seller who will trust you enough to carry back a second or third mortgage. A seller who will trust you enough to sell to you on terms you can live with. It really works.

I remember a young man in Denver who was just starting in real estate. He owned a lot of houses and was moving into commercial property. He decided that a particular piece of property in downtown Denver was likely to show the greatest increase in value. It was just a small commercial building. The trouble was, it wasn't for sale.

Well, the young man found out who the owners were (they happened to be a large corporation), went to the director and members of the board, and said he wanted to buy. He had a brag book, and although he was young and new to the business, he was determined.

They said "Hey, kid, you're crazy. We don't want to sell."

But every few months he kept going back. He did this for a few years, and then one day the corporation got into desperate financial straights. It needed money badly, and the board decided one way to get it was to sell that building.

Who do you think was the first person they called? Do you think they went to a broker or an attorney? Someone said "Hey, remember that kid who wants to buy? He seems pretty honest, and smart. Let's give him a call."

Our investor friend arranged the financing, bought the property, leveled the old building and put up a highrise. His profit was over $1 million.

The reason for his success was that the seller recognized him as a friend. His homework paid off.

There's another creative aspect to dealing with a seller, and that's *closing the deal.*

Even after you've got the seller's confidence, something that you can't identify may produce a snag. There may be some reason that the seller won't finally sign. At this point it can be helpful to look at the four basic types of seller.

Type A: The Driver.   This seller has a high energy level. He or she is aggressive, ready for every challenge, full of self-confidence and always convinced of being right. The *greatest fear of this seller is being taken advantage of.* If this seller balks at signing, you must constantly show that you are not taking advantage. Show that an outside appraisal is being made, that you are paying full price, and so on.

Type B: The Social Expert.   This seller is outgoing and fun to be around. He or she is a good talker and upbeat. But they are lousy at technical work and details. Their *greatest fear is loss of social recognition.*

I've seen such sellers refuse to sign because they thought their neighbors would find out they sold for $20,000 less than the going market! Convince these sellers that the neighbors will never know and they'll come through.

Type C: Mr. and Mrs. Steadfast.   This seller has unbelievable loyalty and is as steady as the Rock of Gibralter. Chances are he or she has been in the same house for 59 years and has worked at the same job for nearly as long. This person's *greatest fear is loss of security.* Show them the proper documentation, the recording procedure, how they are protected, and they'll move.

Type D: The Perfectionist.   This seller is very analytical. If an optimist would say that a glass of water was half full while a pessimist would say it was half empty, an analyst would say that it was too close to call! This person's *greatest fear is making a mistake.*

Since this person has trouble making a decision, give him or her facts, facts, and facts. Eventually they'll figure they have enough to work with, and move.

The bottom line is that every seller has a little of every type in them. If you assume a seller has all four characteristics and deal with all four, they will usually go along with your deal.

PUTTING AGENTS TO WORK FOR YOU

Perhaps you have found what I just said does make sense to you. But then you thought, I just don't have the energy and time to do that. I may want to, but I know that I won't.

If you are in that situation, what do you do?

The answer is that, *instead of farming property, you farm agents!*

All the agents in the area you are considering will be farming property. So you just farm one step removed. Of course, you are going to have to pay a commission to the agent who has done the work. But it is money well-spent. Some of the most successful investors have real-estate licenses and can take commissions. But they pay commissions to agents 100 percent of the time. *Commissions provide dimes. Investing provides dollars.*

Here's how you farm for agents. Go into a real-estate office and ask to talk with two people.

The first person you want to talk with is the top lister in the office. This person is usually a good talker and understands motivation. You ask this person to show you his or her listings. Then ask about which sellers are motivated. Find out what has assumable financing, which sellers will carry back mortgages. This person can do for you what it would take you many hours of pounding the pavement to do for yourself.

The second person you want to talk with is the top seller. The person who is tops in sales is the one who can close deals for you.

Many people are under the mistaken impression that everyone in real estate handles both listings and sales. Often that's not the case. Often agents find that their talents lie in one of two different areas—listing or selling. Some top agents specialize. Budge Offer, who sold the most residential property (over $28 million) in the country last year, *listed* very few houses. He did it through selling.

The office's top lister will be glad to show you the listings because, if you buy, there's a listing commission in it for him or her.

But the top seller is going to wonder about you. You might be interested in FSBOs. If you go out and find a "for sale by owner," he or she is not going to get anything.

At this time, you tell this top salesperson that you want her or him to work for you. And to prove it, you agree to pay a selling commission (half the full commission rate).

You won't believe the motivation this will generate. When the agent realizes that he or she is going to get paid regardless of what you buy, the motivation to get out there and find a property is tremendous. The agent will move to get your results and to collect that commission. (Remember, if the agent happens to find a listed house for you, the seller will end up paying that commission anyway. Nevertheless, to get the right house, you should be prepared to pay a fee yourself.)

Here's the wording to add in the contract to have the seller pay your broker's fee: "Seller acknowledges that (name of broker) represents buyer and is acting as buyer's broker. Sales price is to be reduced by 3 percent in escrow." Hence, the seller pays your broker's fee!

A buyer's commission isn't as terrible as most people think. It is usually half the regular full commission. If the regular commission happens to be 6 percent, a buyer's commission is 3 percent. On a $100,000 property it is $3000. Just take whatever money you were going to put into the property and reduce it by $3000. That goes to the agent for getting you the property you couldn't get by yourself.

FIND THE MUSCLE!

There comes a time in many deals when there is one factor that can make or break the deal. Usually it has to do with financing. You need a loan from a lender to buy the house. But a lender won't make the loan. So this house, which you're sure is the best deal you've ever had, made in heaven, is about to be lost.

Or is it? The answer may lie in *finding the muscle*. You, today, have relationships and the ability to obtain loans that you don't even know about. The reason is that most of us are not used to thinking in terms of using the muscle. And sometimes we don't realize the total amount of muscle we have.

I think the best way to explain finding the muscle is to tell a story.

As I've mentioned before, I used to be a stockbroker, and at that time I went through my sports-cars stage. I wanted to drive one of every type of sports car there was.

The first sports car I bought was just 36 inches off the ground and it would go 190 miles an hour. I needed insurance for the car. But when I called the insurance agent I had dealt with for six or seven years and he heard the horsepower and the make he said, "Oh boy, I don't think my company will want to insure that car. If we do insure it, the rates are going to be $1300 a year. I'll call you back tomorrow and let you know."

The next day he said "I just called and got final word. They will not touch that car with a ten-foot pole."

My brother-in-law is in the insurance business and he's been trying to get me to do business with him for some time. So I called him up and said, "Brother-in-law dear, happy to tell you I'm now going to give you the business."

I told him about the car and he said, "Oh, I don't know about this. It's going to be very expensive and I don't know if they'll take it."

He called his company, then called me back and said "Nope, they will not insure the car."

Two days later I was meeting with an attorney. I said to him, "You've got lots of different kinds of cars and I need insurance. Who do I contact?"

He gave me a phone number, but when I heard the phone answered, I realized it was my own company, which had already turned me down. I asked myself "What am I going to say?"

I decided to simply tell what I needed and see what would happen.

The insurance person had never met me. Never heard of me. I told him about the car and said I needed some insurance. He said "I might be able to do something. I'll call and let you know tomorrow."

The next day he called back and said "Hal, we have the insurance for you. Your premium will be $480 a year."

Can you imagine my surprise?

I said "I didn't tell you this earlier, but I had already been turned down by your company after doing business with them for six or seven years. What's the difference? Why, my agent couldn't get the coverage for $1300, and you got it for $480!"

His answer was short and simple. He said "I've got the muscle."

"What do you mean, you've got the muscle?"

"I'm important to my company. Your agent is not."

That opened up a whole new area of thought for me. If it can make that much difference in terms of money and performance when you've got muscle in insurance, I wondered if it did in real estate? I began looking around, and soon realized that it did.

There are all kinds of areas where having the muscle makes a difference. As you expand your real-estate horizons, you will discover them. But I want to give one example that I feel best illustrates having muscle in real estate.

It occurred not long ago. When working with a client we came across a property in a certain city of California where lenders just don't like to go. There are some racial problems there. The neighborhoods are not the best. Worst of all, from a lender's viewpoint, this was not going to be an owner-occupied house. The buyer was planning to rent it out.

I called up lender after lender and all said no. So I got in the car and went down to a local savings and loan. I asked to talk with the branch manager. I told him where the house was and that we needed a $50,000 loan on it. You know what his answer was? It was no.

Then I asked him another question. "Would you make the loan on this property if we deposit $10,000 in your savings and loan?"

His answer was "Hmmm."

What did that hmmm tell me? Turning that no from an S & L into a yes involves finding the right button. It involves finding out what they want. What the S & L manager wanted was deposits.

Fine, we were able to make the deal.

But it's not very creative if, every time we have to make a $50,000 loan, we have to make a $10,000 deposit.

The broker I was working with, however, did find a creative way of handling this. He asked himself, is there anybody I know who has $10,000 in a savings and loan?

The answer was that he knew a few. He went to them and said, "I will pay you 2 points (2 percent) if you will move that money from where you have it now to the S & L I want it to be in."

What was their reaction? Sure they'd move it. Both S & Ls paid the same interest rate. Both offered the same security. But by moving, they stood to gain 2 points, or $200. They were happy to make the move.

It worked so well for this broker that he put a little ad in the paper. It read "I will pay a premium of 2 points to anybody who will move money." Within three weeks he had a list of 18 people who would move money!

Think about it. What's $200 when you're buying a house worth $60,000 or more? It's less than one month's negative. It's cheap.

What worked for this broker can work for you. You too can find the muscle to get lenders to work for you when you need to arrange financing. And it isn't limited to financing. It works in all aspects of real estate.

Finding the muscle really means finding out what the person wants who is critical to making the deal. Then find a way to give it to him or her and you'll get your investment house.

So, these are the ways to get started in real estate. *Find a mentor* and work with that person. *Buy books and tapes* and absorb what they offer. *Pick a good piece of property* in the middle of the diamond. *Farm an area. Make up a brag book. Establish relationships with sellers,* so that when it's time to ask them to carry financing, they'll trust you. *Learn to analyze sellers* so you can get them to move.

If you need to, *farm agents.* Do what it takes to get good agents working for you, even if it means paying an agent to be a buyer's broker.

Perhaps most important, when it really counts, *find the muscle!*

12

WHERE YOU SHOULD INVEST YOUR MONEY

**The decade of the dumb millionaire is over. . . .
There is an easier, better and quicker way to do most
everything; now as ever before we should seek those easier
ways and methods.
—Gustav Metzman**

It wasn't long ago that you could buy real estate almost anywhere in the country and feel fairly sure that it was going to go
up in price. Today that is simply not true. Some areas will do
well, while others will go downhill.

How do you tell the good areas from the bad ones? More
precisely, how do you know which areas have the greatest potential for appreciation? Even more critical, what investments
should you make in the good areas and what can you do if it
turns out that the best areas aren't where you happen to live?

HOW TO DETERMINE A HIGH-POTENTIAL AREA

What makes one area more likely to do well than another. The
answer to this came home to me in a graphic way within the
past year. I owned a business with two other fellows in Los
Angeles. I helped to organize and finance the business, while
they actually operated it.

One day one of my partners called to say "I'm going to get my kids and wife out of the smog and congestion of Los Angeles. We're leaving."

Within a few weeks he had sold his home, packed up and moved to the little town of Oakhurst just outside Yosemite Valley in the Sierra mountains of California. The town had a population of only about 3000 people.

"Why do you want to go there?" I asked. "What will you do for a living?"

"I'll open a pizza stand," he answered.

I thought he was kidding until he asked me to go up and help him analyze the area and suggest possible approaches for financing the pizza parlor.

After looking at the area, I said "No way will a pizza stand make it. There just isn't a big enough population base to support it."

But, he went ahead anyway and put up his pizza stand, Danny's Red Devil Pizza.

Shortly after that I got a call from the other partner, who we'll call Sid. Sid said he too was fed up with L.A. He had a chance to buy a complete country club dirt cheap in Buffalo, New York. If he could swing the financing, he was going to buy it. So we had two going-away parties.

That was all about a year and a half ago. Recently the Buffalo partner returned to Los Angeles. He had lost his initial investment on the country club and had to give it up.

On the other hand, Danny's Red Devil Pizza is going great guns. He has opened up new outlets and is franchising his pizza operation throughout California, specializing in small cities. If you drive today through small towns in California you can eat there.

Why was one successful and the other not?

Of course it could have been that one was enterprising while the other wasn't. But, I don't think that was the case. I had been partners with both and they were both good businessmen.

It could have been that one had a better idea than another. But at the time I didn't think so. A pizza parlor in a small town?

IMPORTANT FACTORS TO CONSIDER

There were, of course, many factors. But, one of the biggest was something as simple as *weather*. It snows a lot in Buffalo. And maintaining a country club in all that snow was very difficult. On the other hand, the sun shines a lot in Oakhurst. And a lot of people come through there, enjoying the pleasant weather and looking for a good place to eat.

Weather makes a difference in lots of other things, and particularly in real estate. It's a fact of life that those states with harsh winters are, in general, losing population. I'm speaking about the cities of the Midwest and Northeast.

On the other hand those in the Sun Belt (California, Texas, Florida and states in between) are gaining population. It could be the high costs of heating oil or the availability of land or a dozen other factors. But people are moving to warmer climates. And for real estate that means increased demand and prices in the Sun Belt. And reduced demand and slower-moving prices up North. Our country has gone from an industrial society to a thinking one. People have found they can think just as well in Florida as they can in Newark!

POPULATION SHIFTS 1970–79

[IIIII] POPULATION INFLOW (more than 2% in-migration)
[≡] POPULATION STABLE (between ±2% migration)
[ ] POPULATION OUTFLOW (greater than 2% out-migration)

Americans are on the move, mainly headed West and South. The influx has created heavy demand for mortgage money in those areas. (Source: U.S. Bureau of the Census.)

I'm not saying that weather is the *only* thing to watch for when making a real-estate investment. There are other factors to look at very closely.

1. Employment base. It is vital that you invest in an area that has a good employment base. When times are good, all areas will prosper. But, when times are bad, only those with good employment bases will continue to thrive, while those that are luxury areas may suffer.

Of course, it's important that the employment base be founded in growth industries. White-collar, high-technology industries are best. Some blue-collar industries can be trouble. For example, Detroit has a strong employment base—the auto industry. But no one would say that Detroit is a prime area for investing in real estate.

Growth Industries for the 80's

Oil & natural gas
Oil field supply & service industries
  (Drilling rigs, pipelines, drilling bits, measuring devices)
Coal mining
Energy conservation (oil shale, etc.)
Computers
Semiconductors
Software
Consumer electronics (home games, videocassettes, cable TV,
  home computers)
Defense
Crime related companies (security devices, telephone & radio
  monitoring)
Medical instruments
Radio, TV broadcasting
Factory equipment (Reagan tax cuts)
Drug, health care & surgical supply
Genetic engineering

2. Low-crime area. The issue for the 1980s is going to be crime. We are in the midst of an unprecedented crime wave in this country and people are sensitive to it. They are looking for areas where they can live with safety, security and peace of mind.

That translates into picking investment areas where there is a lower-than-average crime rate. Use yourself as an example. Would you like to live in a high-crime area or a low one? Where would you have the best chance of renting an investment house?

3. Quality of life. Is this an area that offers the quality of life that would appeal to you when you get ready to retire? The best place for investment is where there is a good environment. This means that it is clean and attractive, the houses are cheery, the people tend to be friendly. If it also offers easy access to recreational and cultural activities, so much the better.

4. Relatively reasonable pricing. We have already talked about buying a home at or below the median price. We want to select an area that has affordable housing. The way to do this is to find out what the statewide median price for housing is. Then check out the areas you're interested in. Are they at, or close to, the median? Can you buy a three-bedroom, two-bath house in a nice area at or near the median price? If you can, then you have met this criterion.

In the future, affordable housing will become a crucial factor in the decisions by business on where to locate. Companies will want to be assured that an adequate supply of reasonably priced housing exists for their employees.

5. The cost of living. Many people would like to live in the Los Angeles or New York area. But the cost of living in these areas is so high that they go elsewhere. Finding an area that has a reasonable cost of living is an important factor to consider.

6. Relatively low property taxes. This relates both to the monthly payment you'll have to make, and to the potential for

"SMOG" RATINGS

Severity level (PSI>100)	SMSA	"Unhealthful," "very unhealthful," and "hazardous" (PSI>100) (Number of days)		"Very unhealthful" and "hazardous" (PSI>200)	
		3-yr avg	Min/max annual	3-yr avg	Min/max annual
More than 150 days	Los Angeles	242	206–268	115	95–142
	New York	224	174–273	51	14–87
	Pittsburgh[a]	168	168	31	168
	San Bernardino Riverside Ontario	167	145–182	83	68–108
100–150 days	Cleveland	145	60–280	35	17–52
	St. Louis	136	119–164	29	17–44
	Chicago	124	81–150	21	14–31
	Louisville	119	94–160	12	8–14
60–93 days	Washington, D.C.	97	70–147	8	3–15
	Phoenix[b]	84	75–93	10	5–14
	Philadelphia	82	79–87	9	7–10
	Seattle	82	82–95	4	2–5
	Salt Lake City	81	81–110	18	9–25
	Birmingham[b]	75	83–100	19	8–29
	Portland	75	90–81	3	2–5
	Houston	69	50–94	16	11–24
	Detroit	65	67–68	4	2–5
	Jersey City[b]	65	55–74	4	0–8
	Baltimore	60	34–79	12	2–25
	San Diego	52	38–74	6	4–9

[a] Based on 1 year of data only.
[b] Based on 2 years of data only.

Quality of life includes breathable air. Those areas with bad air quality are simply less desirable. Here's a ranking of 40 Standard Metropolitan Statistical areas between 1976 and 1978 with regard to air quality.

Severity level (PSI>100)	SMSA	"Unhealthful," "very unhealthful," and "hazardous" (PSI>100) (Number of days)		"Very unhealthful" and "hazardous" (PSI>200)	
		3-yr avg	Min/max annual	3-yr avg	Min/max annual
25–49 days	Cincinnati	45	30–63	2	1–4
	Dayton	45	32–65	2	1–2
	Gary Hammond East Chicago	36	27–50	8	1–16
	Indianapolis	36	17–49	2	1–3
	Milwaukee	33	32–34	6	3–8
	Buffalo	31	23–40	5	3–8
	San Francisco	30	22–45	1	0–1
	Kansas City	29	7–55	6	1–9
	Memphis	28	22–37	2	0–3
	Sacramento	28	19–38	2	0–3
	Allentown[a]	27	27	1	27
0–24 days	Toledo	24	15–32	2	1–5
	Dallas	22	6–35	1	1–2
	Tampa	12	5–19	1	0–2
	Akron[b]	10	5–14	0	0–0
	Norfolk[b]	9	9–9	0	0–0
	Syracuse	9	7–12	1	0–2
	Rochester	6	4–8	0	0–0
	Grand Rapids	5	2–8	0	0–1

TYPICAL BUDGET EXPENSES IN DIFERENT AREAS OF THE COUNTRY

(per year)

Area	Medical Care	Other Family Consumption
METROPOLITAN U.S.A.	1,396	1,894
Northeast:		
Boston	1,251	2,012
New York	1,383	1,970
Philadelphia	1,449	1,866
Pittsburgh	1,242	1,912
North Central:		
Chicago	1,478	2,071
Cincinnati	1,297	1,766
Detroit	1,433	1,831
Milwaukee	1,332	1,883
Minneapolis/St. Paul	1,159	1,935
St. Louis	1,217	1,799
South:		
Atlanta	1,207	1,757
Baltimore	1,293	1,855
Dallas	1,487	1,802
Houston	1,593	1,808
Washington, D.C.	1,408	2,003
West:		
Denver	1,257	1,964
Los Angeles	1,761	1,713
San Diego	1,625	1,869
San Francisco	1,587	1,921
Seattle	1,503	1,986

Other Items	Social Security & Disability	Personal Taxes
1,637	1,611	8,340
1,796	1,588	10,942
1,758	1,618	13,150
1,648	1,599	8,628
1,584	1,588	7,106
1,643	1,588	7,048
1,565	1,588	6,844
1,618	1,588	7,649
1,603	1,588	8,907
1,578	1,588	9,495
1,571	1,588	6,790
1,525	1,588	6,565
1,606	1,588	8,723
1,567	1,588	5,209
1,592	1,588	5,433
1,661	1,588	9,874
1,606	1,588	7,224
1,613	1,702	7,190
1,616	1,702	7,580
1,683	1,702	8,717
1,657	1,588	6,073

an employment base. If taxes are low, industries will be inclined to come in and build factories. This will improve the employment base. If taxes are high, industries may be chased out of the area, weakening employment.

7. Mixed ages. For investment you want an area that is attractive to a wide range of age groups. You want young and old living together, skilled and unskilled workers. This is the mark of a stable community. An unstable community is where there is only one age group whether it be young, middle-aged or old. In a stratified community, people only live there because (for one reason or another) they have to. As soon as they get an opportunity they move out. You don't want to be renting in an area where everybody is just dying to leave.

8. Special situations. This is the hardest to find. But it can be the most important. Special situations can be anything from a change in government policy to the discovery of a valuable resource nearby. The best example that comes to mind is Seattle.

For a time Seattle was a one industry town—Boeing.

In the early 1970s when the demand for Boeing planes dropped, Seattle went into the skids. Housing prices dived to unbelievably low levels. This was a special situation and smart investors bought and bought.

A few years later Boeing came out of it and diversified. In addition, other industries came to town. Seattle suddenly boomed and those who had bought made a fortune on their investment.

Other examples are Anaheim, California, and Orlando, Florida, when Disney moved into these two areas. Speculators who bought early made great amounts of money as prices suddenly rose on surrounding real estate.

Another example that may yet be happening is Palmdale, California. The City of Los Angeles has spent millions of dollars purchasing land and preparing studies for a new airport at Palmdale. Their studies indicate that a minimum of 36,000 new jobs would be created at the desert town if and when the new airport goes in.

Speculators have already gobbled up much of the surrounding land, waiting. They know that Palmdale is a great potential opportunity. It already has a large agricultural base. Edwards Air Force base is nearby. New industries are going in. And when that big new LA airport arrives, Palmdale is going to blossom. They will be there, having bought before the special situation occurred.

These are the factors to look for when selecting an investment area. In a moment we'll examine dozens of cities across the country to see just how they stack up against these criteria. But for now, let's consider what you are going to do, given the location in which you happen to live.

THE AREA WHERE YOU LIVE

1. If you're in an area of high appreciation where you can afford to buy. If you're on top of the pile, my suggestion is that you play the game both ways. If you have many properties, you will want to hang onto what you've got. But if there's going to be good appreciation in your area, you want to take advantage of that too.

The way to proceed is to change the financial setup of your properties. My suggestion is that you convert half of your properties to a very-low-leveraged or cash situation. If possible, own them free and clear.

The advantage here is that, just in case the real estate market should turn way down before it gets better, you won't get hurt. Half your property will be protected against any great slump. And all the while you'll be earning positive cash flow from rental income.

With the other half of your properties, I suggest high leveraging. Leverage them to the hilt. This is in case the market suddenly moves upward. With this highly leveraged property, you'll be in a position to take strong advantage of it.

If you're in the middle of the pile and you're in an area of strong appreciation, I suggest you take advantage of it at once. Use the five-year plan and begin buying single-family homes (or condos) close to home. Begin today to gain your financial freedom.

If you're on the bottom of the pile and you're also in an area of strong potential appreciation, I suggest that you too move at once. Using the lease/option plan we discussed earlier, or being the occupant/landlord in an equity-sharing plan, begin acquiring properties.

No matter where you are in the pile, if you live in an area that promises strong appreciation and that offers you the chance to buy an affordable house, I suggest you act at once before the favorable circumstances in which you find yourself change.

2. If you're not in an area of high appreciation or where there are affordable houses, you can act, too. While it's easy to see what to do if you're in a top area with low-priced homes, it's not quite so easy to see what to do if your area does not promise good appreciation. Or if your area has high-priced homes. What's to be done in that case?

The first thing you have to decide is whether the conditions in your area are so bad that you want to look elsewhere. Or are they (maybe) not quite as good as someplace else, but not so bad that it's worth going far off.

This question is the same, regardless of where you are in the pile.

3. Importance of being close to your investment property. If we assume that you are going to be an active investor (that is that you are going to participate actively in finding your property, renting it out, collecting rents and so forth), you will want to be close by.

Part of your duties will be managerial and maintenance. These can be very simple if the property is located just a few miles away. But if it's five hundred miles away, it can be very difficult. Imagine a tenant five hundred miles away calling you at 11 p.m. to tell you the water heater just burst and there's water flooding the house. What are you going to do, five hundred miles away?

In general, it's better to be in an area of less appreciation without all the ingredients for investment that you might like, but that is closer, than to go to an area of greater appreciation.

AREAS FAR FROM HOME

Let's say you've decided your area has no potential. It's down on appreciation or the houses are simply too expensive to purchase. You've determined that you've got to look elsewhere. How do you do it?

Your number one concern in buying real estate far from home is going to be management. You're going to need someone to take care of the property and solve the problem when the water heater bursts. Here are some solutions:

1. If the area you are in doesn't seem right, slowly work out from it. Don't immediately pick another area five hundred miles away. Try going ten or fifteen miles, then twenty-five miles away. See if there isn't another area relatively close that offers investment potential.

2. If there are no areas that seem promising within a reasonable range, start looking for areas farther away that offer amenities to you. Look at areas where you like to vacation, so part of the time you can use the property as a vacation house, yet can deduct travel costs there and back.

Look at an area where your kids might be going to college. When they go to college, you can hire them to watch the property and deduct their travel expenses there and back.

Look at an area where you go on business and with which you are familiar.

3. Now, if those two ideas aren't working out, ask yourself "Who do I know who lives in an area where I might invest; with whom I would feel comfortable investing?"

It could be a relative, or a high school or college chum, or anyone who for a portion of the investment would look after the property.

4. If you have such a friend or relative, then put an ad in the paper of that city. The ad should read:

> I will pay full price for your property if you will try my terms, phone, box number.

With the response from this ad, you should be on your way.

5. If you don't have someone to watch the property in the city you've chosen, then consider this ad.

> Out-of-town investor looking for sale leaseback—will consider single-family home, duplex, tri-plex or commercial.

The *sale leaseback* simply means that the seller will lease the property back from you. You'll have a built-in, hopefully longterm tenant who will do much of the management and maintenance.

Another idea along these same lines is to buy a home from an older person, then give them a life estate. Let them live in the property as long as they desire. You pay them so much a month and they get to stay there. Your management headaches are over.

6. Finally, if the above ideas do not work out, try this ad:

> Passive investor wants 50 percent equity-sharing interest with active investor.

This works particularly well with doctors or other professionals who happen to own their own building. They may need cash. They'll sell half-interest for that cash. You get half ownership. They stay in the building, owning half and managing it.

I think the point is clear. If you can't find what you want in your own area, look elsewhere. It is possible to be an active investor in areas other than those close to home, if you're careful.

CAUTIONS IN INVESTING OUTSIDE YOUR AREA

This brings up another point which bears mentioning. Don't invest in an area outside your own unless you know the market there. No two markets are the same.

One of the biggest problems I see investors running into is investing blindly out of their area. An example might be an investor from San Francisco, trying to invest in Houston.

Unless that investor realized that:

1. Utility bills can be devastatingly higher in Houston.
2. Interest rates on seller carrybacks are different in Houston and no second mortgages are possible on one's residence in Texas.
3. Foreclosure laws are different—it's possible to lose everything in just twenty-one days in Texas.
4. Rents per square foot, construction costs, etc. are vastly different from San Francisco to Houston.
5. Houston has no zoning laws so a factory could go in next door tomorrow.

The methods of buying away from home are roughly the same as before. If you're on top of the pile, you have a bigger choice. I would, however, keep the "1-percent rule" in mind.

The 1-percent rule states that whatever kind of residential property you buy, try to keep the monthly unit rental figure as close to 1 percent of the sale price as possible.

For example, if you buy a condominium that rents for $600 a month, try to pay as close to 1 percent or $60,000 as possible. If that doesn't seem possible, then perhaps you should go to a different area where it is possible.

If you're in the middle or the bottom of the pile, lease/option and equity sharing may be the answer for you. In some cases these work better away from home (if you've got the right partner) than they do close by.

OTHER ALTERNATIVES

Finally, if you don't like investing in your area, yet you also don't find the methods I've just suggested for investing elsewhere suitable, you might consider becoming a passive investor. A *passive investor* is one who invests through limited partnerships in properties, often outside his or her area.

Passive Investing Outside Your Area

Group investments are popular and have been growing by leaps and bounds in recent years. Many specialize in particular kinds of property. For example, some large public offerings specialize in Sun Belt area properties only. Others buy just apartment houses in the Sun Belt. Some buy just homes in the Sun Belt.

These group investments are called *limited partnerships* and most people are somewhat familiar with them.

Large limited partnerships are also called *registered* because they must register with their state securities commissioner and, depending on their size, sometimes with the federal Securities and Exchange Commission.

These large public limited partnerships are available through virtually every major stock brokerage firm. (E.F. Hutton in 1980 had over 50 percent of its business in areas other than the sale of stock. A large part of it was in the sale of real-estate products.)

Public limited partnerships, or *syndicates* as they are also called, are a good way of passively investing. You put up a fixed amount of money and the general partner finds the property, manages it and eventually sells it. As a limited partner you have none of these headaches. However, you receive tax benefits in proportion to your share of the partnership as well as any part of the profit.

The problem with public partnerships is the cost of the front end load. By the time the general partner gets paid commissions, appraisals, printing costs and other fees, perhaps 10 to 15 percent of the partners' capital has been used. This is even before a piece of property has been purchased. These costs make turning a profit increasingly difficult.

The small private partnerships are often the best vehicle for a passive investment. They are not registered, nor are they checked by government agencies. They usually involve 35 or fewer partners. If the general partner is well-versed in real estate and is an honest person and a good businessperson, they can succeed and provide handsome returns. On the other hand, if you have a bad general partner, the private limited partnership can be a real concern.

The advantage of the private limited partnership is that there can be less front-end load and there is greater potential for getting into properties with high return. To avoid the problems of a bad general partner, I suggest that you ask these seven questions before getting into any group investment:

Seven Questions to Ask Before Getting Into a Group Investment

1.   How long has the general partner been in business? What is his or her business background? (Make sure he or she wasn't a plumber just twelve months ago.)

2.   What is the general partner's reputation? Don't ask the general partner. The best source is where the general partner banks. Go to your banker and ask him or her to check with the bank and branch that the GP deals with.

(Banker's can do this via their *Morse Code* of ethics. Basically this says that one banker must disclose such information to another banker, but the inquiring banker can't go after the account for at least six months.)

3.   What is the GP's track record? You should see every single limited partnership that the GP has ever put together, not just the successful ones. You should find out the cash raised, the price paid and the profit realized. No honest GP should mind full disclosure here.

4. Who are the accountants and CPAs handling the paper work? You should call them and discuss any aspect of the deal. Remember, as a limited partner, you're putting up the money for their fees. You should have the right to talk with them.

5. Does the GP make any money before you do? He or she shouldn't. If GP's interest is "non-subordinated," GP will make money no matter what. But, if GP's interest is "subordinated," GP must wait for all the limited partners to get their money back first.

6. Does the GP invest his or her own money?

7. What is the front end load?

Where Do You Find Private Limited Partnerships?

The answer is you have to go looking. In the area where you want to invest, contact the real-estate brokers, attorneys, and CPAs. They can direct you to those who are offering these private limited partnerships.

Limited partnerships are basically for the person on top of the pile or in the middle. If the appreciation looks bad where you're living or you can't find a home at a reasonable price to buy, you might consider them. They do require, however, that you come in with cash. Typically such a partnership might have a minimum offering of $5000 or $10,000.

This means that, if you're on the bottom of the pile, you're left out. But only out of the partnerships. Remember, if you're on the bottom, you can make up for your lack of money with your energy. You'll just have to become an active investor, as we've already described, in a city far away.

RATING URBAN AREAS AROUND THE COUNTRY

Now, let's consider where the appreciation is going to be. I've selected areas where I personally feel there is a strong likelihood of growth. First I've chosen my Top Ten cities for the United States.

Next I've listed four-star cities and (in many cases) given my reasons why I think these cities will show above-average growth.

Then I've listed three-star cities. These are areas which are not as likely to have expansion, but which still show promise.

Finally, I've listed my "rebound" cities. These are geographical areas where the trend currently is down, but where I believe there is a strong opportunity to make a profit in the right kind of investment. (I'll discuss this in more detail later.)

My ratings are: Average, Above Average, and Below Average appreciation. If we were to plot it on a chart, it would look something like this:

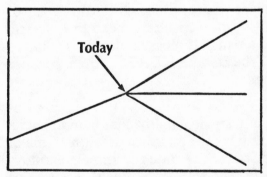

Every city listed will go one of the three directions in terms of real-estate appreciation. The ideal, of course, is to invest in a city where appreciation is headed up. Generally speaking, this comes down to the Frost Belt versus the Sun Belt. Where would you prefer to live: Fort Lauderdale, Florida, or Akron, Ohio? Most people today are picking Fort Lauderdale, primarily because of the better weather. Growth is occurring in Fort Lauderdale, not in Akron. Therefore, I've given Fort Lauderdale a better rating. I believe real-estate appreciation will be far higher there.

I'm going to list my top ten cities for growth and price appreciation, but before I do, I want to give an example of why I chose them. One of the top ten cities on my list is Sacramento, California. Here's why I chose Sacramento.

How a Top Ten City is Chosen

1.   Sacramento has large base of affordable housing. You can buy a three-bedroom tract home for about $65,000 with good financing. (Remember, people have been buying FHA financing with only 3 percent down. Now, when they sell, you can take over this financing.)

2.   Sacramento has the lowest utility costs in the state. Electric generating plants were built years ago when prices were low. Public utilities must pass their savings through to their customers. That gives the city one of the lowest utility costs of any city in the country. Not only does this mean low electric bills for homeowners and tenants, it means industry is going to want to come in. It makes the area attractive for retirees because of the lower cost of living.

3.   There is a strong and stable employment base in Sacramento. The city is the capital of the largest state (in terms of population) in the United States. The state government employs tens of thousands of people. The state government is not going to go away. And even in hard times it continues to employ people.

Additionally, because there is lots of wide open land around Sacramento, high-technology equipment plants such as Hewlett-Packard are moving in. For every one new job they create directly, up to four more jobs are created indirectly.

4.   The projected growth of Sacramento is that it will have a population of 1.2 million by 1990. That's up from 900,000 today. (Compare that to San Francisco, for example, which is expected to decline in population by 1990, yet has the highest housing costs in the country.)

5. Sacramento has a good climate. You don't have to worry about snow in Sacramento. This means there is a broad mix of people, young and old, who live there because the city offers a pleasant and attractive lifestyle. It has rivers, it is near the Lake Tahoe recreational area and it is appealing to retirees.

6. There is a special situation with regard to Sacramento. I always believe in investing where the "smart bankers" go. One smart banker I've followed is Westland Bank. They have a strong management team and a bright president.

Westland's bank first opened its offices in Orange County, California, a number of years ago. Then Orange County housing exploded. Westland bank moved to the San Jose/Santa Clara market and it boomed. Next they went to the San Diego market and it took off. Most recently they've opened an office in Sacramento.

Does Westland bank have a crystal ball? Maybe. But more than that, they are a specialty bank. They don't cater to the general public. They cater to builders and developers. And, naturally, they go where the builders and developers are. Right now the smart money is moving to Sacramento, and they are there too.

Those are some of the reasons I've picked Sacramento. This example will give you an idea of how I used the criteria I mentioned earlier to pick my first and second Top Ten cities. Please keep in mind that I don't have a crystal ball. I could be off base on a couple and they could turn out to be losers. But I don't think so, and in many of these cities I'm investing my own money because I believe in their potential.

TOP TEN CITIES

These are the best cities in which to buy real estate for appreciation:

1. Tampa Bay/St. Petersburg, Florida
2. San Diego, California
3. Ft. Lauderdale, Florida
4. Houston, Texas
5. Riverside/San Bernardino/Ontario, California
6. Orlando, Florida
7. Denver, Colorado
8. Phoenix, Arizona
9. Sacramento, California
10. Salt Lake City, Utah

SECOND TEN CITIES

11. Anaheim/Santa Ana/Garden Grove, California
12. Dallas, Texas
13. Albuquerque, New Mexico
14. Raleigh, North Carolina
15. Seattle, Washington
16. San Antonio, Texas
17. Portland, Oregon
18. Minneapolis, Minnesota
19. Tucson, Arizona
20. Tulsa, Oklahoma

FOUR STAR CITIES

ALBUQUERQUE Slightly above average. I may be prejudiced since my parents live in Albuquerque, but I believe this city is going to have above-average price appreciation. It has a diversified economy, is in a beautiful region and has an excellent university.

ATLANTA   Slightly above average in the city, but well above average in counties nearby. Atlanta is the hub of commerce and finance for the South. It has the second busiest airport in the world. To get to anywhere in the South, you first have to fly through Atlanta. It's an old joke in the South that when you die and go to heaven, you first have to stopover in Atlanta. The city has a new rapid-transit system. The people are friendly and there's a good climate. The cost of living is lower than the national average.

Negatives for Atlanta include:

1.   A financial crisis currently occurring in the city.
2.   A relatively high crime problem.
3.   Worst drivers (statistically) in the South.

Outside Atlanta is an area I like. In particular, *Gwinett County* has a nice mix of houses in various price ranges. The area offers:

1.   One of the highest educational systems in the South.
2.   Nice properties available at reasonable prices.
3.   Lower taxes because much of the county is unincorporated.

I think Atlanta is terrific. I love the people there.

DALLAS   Above average. Dallas, like Houston is part of the new and growing Texas.

DENVER   Above average. Denver is at the heart of energy exploration and recreation. It appeals to the young, upwardly mobile worker. It has a large employment base.

EL PASO   Above average. Much of El Paso's growth will come from its close proximity to Juarez, Mexico. Major manufacturing companies are locating in Juarez because of the unbelievably low labor costs. Employees are coming across the border to spend their money in El Paso.

FT. LAUDERDALE Above average. A recent *U.S. News and World Report* study pinpointed Ft. Lauderdale as the city with the strongest growth potential in the U.S. through 1990.

HONOLULU Above average. Prices will continue to climb because of Canadian and Japanese buying demand. During a recession this city could drop back down to a three-star because of its too strong dependence on tourism. Too many people own second homes here that could easily go into foreclosure. Additionally, high prices and crime are problems.

HOUSTON Above average. Houston should gain an additional one million people by 1990. There are more new millionaires in Houston than anywhere outside of Saudi Arabia. Property taxes are low, living costs are modest, and the city has a balanced budget. Houston is rapidly becoming the new cultural center of the South. Additionally the city has a very low unemployment rate and there is no state or local income tax.

Negatives include quick foreclosures. If you don't make the monthly payment you can lose your property in three weeks.

KANSAS CITY Above average. Kansas City has a good solid economy. It will not have spectacular appreciation, but it should be steady.

MINNEAPOLIS Above average. Minneapolis is a beautiful city. Here are some of the reasons I've picked this city in the Frost Belt:

1. One of the lowest crime rates in the country.
2. A broad and strong employment base in the white-collar high-technology area, including Honeywell, Control Data, and IBM.
3. Median price for a home is still reasonable.
4. People are strong, healthy, robust and resilient.
5. Excellent university, which creates an intellectual stimulus for the entire community.

The quality of life Minneapolis offers keeps it an All-American city and makes for future potential.

OKLAHOMA CITY Slightly above average. Oklahoma City is one of the centers of energy in the United States. The state has one of the lowest unemployment rates in the country.

ORLANDO Above average. Disney World caused development in this area and makes it a still-growing region.

PHOENIX Above average. Phoenix has a great, diversified economy. There are high-technology companies moving in. It is the mecca of the Sun Belt.
Negatives include a high crime rate. But this could be misleading, since the Phoenix police report every crime committed.

PORTLAND No city in the country has residents that work so hard at keeping a good thing to themselves. They do not want the rest of us up there! It is a well-managed city, and it is one of the most attractive areas to retire to.

RIVERSIDE/SAN BERNARDINO/ONTARIO Above average. This area has the most affordable housing left in Southern California. It also boasts a strong business base.

SACRAMENTO Above average (see earlier discussion of Sacramento).

SALT LAKE CITY Above average. This city has good demographics. It is one of the cleanest cities in the U.S., has a low crime rate, nice people, and is a good place to live.

SEATTLE Above average. The recovery of Boeing and the diversification of the city into other industries make this a great investment target.

SAN ANTONIO Above average. Like El Paso, this city will benefit from Mexico's newfound growth (currently at an incredible 8.3% real growth per year). And it's just begun. Statistics indicate that Southwestern cities with a high Mexican-American population will have higher-than-average appreciation.

SAN DIEGO Above average. This is a great city to retire to. (If enough of you buy this book, you may see me there!) San Diego has an ideal climate, it has culture and a variety of entertainment. It has all the benefits of Los Angeles, without the smog and congestion. With recreation and great weather, it is the U.S. mainland's answer to Hawaii.

Appreciation should be well above average in northern San Diego county. Closer in to San Diego, in areas such as Chula Vista and El Cajon, there are still reasonably priced properties available.

SAN JOSE Slightly above average. This is the area known as "Silicon Valley" for the high-technology industries located there. Overbuilding may slow its growth somewhat in the near future.

TAMPA BAY/ST. PETERSBURG Well above average. One of the fastest growing economic centers in the U.S. It is a major port and industrial center for Florida's West Coast. It also has great appeal to retirees as well as tourists. One county in the area (Pasco County) has seen a growth rate of 78 percent!

The tax situation is favorable, the area has an excellent airport, and energy and labor costs are lower than average. Demand for housing is strong in the area and vacancies are low.

If you can maintain your income and move into this area, you can probably get a far better house than you were living in before. Here's a sample of the costs of housing:

City	Typical house cost
Tampa/St. Pete	$ 68,000
Miami	117,000
Orlando	63,000
San Francisco	202,000
San Diego	140,000

TUCSON Above average.

TULSA Above average. Should do better than Kansas City or Oklahoma City.

These, then, are my four-star cities—the stars that should show the highest appreciation. My next group of cities are my three stars. Appreciation here should still be fairly good.

THREE STAR CITIES

BALTIMORE   Below average.

BIRMINGHAM   Average.

BOSTON   Average.

CHICAGO   Slightly below average.

CINCINNATI   Average. Culturally the city has good variety. It also has a low cost of living and below-national-average unemployment. It has a good city-manager type of government and consistently has operated in the black. In a recent study of crime in 30 cities, Cincinnati came out as the fourth lowest. The negatives include air pollution.

COLUMBUS   Below average.

HARTFORD   Average.

INDIANAPOLIS   Average.

JACKSONVILLE   Above average.

LOS ANGELES   Slightly above average. Because of busing, much of the Anglo population moved outside of the city limits. In Greater L.A. there are excellent investment opportunities and should provide above-average appreciation. Within the city the ethnic mixture is:

> 46 percent Anglo
> 34 percent Hispanic
> 13 percent black
> 5 percent Asian

Negatives include:

1. Crime. (The murder rate in L.A. is higher than in New York, Chicago, Philadelphia, or Detroit.)
2. Smog.
3. The high cost of housing.
4. The lack of water for expansion.

LOUISVILLE   Slightly above average.

MADISON   Above average.

MEMPHIS   Slightly above average.

MIAMI   Above average. Miami is senior citizen's haven. The life expectancy for Florida residents is the highest in the U.S. and 17 percent of Miami is over 65 years in age. (The city has been called God's Waiting Room.)

Mortgage money is readily available in Miami. The amount of money in savings and loans in the area per capita is $4776. The nationwide average is only $2399.

The port of Miami is expanding to allow 90-foot super freighters in. By 1984 a $795 million rapid-transit system should be in operation. Right now the city is the commercial and financial gateway to Latin America.

The demographics include, besides retirees, a strong influx of Cubans and Haitians. This has meant that there is strong foreign buying of real estate here. In 1980, 42 percent of major real estate transactions in Miami were made by foreign investors, many with all cash! The result of all this is that appreciation in Miami should be above average.

Negatives for the city include:

1. Retirees do not support new schools, parks, etc. They tend to vote no on new bond measures.
2. The population base is not attractive for major corporate headquarters.
3. Crime is above average.

From a personal viewpoint, if you are going to invest in Florida, I would advise Ft. Lauderdale, Tampa or Orlando over Miami.

MILWAUKEE Slightly below average.

NASHVILLE Above average.

NEW ORLEANS Slightly above average.

NEW YORK Average.

OMAHA Average.

PHILADELPHIA Below average.

PITTSBURGH Below average. Unlike its image, Pittsburgh is not just another dirty industrial city. It has a low cost of living, a low crime rate, and people get very involved in the city. They strongly support its athletic teams, the Steelers and Pirates. But prices are not going to explode.

RICHMOND Average.

ROCHESTER Below average.

SAN FRANCISCO Slightly above average. The energy crisis will probably help S.F. It is cheaper to remodel an old house than to build new. It is the most expensive place to live in the continental U.S., in terms of housing prices.

SANTA FE Above average.

ST. LOUIS Average. St. Louis is our twelfth largest city and is being revitalized. There are strong neighborhoods, a diversified economy, and unemployment is under the national average. The cost of living here is $2300 lower than the national average.

WASHINGTON Too close to call. Washington is subject to the political whims of the party in power. Housing values went up when the Republicans took office. Does that mean sellers felt they had more money than the Democrats?

REBOUND CANDIDATES—THE BOTTOM SIX

Finally we come to my list of rebound candidates. These are cities which seem to be going down. But when things look the bleakest, that is often the time to buy. These cities offer something that other cities do not. They offer positive cash flow. In order to sell, many sellers will make very attractive loans. They will offer long terms at low interest. Prices are also low. For income return, you can't beat many of these cities. And if a turnaround should occur, the investor will be well-situated to take advantage of it.

AKRON Below average. This is an industrial city on the decline. Those industries located in the city tend to be either slow-growth or no-growth.

BUFFALO Below average. Less sun than almost any other city in the U.S. It's not attractive for retirees. Even strong, healthy athletes in the NFL wince when they are traded to Buffalo.

CLEVELAND Below average. The same basic problem as Akron, but after being on the verge of bankruptcy, the city has come back. It is the best rebound candidate.

DAYTON Below average. Problems similar to Akron. The biggest industry in town is jury duty!

DETROIT Below average. This city has long had unemployment above the national average. During recessions, because of its dependence on auto manufacturing, it is hit harder. During the recession of 1975, Detroit's unemployment hit 23.8%. It also has one of the highest crime rates of any U.S. city.

NEWARK Well below average.

COST COMPARISON CHART

To further help you find a good place to invest, the accompanying chart lists comparative prices of housing for most of the country's major cities. Each column gives a particular price range. To use the chart, just locate a city and a column, then find another city and check the same column. The prices shown are what comparable houses would sell for in each city.

For example, a $63,000 house in Akron, Ohio (line one, first column) would be worth $72,000 in Wilmington (last line, first column).

If you're going to invest in real estate, the key to your success may well be location.

We've looked at many different cities across the country and given their potential. We've also considered investing close by, or if the potential seems weak, investing farther away.

The important thing to remember is that location is critical. You want to find an area where property will appreciate rapidly so that you can show a profit. You want to be in an area that has more money than homes, not the other way around.

If you can, stick close to home. But if you can't, consider looking far away from home by using some of the techniques suggested earlier.

No matter where you are in this country, there is a place for you to invest. The challenge is to find the right one.

Akron, OH	$ 63,000	$ 70,000	$ 77,000	$ 84,700	$ 93,170
Albany, NY	55,250	62,500	68,750	75,625	83,187
Albuquerque, NM	58,500	65,000	71,500	78,650	86,515
Anchorage, AK	88,650	98,500	108,350	119,185	131,103
Atlanta, GA	82,800	92,000	101,200	111,320	122,462
Austin, TX	78,300	87,000	95,700	105,270	115,797
Baltimore, MD	67,500	75,000	82,500	90,750	99,825
Billings, MT	81,000	90,000	99,000	108,900	119,790
Birmingham, AL	72,000	80,000	88,000	96,800	106,480
Boise, ID	64,800	72,000	79,200	87,120	96,832
Boston, MA	76,500	85,000	93,500	102,850	113,135
Buffalo, NY	54,900	61,000	67,100	73,810	81,191

Burlington, VT	60,300	67,000	73,700	81,070	89,177
Calgary, Alberta, Canada	85,500	95,000	104,500	114,950	126,446
Charleston, WV	88,200	98,000	107,800	118,580	130,438
Charlotte, NC	79,200	86,000	96,800	106,480	117,128
Cheyenne, WY	54,000	60,000	66,000	72,600	79,860
Chicago, IL	72,000	80,000	88,000	96,800	106,480
Cincinnati, OH	72,000	80,000	88,000	96,800	106,480
Cleveland, OH	81,000	90,000	99,000	108,900	119,790
Colorado Springs, CO	60,750	67,500	74,250	81,675	89,842
Columbia, SC	64,350	71,500	78,650	86,515	95,166
Columbus, GA	80,910	89,900	98,890	108,779	119,656
Columbus, OH	72,000	80,000	88,000	96,800	106,480
Dallas, TX	121,500	135,000	148,500	163,350	179,685
Dayton, OH	67,500	75,000	82,500	90,750	99,825
Denver, CO	85,500	95,000	104,500	114,950	126,445
Des Moines, IA	73,800	82,000	90,200	99,220	108,142
Detroit, MI	81,000	90,000	99,000	108,900	119,790
El Paso, TX	72,000	80,000	88,000	96,800	106,480
Eugene, OR	76,500	85,000	93,500	102,850	113,135
Fairbanks, AK	90,000	100,000	110,000	121,000	133,100
Fairfield Co, North Conn.	90,000	100,000	110,000	121,000	133,100
Fairfield Co, South Conn.	141,300	157,000	172,700	189,970	208,967
Fargo, ND	76,500	85,000	93,500	102,850	113,135
Ft. Lauderdale, FL	94,500	105,000	115,500	127,050	139,755
Ft. Wayne, IN	63,000	70,000	77,000	84,700	93,170
Ft. Worth, TX	76,500	85,000	93,500	102,850	113,135
Fresno, CA	84,150	93,500	102,850	113,135	124,448
Grand Rapids, MI	79,470	88,300	97,130	106,843	117,527
Great Falls, MT	67,500	75,000	82,500	90,750	99,825

Harrisburg, PA		60,750	67,500	74,250	81,675	89,842
Hartford, CT		76,500	85,000	93,500	102,850	113,135
Honolulu, HI		207,000	230,000	253,000	278,300	306,130
Houston, TX		81,000	90,000	99,000	108,900	119,790
Indianapolis, IN		81,000	90,000	99,000	108,900	119,790
Jackson, MS		67,500	75,000	82,500	90,750	98,825
Jacksonville, FL		73,800	82,000	90,200	99,220	109,142
Kansas City, KS		67,500	75,000	82,500	90,750	99,825
Las Vegas, NV		72,000	80,000	88,000	96,800	186,480
Little Rock, AR		67,500	75,000	82,500	90,750	99,825
London, England		126,000	140,000	154,000	169,400	186,340
Los Angeles, CA		144,000	160,000	176,000	193,600	212,960
Louisville, KY		81,000	90,000	98,000	108,800	119,790
Madison, WI		67,500	75,000	82,500	90,750	99,825
Manchester, NH		76,500	85,000	93,500	102,850	113,135
Memphis, TN		76,600	85,000	93,500	102,850	113,135
Miami, FL		117,000	130,000	143,000	157,300	173,030
Milwaukee, WI		81,000	90,000	99,000	108,900	119,790
Minneapolis, MN		112,500	125,000	137,500	151,250	166,375
Mobile, AL		81,000	90,000	99,000	108,900	112,790
Nashville, TN		81,000	90,000	99,000	108,900	119,790
New Orleans, LA		81,000	90,000	99,000	108,900	119,790
New York City, NY	New Jersey Suburban	90,000	100,000	110,000	121,000	133,100
	New York Suburban	117,000	130,000	143,000	157,900	173,000
	Connecticut Suburban	81,000	90,000	99,000	108,900	119,700
	Long Island Suburban	81,000	90,000	99,000	108,900	119,790
Norfolk, VA		49,500	55,000	60,500	66,550	73,205

Oakland, CA	157,500	175,000	192,500	211,750	282,925
Oklahoma City, OK	72,000	80,000	88,000	96,800	105,480
Omaha, NE	67,500	75,000	82,500	90,750	99,825
Orlando, FL	63,000	70,000	77,000	84,700	93,170
Palo Alto, CA	153,000	170,000	187,000	205,700	225,270
Peoria, IL	100,800	112,000	123,200	135,520	149,072
Philadelphia, PA	72,000	80,000	88,000	96,800	106,480
Phoenix, AZ	76,500	85,000	93,500	102,850	113,135
Pittsburgh, PA	70,200	78,000	85,800	94,380	103,818
Portland, ME	76,500	85,000	93,500	102,850	113,135
Portland, OR	108,000	1230,000	132,000	145,200	159,720
Providence, RI	81,000	90,000.	99,000	108,900	119,790
Raleigh, NC	76,500	85,000	93,500	102,850	113,135
Rapid City, SD	58,500	65,000	71,500	78,650	86,515
Reno, NV	108,000	120,000	132,000	145,200	159,720
Richmond, VA	54,000	60,000	66,000	72,600	79,860
Riverside, CA	81,000	90,000	99,000	108,900	119,790
Rochester, NY	64,800	72,000	79,200	87,120	95,832
Sacramento, CA	67,500	75,000	82,500	90,750	99,625
St. Louis, MO	99,000	110,000	121,000	133,100	146,410
St. Paul, MN	112,500	125,000	137,500	151,250	166,375
Salt Lake City, UT	81,000	90,000	99,000	108,900	119,790
San Antonio, TX	81,000	90,000	99,000	108,900	119,790
San Diego, CA	139,500	155,000	170,500	187,550	206,305
San Francisco, CA	202,500	225,000	247,500	272,250	299,475
San Jose, CA	117,000	130,000	143,000	157,300	173,030
San Rafael, CA	180,000	200,000	220,000	242,000	266,200
Seattle, WA	90,000	100,000	110,000	121,000	133,100

Shreveport, LA	85,500	95,000	104,500	114,950	126,445
Sioux Falls, SD	99,000	110,000	121,000	133,100	146,410
Spokane, WA	81,000	90,000	99,000	108,900	119,790
Springfield, IL	76,500	85,000	93,500	102,850	113,135
Stamford, CT	135,000	150,000	165,000	181,500	199,650
Tampa, FL	68,400	76,000	83,600	91,960	101,156
Topeka, KS	81,000	90,000	99,000	108,900	119,790
Toronto, Ontario, Canada	68,400	76,000	83,600	91,360	101,156
Tucson, AZ	76,100	85,000	93,500	102,850	113,135
Tulsa, OK	81,000	90,000	99,000	108,900	119,790
Walnut Creek, CA	139,500	155,000	170,500	187,550	206,305
Washington, D.C.	94,500	105,000	115,500	127,050	139,755
Wichita, KS	90,000	100,000	110,000	121,000	133,100
Wilmington, DE	72,000	80,000	88,000	96,800	106,480

QUESTIONS TO ASK YOURSELF BEFORE YOU BUY

We've looked at many different cities. Obviously the criteria to decide whether or not to invest are similar for all of them. They are the same criteria you use in deciding whether to invest in your own community, even if it's not on one of my lists. Here are ten questions you should ask yourself with regard to *location:*

1. What is the projected growth rate of the city?
2. Is there a strong employment base?
3. Are major employers moving in or leaving?
4. What type of employment is there (manual industries, technical, services)?
5. What's the weather like?
6. Does the area appeal to retirees?
7. What is the crime rate?

8. Does it have sports and recreation appeal?
9. Are incomes in the area anticipated to grow?
10. What's the spread between replacement costs and market costs of housing?

Conclusion

We have seen that there is a wide-scale real-estate crisis occurring. Rapid appreciation in prices, common just a few years ago, has all but disappeared. Lower prices are now starting to appear across the country.

Housing starts are down. High interest rates are keeping buyers out of the market. Delinquency rates and foreclosure rates are edging toward their highest levels since the Great Depression. Builders can't even auction off their current homes; savings and loans, mortgage brokers, and agents are going bankrupt. The problems with real estate are widespread and deep.

But the general economic crisis that real estate is facing may be distinct from your personal crisis related to property.

If you're on top of the pile, chances are you have several properties. You may be facing difficult problems with negative cash flows. Or you may have a big balloon-payment second coming due. Or you may simply be unwilling to take further risks in real estate until the picture clears somewhat.

If you're in the middle or under the pile, your situation is probably different. You don't have an immediate problem caused by the current crisis. Since you're basically out of the investment picture, your big question is "Should I get in now when things are looking bad?"

Whether you're on top of the pile and worried about keeping what you've got, or in the middle, or under and worried about getting started during bad times, you have to consider the *opportunity* that today's market offers you.

We are not in a crisis without end.

Demand for housing is bursting at the seams. Vacancy rates across the country are at all-time lows. The supply of homes is dwindling. Recent tax cuts increase the tax advantages of holding real estate. The old financing of the 1970s and earlier is still in place on millions and millions of homes. It can still be locked in by investors, today.

The opportunity available in the midst of today's real-estate crisis is almost unimaginable.

The next big question for all of us is, how do we act personally, given the bigger picture of opportunity in a real-estate crisis?

This is my answer.

Look around us and see how severe the crisis is in your own particular area of the country, and then take advantage of it.

If you're in the middle of the pile or underneath, carefully examine the area where you live and see if there are single-family houses available that meet the criteria established in the last two chapters. There very well may be owners who are having their own particular financial crisis. They may need to sell, desperately. We can help them, and ourselves, by buying. You may find a "bread-and-butter," working-class area with reasonably low prices just right for renting, and in a relatively crime-free area that promises future growth.

Once you've determined that an area has good investment potential, farm it or farm the brokers who are working it. Become acquainted with sellers and, using devices such as a brag book, establish credibility.

And then buy.

If you're in the middle of the pile and own your home, borrow on the property and begin your five-year plan to financial freedom.

If you're under the pile, use techniques such as lease/option and equity sharing and buy, the aim being to control as much property as possible.

If you're on top of the pile, you may already be in your own personal crisis. High negative and balloon payments may be sinking you.

If that's the case, then use the techniques outlined in earlier chapters to reduce that negative. We take in partners or we dump the dog. Restructure your second, getting longer terms.

We make ourselves "battle ready" to withstand the present economic structure. Once we've done that, we look around our particular area of the country. If rent control seems imminent, we bail out of apartment houses and get into single-family homes. If we don't want management headaches, we get some cash out of our investments and become the "rich uncle" to an investor who's further down in the pile than we are. Because of our experience and our accumulation of property, if we're on top of the pile, we look around our area for good deals such as distressed properties where we can get a good price.

Above all, regardless of where we are in the pile, what we want to do is *act*.

TAKING ACTION

We want to act because if we don't we can get caught in our own special little crisis. If we're on top of the pile and we don't act, we can lose what we've got.

If we're in the middle of the pile and we don't act, we may find our selves locked into just owning one house, in which we live, and never getting anywhere financially. We may look around and say, yes, here's this great big investment that I'm living in. But, where's it getting me? It's a terrible feeling knowing that the potential to get wealthy is at your fingertips, but you just aren't taking advantage of it.

If we're at the bottom of the pile, and we don't act, we miss the last train out for the eighties. If we don't get on board while the market is soft, while sellers are willing to agree to flexible terms, while we can use lease/options and equity sharing, we won't get on board at all. Once the crisis eases and prices turn up, we won't see the kinds of terms that are available today. Sellers, then, simply won't go for the offers that they'll jump at right now.

If we don't act, depending on where we are in the pile, we may not only lose what we have, we may lose the last chance for the rest of this decade to become financially independent.

Acting, however, can sometimes seem to be more difficult than it really is. To help you act, **here are twenty things you should do now to take advantage of the current real-estate crisis:**

1. Buy single-family homes with no-interest loans.

2. Look to buy from people who have big negative cash flows with second mortgages coming due who will sell with 20% to 30% down and a no-interest 2nd mortgage, (or who will accept prepaid interest as the down payment).

3. Prepare for rent control now. Over 2000 cities and counties in the U.S. already have rent control. Structure your rental agreement so that the tenant pays according to increases in taxes, insurance and maintenance (a triple-net lease) so rent control doesn't box you in.

4. Don't buy properties with negative cash flow unless you have two years of reserves set aside in a slush fund to meet it.

5. Look for non-money motivation on the part of sellers. Perhaps the seller has a beautiful rose garden and you'll agree to take wonderful care of it, if they sell.

6. Close escrow the day after rents are due. That way you'll receive a full month's rent (in escrow) whether paid or not.

7. Only buy properties that make economic sense. Don't buy properties just for the tax benefits.

8. Stay out of the luxury rental market. Even during the Great Depression low-rent homes and apartments stayed full.

9. Never accept a balloon payment on a mortgage due in less than five years.

10. Structure financing on the basis of what it will be like for the next buyer.

11. Buy in an area with a good employment base.

12. Buy at or below the median price in your state.

13. Buy a three-bedroom/two-bath home in a working-class tract.

14. Lock in as much fixed-rate, longterm financing as you can, as soon as you can.

15. Find a mentor and get as much education as you can.

16. Find a good area and buy the smaller units as they come on the market. (The trend is to smaller homes and condos.)

17. Buy in a no-growth area where there is, or may be, a building moratorium.

18. Buy in rural areas that will have above-average growth.

19. Set a date that you will become financially independent. (Will it be five years from today?)

20. Buy one house a year for the next five years.

As I close this book, I would like you to consider this little story.

A wise man who lived in Switzerland was known to be able to answer any question. Many people believed him to be the wisest man in the world.

One day a young boy, who happened to be an 11-year-old Smart Aleck, walked up to the wise man and said "Oh Wise Man, I've been told you can answer any question that anyone can ask. Will you please answer this simple question?

"In the palms of my two hands, which are now closed into fists, I hold a little bird. Can you tell me, is the bird alive or dead?"

The wise man thought and thought and thought.

Finally he said, "Young boy, If I were to say alive, you would simply crush the bird and he would die. But, if I were to say dead, you would open your hand and he would fly away.

"You see, young fellow, in the palms of your hands you hold the power of life and death when it comes to that bird."

You see my dear reader, you, with the help of God, hold the power of life and death in the palms of your hands when it comes to your own financial future.

If there were only ten words that I could give you that could help you make the correct choices, they would be: **If it is to be, it is up to me.** You can accomplish more than you have ever dreamed possible.

PRICE LIST

1) **THE DISTRESSED PROPERTY REPORT**
A one-year subscription to the leading report on distressed properties. Featured are in-depth money-making discussions of the various types of foreclosures (e.g. tax sales, I.R.S. sales, sheriff sales, R.E.O.'s, FHA/VA foreclosures) plus real estate tips and recent examples of creative purchases from our readers. **$195.00**

2) **FORECLOSURE SYSTEMS**
Hal Morris will describe in detail various foreclosure wealth-building techniques which will lead you to achieve your highest goals. This all-day seminar is complete with eight tapes and a workbook which will cover how to find a property in foreclosure and buy it; how to buy real estate with little or no money down, no credit required; how to buy wholesale, no real estate license required; how to buy prior, during, and after foreclosure; how to buy Government foreclosed properties; how to deal with R.E.O.'s and much, much more. **$295.00**

3) **EQUITY SHARING**, An Answer for the 80s
This all-day seminar will show you how to achieve maximum leverage when acquiring properties. This is an excellent program for the new investor, first-time home buyer with little or no capital, or the seasoned professional. If you are one of the many people who thought home ownership not possible then Equity Sharing will show you "win-win" techniques for achieving your goals. **$350.00**

4) **HOW TO STOP FORECLOSURE**
Nationally-known authority on foreclosures and host of the nationally-syndicated talk show "Money, Money, Money," Hal Morris will show you how the foreclosure process works whether your property is worth saving, how to negotiate with an institutional lender, how to deal with creditors. A must for those who want the system to work for them. **$14.95**

5) **REAL ESTATE SUPERSTARS**
A collection of tapes featuring six real estate experts personally chosen from Hal Morris's nationally-syndicated television show, "Money, Money, Money." **$69.50**

6) **MILLIONAIRE IN THE MAKING PACKAGE**
All of the above. **$595.00**

ORDER FORM

(These materials are tax deductible)

*To order call (818) 577-7444 with an
American Express, Mastercard, or Visa number
or mail a copy of this form to:*

HAL MORRIS COMPANIES

175 South Los Robles Avenue
Pasadena, California 91101

Please send me: PRICES

(   ) **THE DISTRESSED PROPERTY REPORT** $195.00

(   ) **FORECLOSURE SYSTEMS**   295.00

(   ) **EQUITY SHARING,** An Answer for the 80's   350.00

(   ) **HOW TO STOP FORECLOSURE**   14.95

(   ) **REAL ESTATE SUPERSTARS**   69.50

(   ) **MILLIONAIRE IN THE MAKING PACKAGE** $595.00
(all of the above)   (SPECIAL PRICE)

Name: _____

Address: _____

City/State/Zip: _____

      Visa   Mastercard   American Express   Check
(circle one)

Charge Card Number: _____

Charge Card Expiration Date: _____

Telephone Number: _____

Signature: _____

Please add $2.00 postage for the first order and $1.00 for each additional order.
California Residents add 6½% sales tax.

Total of Order: _____